# 200
# SMALL
# HOUSE PLANS

© 1991 Donald A. Gardner Architects, Inc.

*Design 9645, page 75*

B. NATHAN.

## Selected Designs Under 2,500 Square Feet
*Innovative Plans for Sensible Lifestyles*

## HOME PLANNERS, LLC
**Wholly owned by Hanley-Wood, Inc.**
**Tucson, Arizona**

**Published by Home Planners, LLC**
**Wholly owned by Hanley-Wood, Inc.**

Editorial and Corporate Offices:
3275 West Ina Road, Suite 110
Tucson, Arizona 85741

**Distribution Center:**

29333 Lorie Lane
Wixom, Michigan 48393

**Rickard D. Bailey,** CEO and Publisher
**Cindy Coatsworth Lewis,** Director of Publishing
**Paulette Mulvin,** Senior Editor
**Laura Hurst Brown,** Project Editor
**Paul D. Fitzgerald,** Senior Graphic Designer
**Karen L. Leanio,** Graphic Designer

**Photo Credits**

Front Cover: © Jon Riley, Jon Riley Photography, Inc.
Back Cover: © Bob Greenspan

First Printing, February, 1997

10  9  8  7  6  5  4  3  2

Printed in the United States of America.

Library of Congress Catalog Card Number: 96-078882

ISBN: 1-881955-34-6

*On the front cover:* Design 9645, a charming country-style bestseller with natural
character. See page 75 for a closer look.

*On the back cover:* Design 2974, a cool Rocky Mountain Victorian to build in any
region. For more information, see page 67.

*Design 3652, page 45*

# TABLE OF CONTENTS

### EDITOR'S NOTE

Home is a personal thing—it has to do with our needs and values. Building a home is an investment in lifestyle as well as in land and materials, and the *best* homes breathe with a relaxed spirit and natural character.

These designs, all less than 2,500 square feet, are big on style and comfort and—despite their modest size—luxury. I've selected exterior styles that are strong and distinctive enough to make a statement, and interior plans that are bold and forthright but never showy.

You'll find acres of variety here, from Southwesterns to Cape Cods. But let me take a moment to point out a few of the bestsellers: our prairie-style farmhouse on page 147 (Design 2774), our Rocky Mountain Victorian on page 67 (Design 2974), and a cozy starter home on page 12 (Design 2947). If yours is a growing family, check out our stunning move-up homes starting on page 126.

This selection of homes offers the height of quality and tradition that's been Home Planners' hallmark for 50 years, and introduces a thought: How you feel in a home is as important as how the house looks. Our plans create real homes—homes you can live in and love for years.

# ABOUT THE DESIGNERS

The Blue Ribbon Designer Series™ is a collection of books featuring the home plans of a diverse group of outstanding home designers and architects known as the Blue Ribbon Network of Designers. This group of companies is dedicated to creating and marketing the finest possible plans for home construction on a regional and national basis. Each of the companies exhibits superior work and integrity in all phases of the stock-plan business including modern, trendsetting floor planning, a professionally executed blueprint package and a strong sense of service and commitment to the consumer.

## Design Basics, Inc.

For nearly a decade, Design Basics, a nationally recognized home design service located in Omaha, has been developing plans for custom home builders. Since 1987, the firm has consistently appeared in *Builder* magazine, the official magazine of the National Association of Home Builders, as the top-selling designer. The company's plans also regularly appear in numerous other shelter magazines such as *Better Homes and Gardens, House Beautiful* and *Home Planner.*

## Stephen Fuller/Design Traditions

Design Traditions was established by Stephen S. Fuller with the tenets of innovation, quality, originality and uncompromising architectural techniques in traditional and European homes. Especially popular throughout the Southeast, Design Traditions' plans are known for their extensive detail and thoughtful design. They are widely published in such shelter magazines as *Southern Living* magazine and *Better Homes and Gardens.*

## Alan Mascord Design Associates, Inc.

Founded in 1983 as a local supplier to the building community, Mascord Design Associates of Portland, Oregon began to successfully publish plans nationally in 1985. With plans now drawn exclusively on computer, Mascord Design Associates quickly received a reputation for homes that are easy to build yet meet the rigorous demands of the buyers' market, winning local and national awards. The company's trademark is creating floor plans that work well and exhibit excellent traffic patterns. Their motto is: "Drawn to build, designed to sell."

## Larry E. Belk Designs

Through the years, Larry E. Belk has worked with individuals and builders alike to provide a quality product. After listening to over 4,000 dreams and watching them become reality all across America, Larry's design philosophy today combines traditional exteriors with upscale interiors designed for contemporary lifestyles. Flowing, open spaces and interesting angles define his interiors. Great emphasis is placed on providing views that showcase the natural environment. Dynamic exteriors reflect Larry's extensive home construction experience, painstaking research and talent as a fine artist.

## Larry W. Garnett & Associates, Inc.

Starting as a designer of homes for Houston-area residents, Garnett & Associates has been marketing designs nationally for the past ten years. A well-respected design firm, the company's plans are regularly featured in *House Beautiful, Country Living, Home* and *Professional Builder.* Numerous accolades, including several from the Texas Institute of Building Design and the American Institute of Building Design, have been awarded to the company for excellence in architecture.

## Home Planners

Headquartered in Tucson, Arizona, with additional offices in Detroit, Home Planners is one of the longest-running and most successful home design firms in the United States. With over 2,500 designs in its portfolio, the company provides a wide range of styles, sizes and types of homes for the residential builder. All of Home Planners' designs are created with the care and professional expertise that fifty years of experience in the home-planning business affords. Their homes are designed to be built, lived in and enjoyed for years to come.

## Donald A. Gardner, Architects, Inc.

The South Carolina firm of Donald A. Gardner was established in response to a growing demand for residential designs that reflect constantly changing lifestyles. The company's specialty is providing homes with refined, custom-style details and unique features such as passive-solar designs and open floor plans. Computer-aided design and drafting technology resulting in trouble-free construction documents places the firm at the leading edge of the home plan industry.

## The Sater Design Collection

The Sater Design Collection has a long established tradition of providing South Florida's most diverse and extraordinary custom designed homes. Their goal is to fulfill each client's particular need for an exciting approach to design by merging creative vision with elements that satisfy a desire for a distinctive lifestyle. This philosophy is proven, as exemplified by over 50 national design awards, numerous magazine features and, most important, satisfied clients. The result is an elegant statement of lasting beauty and value.

## Home Design Services, Inc.

For the past fifteen years, Home Design Services of Longwood, Florida, has been formulating plans for the sun-country lifestyle. At the forefront of design innovation and imagination, the company has developed award winning designs that are consistently praised for their highly detailed, free-flowing floor plans, imaginative and exciting interior architecture and elevations which have gained international appeal.

# BRILLIANT BEGINNINGS

## *Beautiful Homes For First-Time Builders*

Few experiences measure up to the joy of building a new home. It's exciting to lay out fresh plans for the first time. Starter homes may be the humble beginnings of a grander scheme, but they may well offer the vigorous spirit of the design of our dreams.

First-time builders generally appreciate amenities such as a clustered bedroom plan—with a nearby nursery or study—a kitchen with breakfast nook, and a spacious family or gathering room. Naturally cozy spaces are important. Recently, a Home Planners customer mentioned he enjoyed stretching out on the living room floor with his golden retriever—in front of a warming fireplace, of course. No problem. (Check out Design 2878 on page 8.)

Economy is an attractive element of these plans. But perhaps the most appealing feature is their flexibility: there's room for change and growth. A study could become a nursery or a third bedroom; a den becomes a media room or home office.

Selecting a design for the first time invites imagination and a bit of instinct, and we pledge to help you find just the right plan. This section offers a sampling of 31 plans for starter homes, but we have many more—thousands more—to choose from. Each promises a happy marriage of style and comfort, and a place you'll simply love for years to come.

## Design 3655

**Square Footage:** 1,418

**L**

If you need a guest or mother-in-law suite, you'll love this compact design. The suite—which could also be used as a home office—enjoys its own courtyard, a cozy fireplace and a private bath. The efficient floor plan also features a spacious living area, which offers patio access and a three-sided fireplace that shares its warmth with a formal dining area with built-in shelves for curiosa. A thoughtfully planned kitchen offers a corner sink with window, as well as easy access from the garage. Clustered bedrooms include a spacious master suite with a whirlpool tub, a double-bowl vanity and twin closets. Two nearby family bedrooms share a full bath.

Cost to build? See page 214 to order complete cost estimate to build this house in your area!

ULTRA TUB

MASTER SUITE
13⁸ x 10⁴
SLOPED CLG

BEDRM
11⁰ x 10⁴
SLOPED CLG

COVERED PATIO

MASTER BATH

LIVING RM
15⁰ x 14⁰
SLOPED CLG

BEDRM
9⁰ x 9⁸
SLOPED CLG

LINEN

BATH

REFG

HVAC  WH

D  W

RANGE

FOYER

9-SIDED FP  SLVS

CURB

KITCHEN
8⁰ x 14⁶

COVERED ENTRY

DINING RM
9¹⁰ x 9⁴
COFFERED CLG

CURB

P  DW

S

GARAGE
19⁴ x 22¹⁰

COURTYARD

BATH

BRICK PLANTER

SLPNG CLG

OFFICE/ GUEST
13² x 11¹⁰

SLVS

BRICK WING WALLS W/POST

Width 44'-8"
Depth 52'-4"

## Design 3659

**Square Footage:** 1,118

**L**

**C**ompact yet comfortable, this home offers many appealing amenities. From the covered front porch, the entrance foyer opens onto the sunlit, octagonal dining room and to the gracious living room which offers a sloped ceiling and access to a rear covered patio. To the left of the foyer is the efficient kitchen that has the added bonus of no cross-room traffic. The luxurious master suite includes a lavish bath complete with a corner tub, a separate shower, a walk-in closet and twin vanities. A secondary bedroom has access to a full hall bath.

DESIGN BY

**Home Planners**

### Floor Plan Labels

- WALK-IN CLOSET
- SHOWER
- LIN
- MASTER BATH
- ULTRA TUB
- **MASTER SUITE** 15¹⁰ x 12⁸ SLOPED CLG
- COVERED PATIO
- **LIVING RM** 15⁰ x 14⁰ SLOPED CLG
- **BEDRM** 9⁰ x 9⁸ SLOPED CLG
- LINEN
- BATH
- REF8
- RANGE
- HVAC WH
- D W
- **KITCHEN** 8⁰ x 14⁸
- CURB
- P DW
- S
- FOYER
- 3-SIDED FP
- SLVS
- CURB0
- COVERED PORCH
- **DINING RM** 9¹⁰ x 9⁴ COFFERED CLG
- RAILING
- RAILING
- **GARAGE** 19⁴ x 22¹⁰

Width 44'-4"
Depth 47'-4"

**QUOTE ONE®**

Cost to build? See page 214 to order complete cost estimate to build this house in your area!

*Photo by Andrew D. Lautman*

This home, as shown in the photograph, may differ from the actual blueprints. For more detailed information, please check the floor plans carefully.

## Design 2878

**Square Footage:** 1,530

**L** **D**

This charming, compact design combines traditional styling with sensational commodities and modern livability. Thoughtful zoning places sleeping areas to one side, apart from household activity. The plan includes a spacious gathering room with sloped ceiling and centered fireplace, and a formal dining room overlooking a rear terrace. A handy pass-through connects the breakfast room with the efficient kitchen. The laundry is conveniently positioned nearby. An impressive master suite enjoys access to a private rear terrace and offers a separate dressing area with walk-in closet. Two family bedrooms, or one and a study, are nearby and share a full bath.

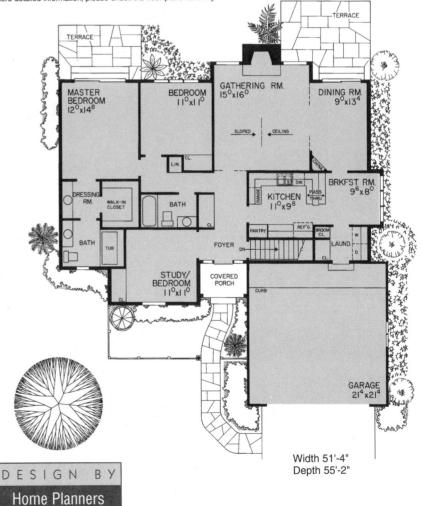

Width 51'-4"
Depth 55'-2"

**QUOTE ONE®**

Cost to build? See page 214
to order complete cost estimate
to build this house in your area!

DESIGN BY

**Home Planners**

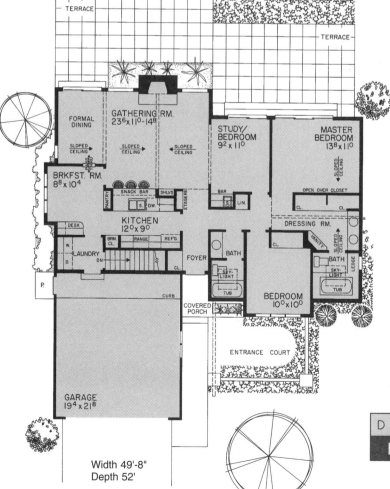

TERRACE

TERRACE

FORMAL DINING

SLOPED CEILING

GATHERING RM.
23⁶x11⁰-14⁸

SLOPED CEILING

SLOPED CEILING

STUDY/ BEDROOM
9²x11⁰

MASTER BEDROOM
13⁸x11⁰

SLOPED CEILING

BRKFST. RM.
8⁸x10⁴

PANTRY

SNACK BAR

SHLVS.

ETAGERE

BAR

OPEN OVER CLOSET

CL.

CL.

S.

D.W.

DESK

KITCHEN
12⁰x9⁰

BRM. CL.

RANGE

REF'G.

BATH

DRESSING RM.

CL.

VANITY

BATH

SLOPED CEILING

LEDGE

W.

LAUNDRY

D.

DN

CL.

FOYER

SKY-LIGHT

TUB

BEDROOM
10⁰x10⁰

SKY-LIGHT

TUB

P.

CURB

COVERED PORCH

GARAGE
19⁴x21⁸

ENTRANCE COURT

Width 49'-8"
Depth 52'

DESIGN BY
Home Planners

# Design 2864

**Square Footage:** 1,387

**L** **D**

Projecting the garage to the front of a house is economical in two ways: by reducing the required lot size and by protecting the interior from street noise. Many other features deserve mention as well. A formal dining area opens to a spacious gathering room with a large, centered fireplace; both areas offer a sloped ceiling. The well-appointed kitchen services an adjacent breakfast room as well as a counter snack bar. Clustered bedrooms offer convenience for families just starting out. Use a third bedroom with wet bar area as a study. Sliding glass doors in three rooms open to the rear terrace.

Cost to build? See page 214 to order complete cost estimate to build this house in your area!

9

## Design 2871

**Living Area:** 1,824 square feet
**Greenhouse Area:** 81 square feet
**Total:** 1,905 square feet

**D**

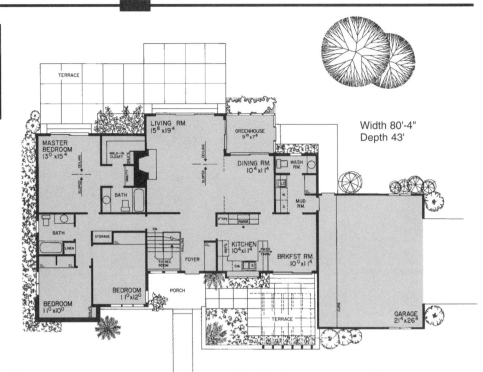

Width 80'-4"
Depth 43'

A greenhouse area off the dining room and living room provides a cheerful focal point for this comfortable three-bedroom Trend home. The spacious living room features a cozy fireplace and a sloped ceiling. In addition to the dining room, there's a less formal breakfast room just off the modern kitchen. Both kitchen and breakfast areas look out onto a front terrace. Stairs just off the foyer lead down to a recreation room. The master bedroom suite opens to a terrace. A mud room and a wash room off the garage allow rear entry to the house during inclement weather.

Cost to build? See page 214
to order complete cost estimate
to build this house in your area!

DESIGN BY
**Home Planners**

This smart design features multi-gabled ends, varied rooflines and vertical windows. Inside, effective zoning offers privacy for sleeping quarters and convenience for living areas. The grand foyer opens to a large, central gathering room with a fireplace, a sloped ceiling, and its own special view of the rear terrace. The modern kitchen features a snack bar and a pass-through to a sunny breakfast room with rear terrace access. The adjacent formal dining room enjoys terrace access and opens to the gathering room. A secluded media room offers built-ins designed to accomodate a sophisticated entertainment center—or start a library! Amenities abound in the master suite, complete with a whirlpool bath, a walk-in closet and knee-space vanity. A two-car garage with sloped ceiling has an additional storage area.

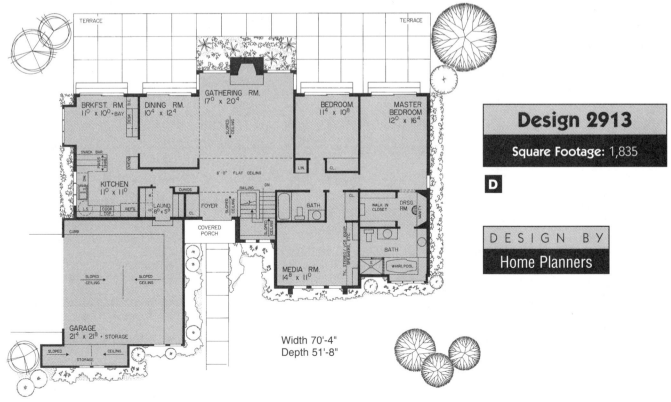

## Design 2913

**Square Footage:** 1,835

D

DESIGN BY
**Home Planners**

Width 70'-4"
Depth 51'-8"

Photos by Andrew D. Lautman

This home, as shown in the photograph, may differ from the actual blueprints. For more detailed information, please check the floor plans carefully.

## Design 2947

**Square Footage:** 1,830

**L** **D**

This charming, one-story traditional home greets visitors with a covered porch. A galley-style kitchen shares a snack bar with the spacious gathering room, where a fireplace is the focal point. An ample master suite offers a luxury bath with a whirlpool tub and a separate dressing room. Two additional bedrooms—one could double as a study—are located at the front of the home.

Width 75'
Depth 43'-5"

DESIGN BY
**Home Planners**

QUOTE ONE®
Cost to build? See page 214 to order complete cost estimate to build this house in your area!

## Design 3332

**Square Footage:** 2,203

# QUOTE ONE®

Cost to build? See page 214
to order complete cost estimate
to build this house in your area!

**N**othing warms a traditional-style home quite as wonderfully as a country kitchen with a fireplace. Additional features include a second fireplace (with raised hearth) and a sloped ceiling in the living room, a nearby dining room with an attached porch, and a snack bar pass-through in the kitchen. A clustered bedroom plan offers two family bedrooms, which share a full bath and a grand master suite with rear terrace access, a walk-in closet, a whirlpool tub and a double-bowl vanity. A handy washroom is near the laundry, just off the two-car garage. A second terrace is located to the rear of this area.

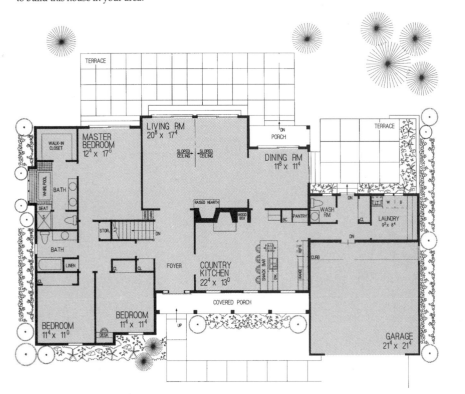

DESIGN BY

**Home Planners**

Width 77'-2"
Depth 46'-6"

## Design 8177

**Square Footage:** 1,834

DESIGN BY
**Larry E. Belk Designs**

**R**eminiscent of America's farmhouses, this home comes complete with a front covered porch perfect for those hot summer evenings. Inside, the foyer opens to the great room, with a matching pair of double French doors flanking the fireplace and leading out to the rear porch. The dining room adds a formal flair with square columns and arched openings. An angled counter design in the kitchen opens the area to the great room and provides a convenient pass-through. The master bedroom features a coffered ceiling and an enormous walk-in closet. Amenities that include a double vanity, a corner whirlpool tub and a separate shower highlight the master bath. Nearby, bedrooms 2 and 3 complete the plan. Please specify crawlspace or slab foundation when ordering.

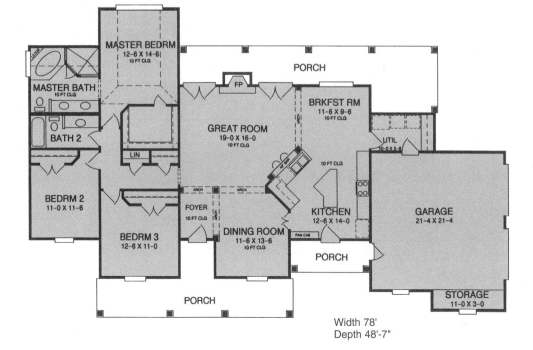

Width 78'
Depth 48'-7"

## Design 3460

**Square Footage:** 1,389

**L**

Width 44'-8"
Depth 54'-6"

FAMILY RM
VAULTED CLG
12⁴ x 12⁰

MASTER BEDRM
VAULTED CLG
13⁰ x 12⁰

MASTER BATH

BEDRM
VAULTED CLG
10⁰ x 10⁸

SNACK BAR
PANTRY
KIT
12⁴ x 10⁰
SINK
DW
REFS
LAUNDRY
D W

LINEN
BATH

BEDRM
VAULTED CLG
10⁰ x 10⁸

COVERED PORCH

DINING

LIVING RM
VAULTED CLG
13¹⁰ x 19⁰

PLANT SHELF ABOVE

F.U.
W.H.

ENTRY
HALF WALL
CURB

COVERED PORCH

GARAGE
21⁴ x 23⁸

**DESIGN BY**

**Home Planners**

**QUOTE ONE®**

Cost to build? See page 214 to order complete cost estimate to build this house in your area!

**A** double dose of charm, this special farmhouse plan offers two elevations in its blueprint package—one showcases a delightful wraparound porch. The formal living room has a warming fireplace and a sunny bay window. The kitchen separates this area from the more casual family room. In the kitchen, you'll find an efficient snack bar as well as a pantry for additional storage space. Three bedrooms include two family bedrooms which share a full bath, and a lovely master suite with a private bath. Notice the location of the washer and dryer—convenient to all of the bedrooms.

## Design 7601

**Square Footage:** 1,787
**Bonus Room:** 326 square feet

A neighborly porch as friendly as a handshake wraps around this charming country home. Inside, cathedral ceilings promote an aura of spaciousness. To the left of the foyer, the great room offers a fireplace and built-in bookshelves. A unique formal dining room separates the kitchen and breakfast area. Enjoy outdoor pursuits—rain or shine—from the screen porch. The private master suite features a walk-in closet and a luxurious bath—two additional bedrooms, one with a walk-in closet, share a skylit bath. A second-floor bonus room is available to develop later as a study, home office or play area. Please specify basement or crawlspace foundation when ordering.

DESIGN BY

**Donald A. Gardner,**
**Architects, Inc.**

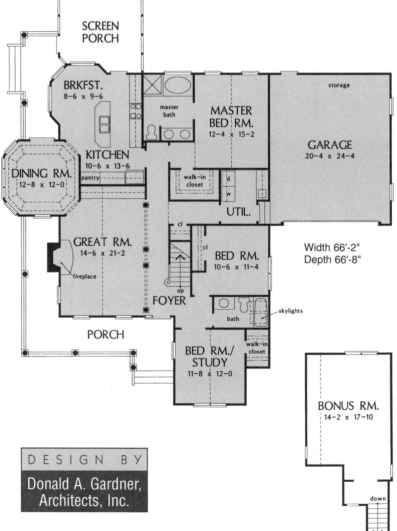

SCREEN PORCH

BRKFST.
8-6 x 9-6

master bath

MASTER BED RM.
12-4 x 15-2

storage

GARAGE
20-4 x 24-4

KITCHEN
10-6 x 13-6

pantry

DINING RM.
12-8 x 12-0

walk-in closet

UTIL.

GREAT RM.
14-6 x 21-2

fireplace

cl

cl

BED RM.
10-6 x 11-4

Width 66'-2"
Depth 66'-8"

up

FOYER

bath

skylights

PORCH

BED RM./ STUDY
11-8 x 12-0

walk-in closet

BONUS RM.
14-2 x 17-10

down

B. NATHAN

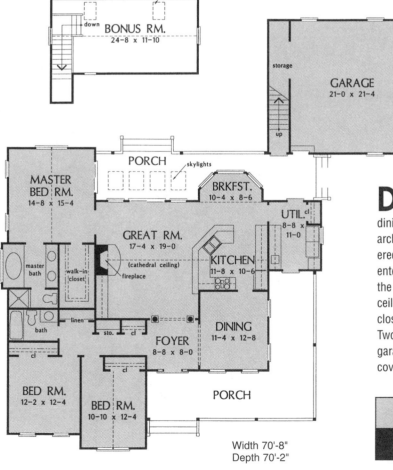

attic stor.          skylights

down    **BONUS RM.**
24-8 x 11-10

**GARAGE**
21-0 x 21-4

storage

up

**PORCH**    skylights

**MASTER
BED RM.**
14-8 x 15-4

**BRKFST.**
10-4 x 8-6

**UTIL.** cl
8-8 x
11-0

**GREAT RM.**
17-4 x 19-0

(cathedral ceiling)

fireplace

**KITCHEN**
11-8 x 10-6

master
bath    walk-in
closet

linen

bath    sto.    cl

**FOYER**
8-8 x 8-0

**DINING**
11-4 x 12-8

**BED RM.**
12-2 x 12-4

**BED RM.**
10-10 x 12-4

**PORCH**

Width 70'-8"
Depth 70'-2"

Quote One®

Cost to build? See page 214
to order complete cost estimate
to build this house in your area!

D E S I G N   B Y

**Donald A. Gardner,
Architects, Inc.**

**D**ormers, arched windows and covered porches lend this
home a country appeal. Inside, the foyer opens to the
dining room on the right and leads through a columned
archway to the great room, warmed by a fireplace. The covered, skylit rear porch provides opportunities for outdoor
entertaining. The open kitchen easily serves the great room,
the bayed breakfast area and the dining room. A cathedral
ceiling graces the master bedroom, which offers a walk-in
closet and a private bath with dual vanity and whirlpool tub.
Two additional bedrooms share a full bath. A detached
garage with a skylit bonus room is connected to the rear
covered porch.

# Design 9764

**Square Footage:** 1,815

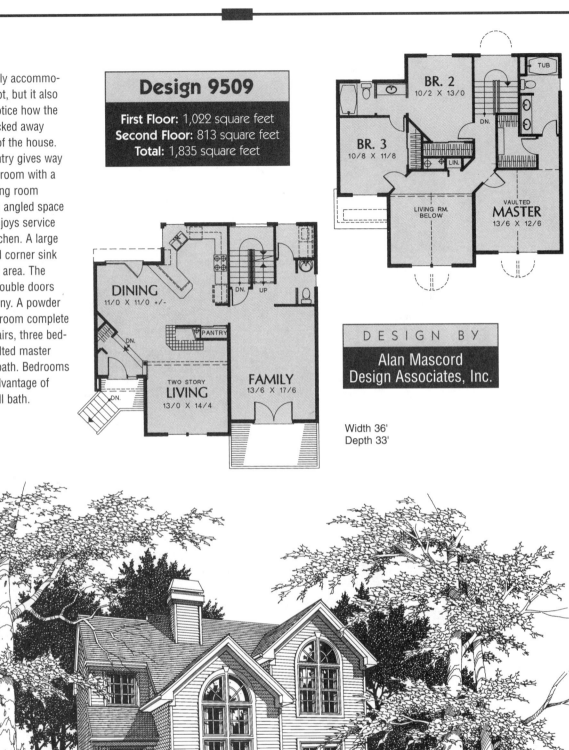

This house not only accommodates a narrow lot, but it also fits a sloping site. Notice how the two-car garage is tucked away under the first level of the house. The angled corner entry gives way to a two-story living room with a tiled hearth. The dining room shares an interesting angled space with this area and enjoys service from the efficient kitchen. A large pantry and an angled corner sink add character to this area. The family room offers double doors to a refreshing balcony. A powder room and a laundry room complete the main level. Upstairs, three bedrooms include a vaulted master suite with a private bath. Bedrooms 2 and 3 each take advantage of direct access to a full bath.

## Design 9509

**First Floor:** 1,022 square feet
**Second Floor:** 813 square feet
**Total:** 1,835 square feet

BR. 2
10/2 X 13/0

BR. 3
10/8 X 11/8

TUB

DN.

LIN.

LIVING RM. BELOW

VAULTED MASTER
13/6 X 12/6

DINING
11/0 X 11/0 +/-

DN.

UP

DN.

PANTRY

TWO STORY
LIVING
13/0 X 14/4

FAMILY
13/6 X 17/6

DN.

DESIGN BY

Alan Mascord
Design Associates, Inc.

Width 36'
Depth 33'

## Design 9235

**First Floor:** 919 square feet
**Second Floor:** 927 square feet
**Total:** 1,846 square feet

## QUOTE ONE®

Cost to build? See page 214
to order complete cost estimate
to build this house in your area!

This wonderful design begins with a quintessential wraparound porch. Explore further and find a two-story entry with a roomy coat closet and a plant shelf above. The island kitchen with a boxed window over the sink is adjacent to a large bay-windowed breakfast room. The great room includes triple windows and a warming fireplace. A powder bath and laundry room are conveniently placed on the first floor. Upstairs, the large master suite contains His and Hers walk-in closets, corner windows and a bath area featuring a double vanity and a whirlpool tub. Two pleasant secondary bedrooms offer interesting angles. A third bedroom in the front features a volume ceiling and an arched window.

DESIGN BY
Design Basics, Inc.

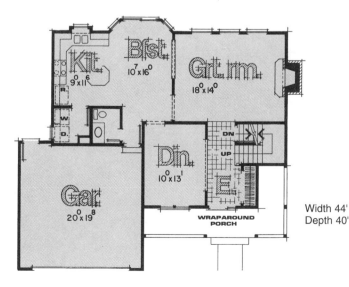

Width 44'
Depth 40'

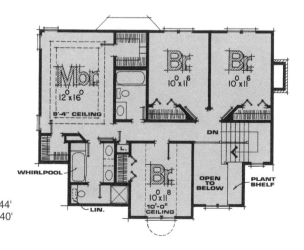

The true meaning of "less is more" is apparent in this two-story narrow-lot home. Creative use of space makes this home appear much larger than it actually is. Enter the formal living areas—a bayed living room and a columned dining room—to the right of the foyer. Informal living areas occupy the rear of the plan. A family room with a warming fireplace shares space with an efficient, L-shaped kitchen with a cooktop island and a sunny eating nook. The second floor contains the sleeping zone with three family bedrooms and a master suite, which is highlighted by a vaulted ceiling and a walk-in closet. The master bath features a shower and a double-bowl vanity.

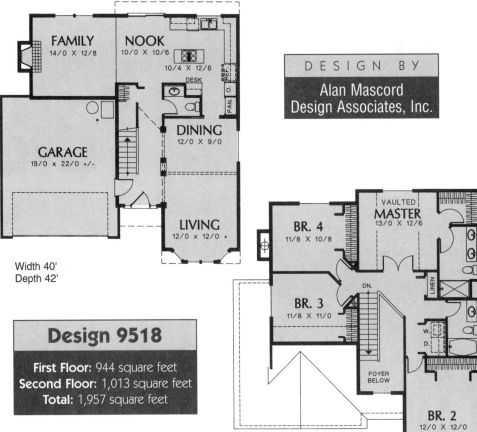

FAMILY
14/0 X 12/8

NOOK
10/0 X 10/6

10/4 X 12/6

DESK

PAN.

GARAGE
19/0 x 22/0 +/-

DINING
12/0 X 9/0

LIVING
12/0 X 12/0 +

Width 40'
Depth 42'

DESIGN BY
Alan Mascord
Design Associates, Inc.

VAULTED
MASTER
13/0 X 12/6

BR. 4
11/8 X 10/8

LINEN

DN.

BR. 3
11/8 X 11/0

W.

D.

FOYER
BELOW

BR. 2
12/0 X 12/0

## Design 9518

**First Floor:** 944 square feet
**Second Floor:** 1,013 square feet
**Total:** 1,957 square feet

# Design 9593

**First Floor:** 968 square feet
**Second Floor:** 837 square feet
**Total:** 1,805 square feet

Stone piers add character to the charming covered porch that welcomes you into this three-bedroom home. Inside, a columned hallway provides a graceful entrance into the formal living and dining rooms from the two story foyer. A nearby L-shaped kitchen conveniently serves both the formal dining room and the casual bay-windowed breakfast nook. Board games, good books and lively conversation are just a few of the family pursuits that will be enjoyed in a comfortable family room warmed by the glow of the fireplace. Upstairs, two secondary bedrooms share a full hall bath. Double doors provide entry into a luxurious master suite designed to transport you into a world of relaxation. A walk-in closet and a soothing master bath complete this quiet retreat. Laundry facilities handily accommodate the family's needs and complete the second floor.

DESIGN BY
Alan Mascord
Design Associates, Inc.

**NOOK**
10/0 X 12/6
(9' CLG)
10/4 X 12/6 +/-

**VAULTED FAMILY**
13/0 X 12/8

DESK

**DINING**
12/0 x 9/0
(9' CLG)

**GARAGE**
19/0 x 22/0

**LIVING**
12/0 x 12/0
(9' CLG)

UP

**PORCH**

Width 40'
Depth 46'

**VAULTED MASTER**
13/0 X 12/6

LINEN

**BR. 3**
10/8 x 11/0

DN

**BR. 2**
12/0 X 10/0

## Design 8229

**Square Footage:** 1,955

A finely detailed covered porch and arch-topped windows announce a scrupulously designed interior, replete with amenities. A grand foyer with 10-foot ceiling and columned archways set the pace for the entire floor plan. Clustered sleeping quarters to the left feature a luxurious master suite with a sloped ceiling, corner whirlpool bath and walk-in closet, and two family bedrooms which share a bath. Picture windows flanking a centered fireplace lend plenty of natural light to the great room, which is open through grand, columned archways to the formal dining area and the bay-windowed breakfast room. The kitchen, conveniently positioned between the dining and breakfast rooms, shares an informal eating counter with the great room. A utility room and walk-in pantry are tucked neatly to the side of the plan. Please specify crawlspace or slab foundation when ordering.

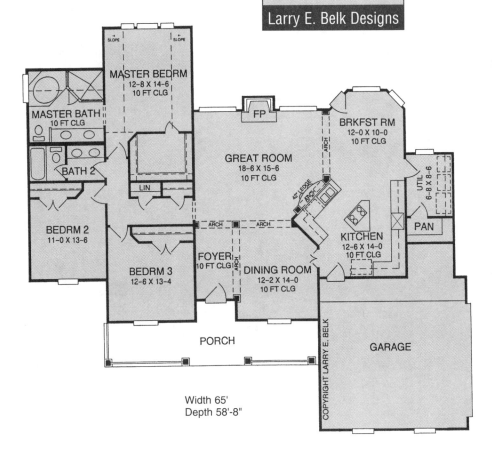

Width 65'
Depth 58'-8"

## Design 8180

**Square Footage:** 1,862

### DESIGN BY
## Larry E. Belk Designs

This charming traditional has all the amenities of a larger plan in a compact layout. Ten-foot ceilings give this home an expansive feel. An angled eating bar separates the kitchen and great room while leaving these areas open to one another for family gatherings and entertaining. The master bedroom includes a huge walk-in closet and a superior master bath with a whirlpool tub and separate shower. A large utility room and an oversized storage area are located near the secondary entrance to the home. Two additional bedrooms and a bath finish the plan. Please specify crawlspace or slab foundation when ordering.

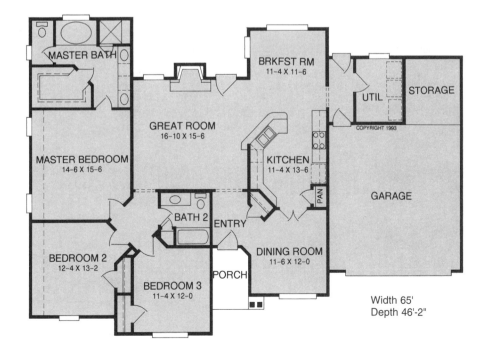

MASTER BATH

BRKFST RM
11-4 X 11-6

UTIL

STORAGE

COPYRIGHT 1993

GREAT ROOM
16-10 X 15-6

MASTER BEDROOM
14-6 X 15-6

KITCHEN
11-4 X 13-6

GARAGE

BATH 2

ENTRY

PAN

BEDROOM 2
12-4 X 13-2

DINING ROOM
11-6 X 12-0

PORCH

BEDROOM 3
11-4 X 12-0

Width 65'
Depth 46'-2"

## Design 8181

**Square Footage:** 1,500

This bestselling traditional home is compact in size but packed with all of the amenities you'd expect in a larger home. The foyer opens to a formal dining room with a classic bay window. The adjacent kitchen opens to a breakfast nook and shares an angled eating bar with the living room, which offers a cozy fireplace flanked by picture windows. The master suite features His and Hers vanities, a whirlpool tub/shower combination and a walk-in closet. Ten-foot ceilings in the major living areas as well as in two of the bedrooms contribute an aura of spaciousness to this plan. Please specify crawlspace or slab foundation when ordering.

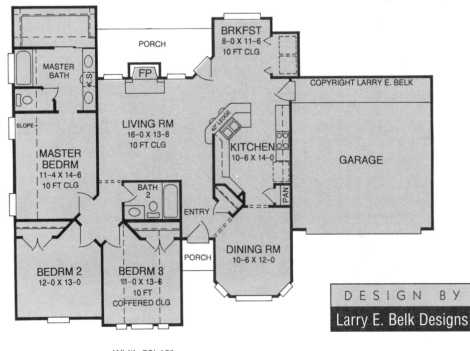

Width 59'-10"
Depth 44'-4"

DESIGN BY
Larry E. Belk Designs

Bath

Porch

Breakfast
10' x 10'

2-Car Garage

Master Bedroom
13'-8" x 16'
11' Vaulted Clg.

Dining
11'-4" x 13'-8"
10' Clg.

Kitchen
12' x 13'-4"

42" Wall

Util.

Living Room
18'-4" x 17'
9'-6" Clg.

Width 64'
Depth 50'-10"

Bath 2

Bedroom 2
11'-4" x 10'-4"

Foyer

Bedroom 3
11'-4" x 10'-8"
10' Clg.

8' Clg. Throughout
Unless Otherwise Noted

**N**o slouch on amenities, this plan is a popular choice with those just starting out. High ceilings in the dining room and the master suite add a sense of space. A decorative front wall separates the formal dining area from the foyer while preserving the openness of the area. A bay-windowed breakfast room adjoins the kitchen area and opens to a rear porch for outdoor dining. Sleeping quarters include a master suite with vaulted ceiling, walk-in closet, glass-surrounded tub and separate shower, as well as two family bedrooms which share a full bath. The laundry area is conveniently located near the bedrooms.

DESIGN BY

Larry W. Garnett
& Associates, Inc.

## Design 9028

**Square Footage:** 1,707

QUOTE ONE®

Cost to build? See page 214
to order complete cost estimate
to build this house in your area!

Copyright 1992 Stephen S. Fuller, Inc.

## Design 9872

**Square Footage:** 1,815

This stately European home offers an easy-care stucco exterior with finely detailed windows and a majestic front door that furthers a graceful presence. Inside, a grand, columned foyer opens to both the formal dining room and the great room with a vaulted ceiling and a fireplace. The spacious, well-appointed kitchen, open to a breakfast room and adjacent to the formal dining area, makes serving and entertaining easy and delightful work. Nestled away at the opposite end of the home, the master suite combines perfect solitude with elegant luxury. Features include a double door entry, tray ceiling, niche detail and private rear deck. Two additional bedrooms, a full bath and a powder room accomodate other members of the family as well as guests. This home is designed with a basement foundation.

DESIGN BY
**Design Traditions**

PORCH

BREAKFAST
10'-0" X 10'-0"

GREAT ROOM
16'-0" X 18'-0"

MASTER BEDROOM
15'-0" X 14'-0"

W.I.C.

MASTER BATH

POWDER

KITCHEN
14'-0" X 11'-4"

DINING ROOM
10'-6" X 13'-0"

FOYER
5'-0" X 9'-0"

BEDROOM
NO. 3
10'-6" X 10'-0"

BEDROOM NO. 2
11'-2" X 11'-0"

BATH

LAUND
5'-2" X 10'-6"

DN.

TWO CAR GARAGE
20'-4" X 19'-4"

Width 60'
Depth 58-6"

**QUOTE ONE®**
Cost to build? See page 214
to order complete cost estimate
to build this house in your area!

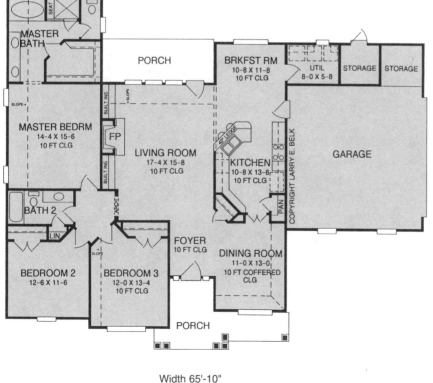

MASTER
BATH

PORCH

BRKFST RM
10-8 X 11-8
10 FT CLG

UTIL
8-0 X 5-8

STORAGE

STORAGE

MASTER BEDRM
14-4 X 15-6
10 FT CLG

FP

LIVING ROOM
17-4 X 15-8
10 FT CLG

KITCHEN
10-8 X 13-6
10 FT CLG

GARAGE

COPYRIGHT LARRY E. BELK

BATH 2

LIN

FOYER
10 FT CLG

BEDROOM 2
12-6 X 11-6

BEDROOM 3
12-0 X 13-4
10 FT CLG

DINING ROOM
11-0 X 13-0
10 FT COFFERED
CLG

PORCH

Width 65'-10"
Depth 53'-5"

## Design 8183

**Square Footage:** 1,890

This classic home exudes elegance and style and offers sophisticated amenities in a compact size. Ten-foot ceilings throughout the plan lend an aura of spacious hospitality. A generous living room with a sloped ceiling, built-in bookcases and a centerpiece fireplace, offers views as well as access to the rear yard. The nearby breakfast room shares an informal eating counter with the ample kitchen, which serves the coffered-ceiling dining room through French doors. Three bedrooms include a sumptuous master suite with windowed whirlpool tub and walk-in closet, and two family bedrooms which share a full bath. Please specify slab or crawlspace foundation when ordering.

### DESIGN BY
### Larry E. Belk Designs

The lines of this traditional home are very clean, with classical detailing that defines elegance. Columns, brickwork and shuttered windows remind us of the best homes of turn-of-the-century America. Inside, contemporary amenities prevail. A columned foyer opens to the right to a formal dining room with French doors to a thoroughly modern kitchen. To the left of the foyer, a convenient powder room accomodates guests. Directly ahead, the foyer leads to a wide open living area that shares the warmth of a hearth, centered in the great room, framed by glass and light. This area is particularly well-suited to entertaining—both formally and informally—with an open kitchen and bay-windowed breakfast nook as well as access to the rear deck. Upstairs, the master suite features a tray ceiling, whirlpool tub, twin lavatories and compartmented toilet. Bedrooms 2 and 3 each have separate access to a full bath. The laundry room is found on this level, convenient to any of the bedrooms. This home is designed with a basement foundation.

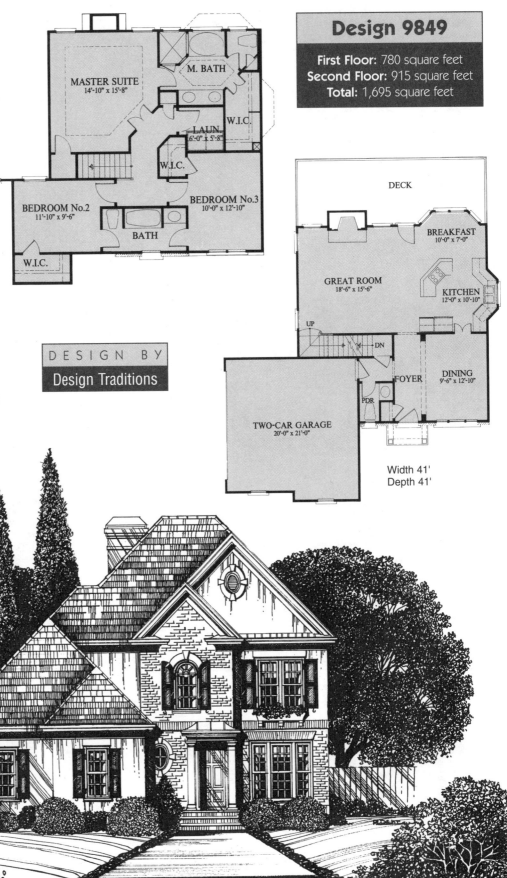

## Design 9849

**First Floor:** 780 square feet
**Second Floor:** 915 square feet
**Total:** 1,695 square feet

MASTER SUITE
14'-10" x 15'-8"

M. BATH

W.I.C.

LAUN.
6'-0" x 5'-8"

W.I.C.

BEDROOM No.2
11'-10" x 9'-6"

BEDROOM No.3
10'-0" x 12'-10"

BATH

W.I.C.

DESIGN BY
Design Traditions

DECK

BREAKFAST
10'-0" x 7'-0"

GREAT ROOM
18'-6" x 15'-6"

KITCHEN
12'-0" x 10'-10"

UP

DN

FOYER

DINING
9'-6" x 12'-10"

PDR

TWO-CAR GARAGE
20'-0" x 21'-0"

Width 41'
Depth 41'

Copyright 1992 Stephen S. Fuller, Inc.

MASTER SUITE
14'-10" x 15'-8"

M. BATH

W.I.C.

LAUN.
6'-0" x 5'-8"

BEDROOM No.3
10'-0" x 12'-10"

BEDROOM NO. 2
12'-0" X 14'-0"

BATH

Width 41'
Depth 40'-6"

## Design 9902

**First Floor:** 830 square feet
**Second Floor:** 1,060 square feet
**Total:** 1,890 square feet

DECK

BREAKFAST
10'-0" x 7'-0"

GREAT ROOM
18'-6" x 15'-6"

KITCHEN
12'-0" x 10'-10"

UP

DN

FOYER

DINING
9'-6" x 12'-10"

POWDER

TWO-CAR GARAGE
20'-0" x 21'-0"

PORCH

The pleasing character of this house does not stop with its charming facade. The foyer opens into a large formal dining room on the right and, directly ahead, into the great room. Open planning in the living areas invites formal as well as informal gatherings. The well-equipped kitchen shares natural light from the bay-windowed breakfast nook and opens to the great room, sharing its view of the rear yard. Stairs lead from the great room to the second floor—and here's where you'll find the laundry! The master suite spares none of the popular amenities: full bath with double vanity, shower and tub, walk-in closet. Bedrooms 2 and 3 share a full bath. This home is designed with a basement foundation.

**D**ouble columns provide special interest for this lovely traditional home. A separate entry into the den creates a perfect setup for use as an office or home-operated business. The foyer leads to a central hall connecting all areas of the house. The kitchen with central cooktop island opens to the formal dining room which offers access to the rear yard. The dining area opens to a spacious great room with 1½-story ceiling, warming fireplace with extended hearth, built-in bookshelves and generous views of the rear property. A split bedroom plan offers privacy for the first-floor master suite, with vaulted ceiling, whirlpool spa, twin lavatories and walk-in closet. Upstairs, a balcony hall connects two family bedrooms—or make one a study—which share a full bath.

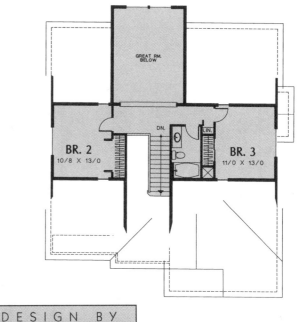

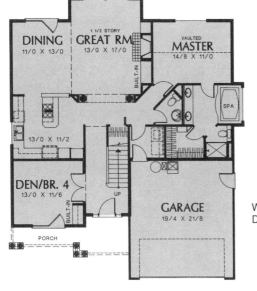

Width 44'
Depth 51'

D E S I G N   B Y

**Alan Mascord**
**Design Associates, Inc.**

## Design 9516

**First Floor:** 1,396 square feet
**Second Floor:** 523 square feet
**Total:** 1,919 square feet

## Design 9282

**First Floor:** 1,042 square feet
**Second Floor:** 803 square feet
**Total:** 1,845 square feet

At 1,845 square feet, this classic two-story home is perfect for a variety of lifestyles. Upon entry from the covered front porch, the thoughtful floor plan is immediately evident. To the right of the entry is a formal volume living room with ten-foot ceiling. Nearby is the formal dining room with a bright window. Serving the dining room and bright bayed dinette, the kitchen features a pantry, Lazy Susan and window sink. Off the breakfast area, step down into the family room with a handsome fireplace and wall of windows. Upstairs, two secondary bedrooms share a hall bath. The private master bedroom has a boxed ceiling, walk-in closet and a pampering dressing area with double vanity and whirlpool.

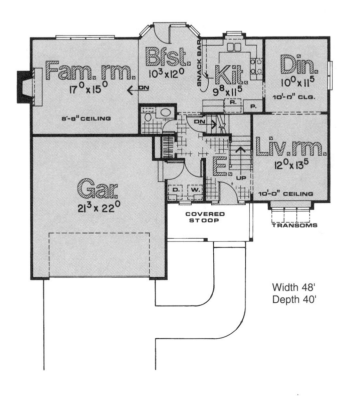

**Fam. rm.**
17⁰ x 15⁰
8'-8" CEILING

**Bfst.**
10³ x 12⁰

SNACK BAR

**Kit.**
9⁸ x 11⁵

**Din.**
10⁰ x 11⁵
10'-0" CLG.

**Liv. rm.**
12⁰ x 13⁵
10'-0" CEILING

**Gar.**
21³ x 22⁰

COVERED STOOP

TRANSOMS

DN

UP

D. W. R. P.

Width 48'
Depth 40'

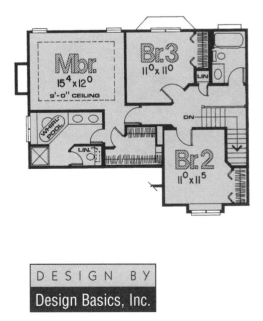

**Mbr.**
15⁴ x 12⁰
9'-0" CEILING

WHIRL POOL

LIN

**Br. 3**
11⁰ x 11⁰

LIN

DN

**Br. 2**
11⁰ x 11⁵

DESIGN BY
**Design Basics, Inc.**

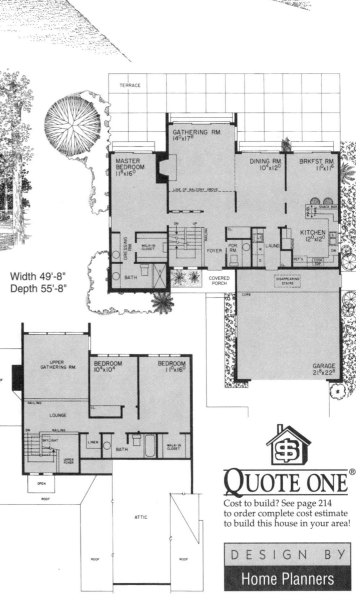

## Design 2905

**First Floor:** 1,342 square feet
**Second Floor:** 619 square feet
**Total:** 1,961 square feet

**L** **D**

All of the livability in this plan is in the back! With this sort of configuration, this home makes a perfect lakefront or beachfront home. The first-floor living areas, except the kitchen, maintain access to the rear terrace via sliding glass doors. However, the kitchen is open to the breakfast room and thus takes advantage of the view. The master bedroom delights with its private bath and walk-in closet. Two secondary bedrooms comprise the second floor. One utilizes a walk-in closet while both make use of a full hall bath. A lounge overlooks the foyer as well as the gathering room below.

Width 49'-8"
Depth 55'-8"

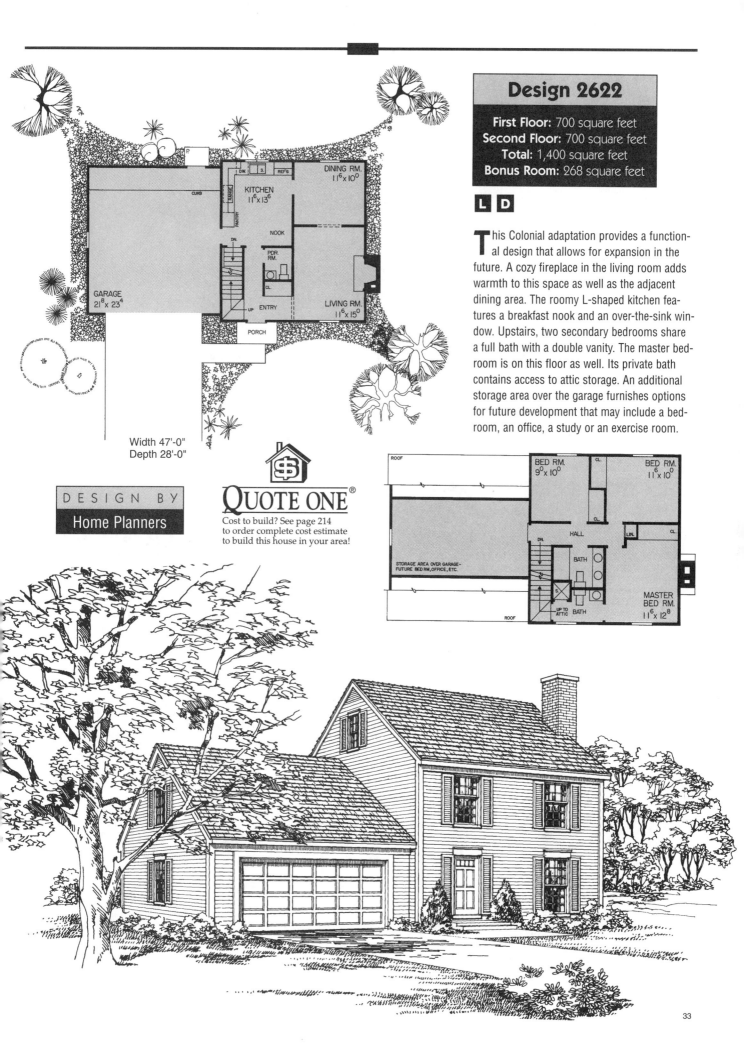

## Design 2622

**First Floor:** 700 square feet
**Second Floor:** 700 square feet
**Total:** 1,400 square feet
**Bonus Room:** 268 square feet

**L** **D**

This Colonial adaptation provides a functional design that allows for expansion in the future. A cozy fireplace in the living room adds warmth to this space as well as the adjacent dining area. The roomy L-shaped kitchen features a breakfast nook and an over-the-sink window. Upstairs, two secondary bedrooms share a full bath with a double vanity. The master bedroom is on this floor as well. Its private bath contains access to attic storage. An additional storage area over the garage furnishes options for future development that may include a bedroom, an office, a study or an exercise room.

DINING RM.
11⁶ x 10⁰

KITCHEN
11⁶ x 13⁶

NOOK

GARAGE
21⁸ x 23⁴

PDR. RM.

ENTRY

LIVING RM.
11⁶ x 15⁰

PORCH

Width 47'-0"
Depth 28'-0"

DESIGN BY
Home Planners

**QUOTE ONE®**
Cost to build? See page 214
to order complete cost estimate
to build this house in your area!

BED RM.
9⁰ x 10⁰

BED RM.
11⁶ x 10⁰

HALL

STORAGE AREA OVER GARAGE—
FUTURE BED RM, OFFICE, ETC.

BATH

LIN.

BATH

UP TO ATTIC

MASTER BED RM.
11⁶ x 12⁸

## Design 2682

**First Floor (Basic Plan):** 1,016 square feet
**First Floor (Expanded Plan):** 1,272 square feet
**Second Floor (Both Plans):** 766 square feet
**Total (Basic Plan):** 1,782 square feet
**Total (Expanded Plan):** 2,038 square feet

**L** **D**

Here is an expandable Colonial with a full measure of Cape Cod Charm. For those who wish to build the basic house, there is an abundance of low budget livability. Twin fireplaces serve the formal living room and the informal country kitchen. Note the spaciousness of both areas. A dining room and a powder room are also on the first floor of this basic plan. Upstairs are three bedrooms and two full baths.

BEDROOM 12¹⁰ x 9⁸
BEDROOM 12¹⁰ x 9⁸
ROOF
DN
LINEN
BATH
BATH
MASTER BEDROOM 11¹⁰ x 14⁰
CL
ROOF

QUOTE ONE®

Cost to build? See page 214 to order complete cost estimate to build this house in your area!

Width 33'-0"
Depth 32'-0"

DESIGN BY
Home Planners

TERRACE
DINING RM. 10⁸ x 12⁰
COUNTRY KITCHEN 20⁰ x 13⁰-15⁸
DN
PDR. RM.
BRM CL
PTRY
P.
LIVING RM. 20⁰ x 13⁰
UP
FOYER
BOOKS
PORCH

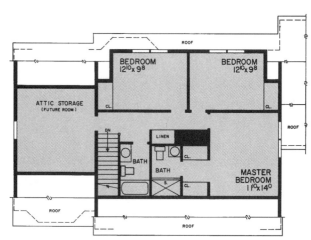

**T**his expanded version of the basic house on the opposite page is equally as reminiscent of Cape Cod. Common in the 17th Century were appendages to the main structure as family size increased or finances improved. This version provides for the addition of wings to accommodate a large study and a garage. Utilizing the alcove behind the study results in a big, covered porch. Certainly a charming design whichever version you decide to build for your family.

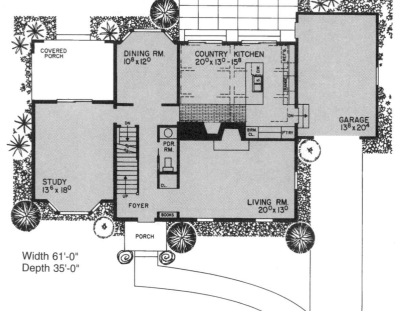

Width 61'-0"
Depth 35'-0"

## Design 2661

**First Floor:** 1,100 square feet
**Second Floor:** 808 square feet
**Total:** 1,908 square feet

**L D**

It would be difficult to find a starter or retirement home with more charm than this. Inside, it contains a very livable floor plan. An outstanding first floor centers around the huge country kitchen which includes a beam ceiling, a raised-hearth fireplace, a window seat and rear-yard access. The living room with its warming corner fireplace and private study is to the front of the plan. Upstairs are three bedrooms and two full baths. Built-in shelves and a linen closet in the upstairs hallway provide excellent storage.

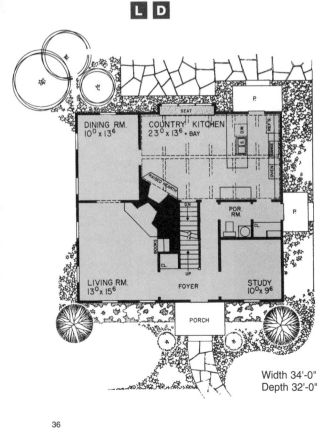

DINING RM.
10⁰ x 13⁶

COUNTRY KITCHEN
23⁰ x 13⁶ + BAY

SEAT

RAISED HEARTH

PDR. RM.

LIVING RM.
13⁰ x 15⁶

FOYER

STUDY
10⁰ x 9⁶

UP

DN

BOOKS

PORCH

ROOF

BATH

BATH

BEDROOM
12⁴ x 11⁰

LINEN

SHLVS

DN

MASTER BEDROOM
13⁰ x 15⁸

WALK-IN CLOSET

BEDROOM
11⁰ x 12⁰

CEILING CLG.

ROOF

Width 34'-0"
Depth 32'-0"

## QUOTE ONE®

Cost to build? See page 214 to order complete cost estimate to build this house in your area!

DESIGN BY
**Home Planners**

# EMPTY-NEST ESPRIT

## *Super "Sunny-Side" Homes*

**H**ere's a vibrant collection of plans, carefully selected for people who are ready to relax and enjoy life! There's no scrimping on style or luxury here. Although the square footages are conveniently modest, sumptuous master suites, split bedroom plans, handy U-shaped kitchens and sunny outdoor areas abound.

Some of our best traditional designs are here; traditional, but with a twist. With classic features such as gables, dormers, wraparound porches and verandas, they don't just look traditional, they look authentic—as if they had been family homes for generations. Some wear a country charm; some sport a spicier, more cosmopolitan appearance.

Our classic Cape Cod, Design 2563 (on the next page), delivers a contemporary floor plan, complete with a farm kitchen and a secluded master suite— all with a timeless appeal. And our bungalow, Design 3499 on page 39, captures a healthy splash of craftsman flavor with its slightly rustic exterior and charming porte cochere.

So go ahead, dream! We'd love to help create your new home and, since we've been doing this for 50 years now, we're able to help you define your vision pretty accurately. Visual appeal and design integrity are proven ingredients in all of our plans, but the most impressive quality is the way you feel when you live in them. Have you ever thought of falling in love with a home?

Photo by Laszlo Regos

This home, as shown in the photograph, may differ from the actual blueprints. For more detailed information, please check the floor plans carefully.

This charming Cape Cod will capture your heart with its warm appeal. From the large living room with fireplace and the adjacent dining room to the farm kitchen with an additional fireplace, the plan works toward livability. The first-floor laundry and walk-in pantry further aid in the efficiency of this plan. The master bedroom is located on this level for privacy and is highlighted by a luxurious bath and sliding glass doors to the rear terrace. A front study might be used as a guest bedroom or a library. Upstairs there are two bedrooms and a sitting room plus a full bath to accommodate the needs of family members. Both bedrooms have access to the attic. A three-car garage allows plenty of room for vehicles and storage space.

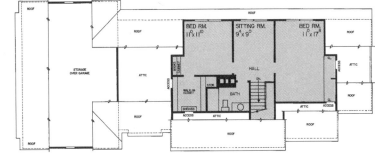

## Design 2563

**First Floor:** 1,500 square feet
**Second Floor:** 690 square feet
**Total:** 2,190 square feet

L D

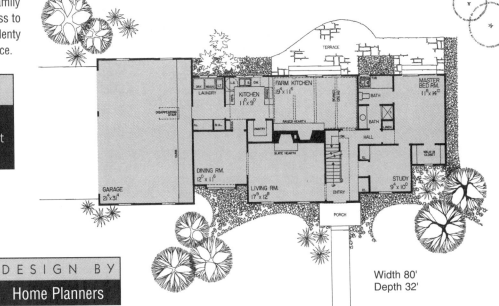

Width 80'
Depth 32'

QUOTE ONE®

Cost to build? See page 214
to order complete cost estimate
to build this house in your area!

DESIGN BY
Home Planners

## Design 3499

**First Floor:** 1,836 square feet
**Second Floor:** 600 square feet
**Total:** 2,436 square feet

If "country" is not a place but a state of mind, then you can enjoy life's simple pleasures anywhere with this stylish country charmer. Rustic rafter tails and double columns highlight the front covered porch of this slightly rugged exterior, but sophisticated amenities abound inside and out—starting with the unique porte cochere and quiet side entrance to the home. The front entry offers a grand tiled foyer which opens to all other areas of the home. To the left, a formal dining room is bathed in natural light from two sets of triple windows. This area is easily served by a well-appointed, roomy kitchen with built-in desk and snack bar, open to a sunny breakfast nook with access to the rear covered porch. A secluded master suite is replete with popular amenities: a garden tub with separate shower, knee-space vanity, dual lavatories and an adjoining study or sitting room. Upstairs, a balcony hall connects two additional bedrooms and a full bath—there's even space for a library or study area!

Width 86'-7"
Depth 54'

**DESIGN BY**
**Home Planners**

**QUOTE ONE®**
Cost to build? See page 214
to order complete cost estimate
to build this house in your area!

## Design 3651

**Square Footage:** 2,213

**L** **D**

This home's two projecting wings with low-pitched, wide, overhanging roofs provide a distinctive note. The compact, efficient floor plan assures convenient living patterns. In the kitchen, a planning desk, an island cooking counter with storage below, double ovens, a pantry, fine counter space and an opening to a handy snack bar capture attention. The open planning of the living and dining rooms provides one big, spacious area for functional family living. The master bedroom has French doors to provide outdoor living potential.

**QUOTE ONE®**

Cost to build? See page 214 to order complete cost estimate to build this house in your area!

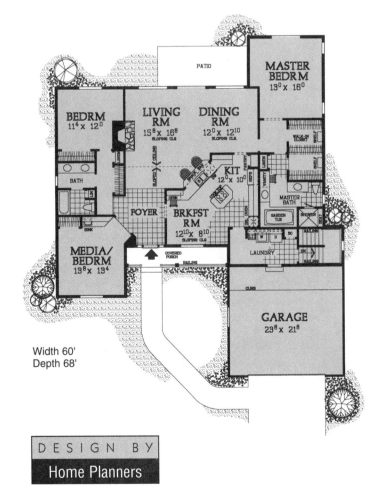

Width 60'
Depth 68'

DESIGN BY
**Home Planners**

C ountry living is the focus of this charming design. A cozy covered porch invites you into the foyer with the sleeping area on the right and the living area straight ahead. From the windowed front-facing breakfast room, enter the efficient kitchen with its corner laundry room, large pantry, snack-bar pass-through to the gathering room, and passage to the dining room. The massive gathering room and dining room feature sloped ceilings, an impressive fireplace and access to the rear terrace. Terrace access is also available from the master bedroom with its sloped ceiling and a master bath that includes a whirlpool tub, a separate shower and a separate vanity area. A study at the front of the house can also be converted into a third bedroom.

## Design 3487

**Square Footage:** 1,835

Width 71'
Depth 43'-5"

DESIGN BY
**Home Planners**

## QUOTE ONE®

Cost to build? See page 214
to order complete cost estimate
to build this house in your area!

This engaging split-bedroom plan promotes casual living both inside and out. Amenities abound starting with the columned entry and elegant foyer, which opens to a spacious living area. The formal dining room, breakfast nook and great room all share generous views to the rear property. Double French doors allow access to the veranda through the great room, complete with a fireplace and a built-in entertainment center—or create a library! The large kitchen includes a walk-in pantry and shares an eating bar with the bay-windowed breakfast nook. A secluded master suite enjoys private access to the screened veranda through lovely French doors, and offers His and Hers walk-in closets and a private bath with glass enclosed shower. Two family bedrooms—or make one a study—share a full bath and offer additional storage space.

DESIGN BY

The Sater
Design Collection

## Design 6600

**Square Footage:** 1,795

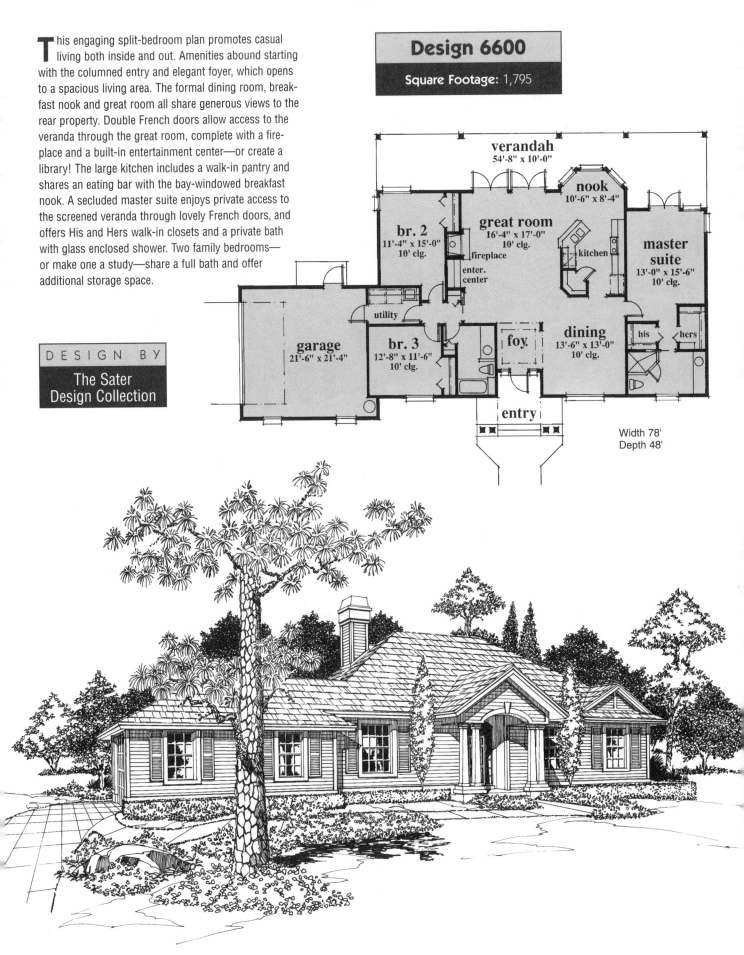

verandah
54'-8" x 10'-0"

nook
10'-6" x 8'-4"

great room
16'-4" x 17'-0"
10' clg.

kitchen

master
suite
13'-0" x 15'-6"
10' clg.

br. 2
11'-4" x 15'-0"
10' clg.

fireplace

enter.
center

utility

his        hers

garage
21'-6" x 21'-4"

br. 3
12'-8" x 11'-6"
10' clg.

foy.

dining
13'-6" x 13'-0"
10' clg.

entry

Width 78'
Depth 48'

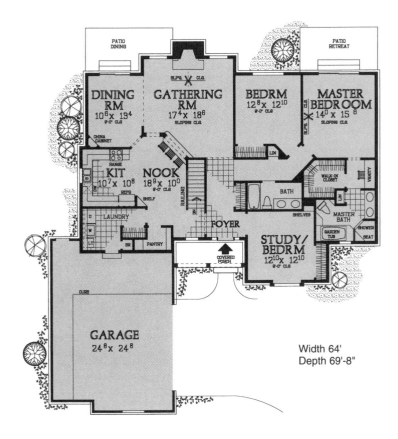

DINING
RM
10⁶ x 19⁴
9'-0" CLG.

GATHERING
RM
17⁴ x 18⁶
SLOPING CLG.

BEDRM
12⁸ x 12¹⁰
9'-0" CLG.

MASTER
BEDROOM
14⁰ x 15⁸
SLOPING CLG.

CHINA
CABINET

RANGE

KIT
10⁷ x 10⁸

REFG.

NOOK
18⁹ x 10⁰
9'-0" CLG.

SHELF

PAINTING

WALK-IN
CLOSET

LIN

VANITY

LIN

BATH

LAUNDRY

FOYER

SHELVES

MASTER
BATH

GARDEN
TUB

SHOWER

SEAT

BR

PANTRY

COVERED
PORCH

STUDY/
BEDRM
12¹⁰ x 12¹⁰
9'-0" CLG.

PATIO
DINING

PATIO
RETREAT

GARAGE
24⁸ x 24⁸

CURB

Width 64'
Depth 69'-8"

## Design 3491

**Square Footage:** 2,098

L D

This is a fine home for a young family or for empty-nesters. The versatile bedroom/study offers room for growth or a quiet haven for reading. The U-shaped kitchen includes a handy nook with a snack bar and easy accessibility to the dining room or the gathering room—perfect for entertaining. The master bedroom includes its own private outdoor retreat, a walk-in closet and an amenity-filled bathroom. An additional bedroom and a large laundry room with an adjacent, walk-in pantry complete the plan.

DESIGN BY
**Home Planners**

## Design 3466

**Square Footage:** 1,800

**L D**

**QUOTE ONE®**

Cost to build? See page 214
to order complete cost estimate
to build this house in your area!

**S**mall but inviting, this one-story ranch-style farmhouse is the perfect choice for empty-nesters—and it's loaded with amenities to please the most particular homeowner. Step into a spectacular foyer, bathed in sunlight streaming through dual clerestories, front and rear. The foyer opens to formal living areas on the left and right and leads to split sleeping quarters toward the rear of the plan. Guests and family alike will enjoy the spacious living room, complete with sloped ceiling, warming fireplace, entertainment center and decorative plant shelves. The formal dining room offers a wet bar, sloped ceiling, built-in shelves and natural light from windows to the front and rear of the plan. A sumptuous master suite boasts a warming fireplace, sloped ceiling, whirlpool bath and separate shower. A family bedroom or guest suite offers a full bath on the opposite side of the plan. The kitchen is replete with popular amenities and shares light with a sunny breakfast nook with access to the entertainment terrace.

**DESIGN BY**

**Home Planners**

Width 89'
Depth 46'-2"

MASTER BEDRM 17⁴ x 14⁰

LIVING RM 17⁰ x 15⁴

DINING RM 10⁰ x 12⁶

BEDRM 14⁴ x 12⁰

WALK-IN CLOSET

LINEN

BATH

MASTER BATH

SHOWER  GARDEN TUB

LAUNDRY

FOYER

KIT 19⁰ x 11²

BEDRM 14⁴ x 14⁴

COVERED PORCH

RAILING

PATIO

SNACK BAR

RANGE  DW  SINK

REF'G  PANTRY

GARAGE 21⁴ x 20⁴

Width 64'-8"
Depth 54'-7"

**QUOTE ONE®**

Cost to build? See page 214
to order complete cost estimate
to build this house in your area!

## Design 3652

**Square Footage:** 2,076

**L** **D**

Small, but so livable, this charming ranch home is great for starters or empty-nesters. The cozy covered porch opens to a tiled foyer and then into the huge kitchen on the right. The kitchen connects to the living room/dining room area via a snack bar. Look for a warming fireplace in the living room and a sunny patio through sliding glass doors in the dining room. Bedrooms are split with two family bedrooms and a full bath on the right and the master suite on the left. A handy laundry room connects the home to a two-car garage.

DESIGN BY

**Home Planners**

## Design 9238

**First Floor:** 1,421 square feet
**Second Floor:** 448 square feet
**Total:** 1,869 square feet

**A**lways a welcome site, the covered front porch of this home invites investigation of its delightful floor plan. Living areas to the back of the house include the great room with see-through fireplace to the bay-windowed breakfast area and hearth kitchen. A clever snack bar, a planning desk and a large corner walk-in pantry highlight this area. The formal dining room offers a built-in hutch for precious china or curiosa as well as a view to the front property through triple windows. A split bedroom plan offers privacy for the luxurious first-floor master suite, which includes a corner whirlpool bath, while two additional bedrooms and a full bath reside upstairs —a perfect plan for empty-nesters.

DESIGN BY
**Design Basics, Inc.**

**QUOTE ONE®**
Cost to build? See page 214 to order complete cost estimate to build this house in your area!

Width 52'
Depth 47'-4"

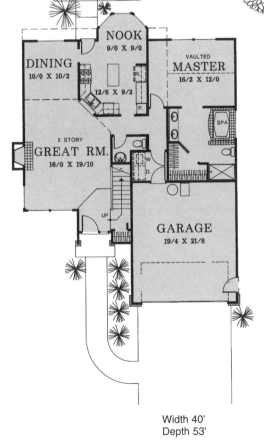

**NOOK**
9/0 X 9/0

**DINING**
10/0 X 10/2

**VAULTED MASTER**
16/2 X 12/0

12/6 X 9/2

2 STORY
**GREAT RM.**
16/0 X 19/10

SPA

UP

**GARAGE**
19/4 X 21/8

Width 40'
Depth 53'

T his split-bedroom plan offers wonderfully open living area, creating a sense of space throughout the interior. Perhaps the highlight of the floor plan is the two-story great room with fireplace and tiled hearth. A complete kitchen with food preparation island shares natural light from the bay-windowed breakfast nook and opens to a formal dining area, adjacent to the great room. The first-floor master suite boasts a vaulted ceiling, whirlpool spa, dual lavatories and walk-in closet. Upstairs are two family or guest bedrooms, which share a full bath, plus bonus space that can be developed in any way you choose.

## Design 9459

**First Floor:** 1,230 square feet
**Second Floor:** 477 square feet
**Total:** 1,707 square feet
**Bonus Room:** 195 square feet

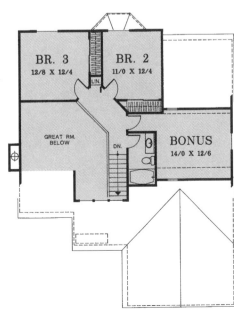

**BR. 3**
12/8 X 12/4

**BR. 2**
11/0 X 12/4

LIN.

GREAT RM.
BELOW

DN.

**BONUS**
14/0 X 12/6

DESIGN BY
**Alan Mascord
Design Associates, Inc.**

## Floor Plan

PORCH

arched window above door

(cathedral ceiling)

BED RM.
11-4 x 10-0

GREAT RM.
15-4 x 17-8

fireplace

cl

lin.

bath

BRKFST.
9-6 x 9-8

UTIL.

w

d

cl

KITCHEN
11-8 x
11-2

MASTER
BED RM.
13-4 x 13-4
(cathedral ceiling)

master
bath

walk-in
closet

lin.

stor.

GARAGE
20-0 x 20-4

BED RM.
11-4 x 11-8

cl

FOYER
5-4 x
11-8

cl

DINING
12-0 x 11-8

PORCH

Width 60'-10"
Depth 51'-6"

DESIGN BY

**Donald A. Gardner,
Architects, Inc.**

## Design 9780

**Square Footage:** 1,561

Special touches such as interior columns, a bay window and dormers add their own special brand of charm to this wonderful country home. Inside, the centrally located great room features a cathedral ceiling, a welcoming fireplace and a clerestory window that fills the room with natural light. Whether entertaining guests or gathering with the family, you'll find that the adjoining kitchen and sun-filled breakfast area combine with the great room to create an open, comfortable space. Split for privacy, the master bedroom provides a quiet getaway. For ultimate relaxation, indulge yourself in a pampering master bath that offers a double-bowl vanity, a separate shower and a whirlpool tub. Two additional bedrooms share a full bath.

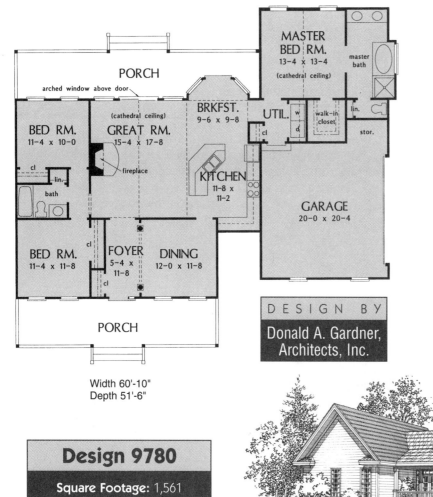

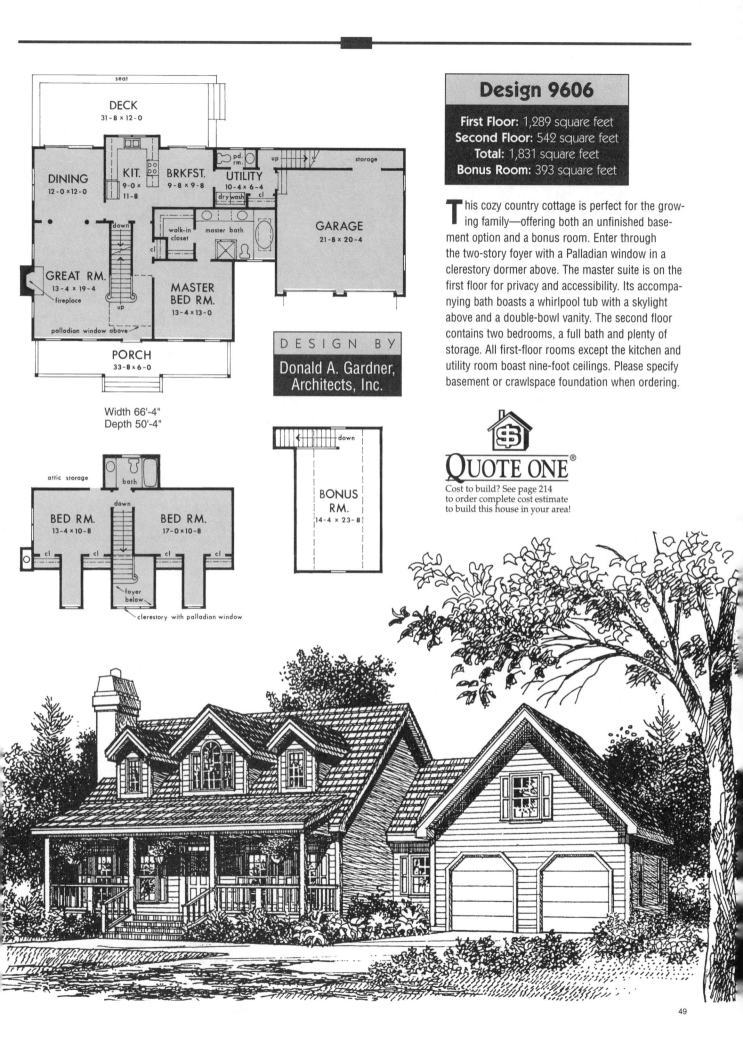

## DECK
31-8 × 12-0

seat

## DINING
12-0 ×12-0

## KIT.
9-0 × 11-8

## BRKFST.
9-8 × 9-8

## UTILITY
10-4 × 6-4

pd. rm.

up

storage

dry wash

cl

walk-in closet

master bath

cl

down

## GREAT RM.
13-4 × 19-4

fireplace

up

palladian window above

## MASTER BED RM.
13-4 × 13-0

## GARAGE
21-8 × 20-4

## PORCH
33-8 × 6-0

Width 66'-4"
Depth 50'-4"

attic storage

bath

## BED RM.
13-4 × 10-8

down

## BED RM.
17-0 × 10-8

cl    cl    cl    cl

foyer below

clerestory with palladian window

down

## BONUS RM.
14-4 × 23-8

# Design 9606

**First Floor:** 1,289 square feet
**Second Floor:** 542 square feet
**Total:** 1,831 square feet
**Bonus Room:** 393 square feet

This cozy country cottage is perfect for the growing family—offering both an unfinished basement option and a bonus room. Enter through the two-story foyer with a Palladian window in a clerestory dormer above. The master suite is on the first floor for privacy and accessibility. Its accompanying bath boasts a whirlpool tub with a skylight above and a double-bowl vanity. The second floor contains two bedrooms, a full bath and plenty of storage. All first-floor rooms except the kitchen and utility room boast nine-foot ceilings. Please specify basement or crawlspace foundation when ordering.

### DESIGN BY
Donald A. Gardner, Architects, Inc.

## QUOTE ONE®

Cost to build? See page 214 to order complete cost estimate to build this house in your area!

## Design 3682

**First Floor:** 1,093 square feet
**Second Floor:** 603 square feet
**Total:** 1,696 square feet

L D

A rustic country style combined with contemporary livability set this plan apart from the rest. Arch-topped dormer windows and a wraparound porch with a balustrade create a welcoming exterior, but the real charm begins within. A tiled foyer opens to a two-story great room with sloped ceiling, raised-hearth fireplace and views of the front property through triple windows. The tiled kitchen and windowed eating nook offer a snack bar, open to the great room, and access to the rear covered porch. An impressive master suite with a walk-in closet, garden tub and separate shower, is snugly tucked away to the side of the first-floor plan. Upstairs, two additional bedrooms and a loft/study with dormer window seat share a full bath as well as the view below to the great room.

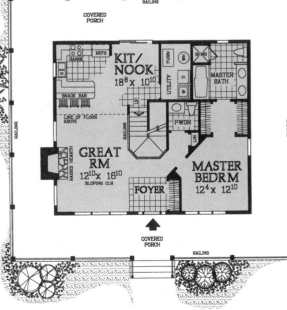

Width 46'
Depth 52'

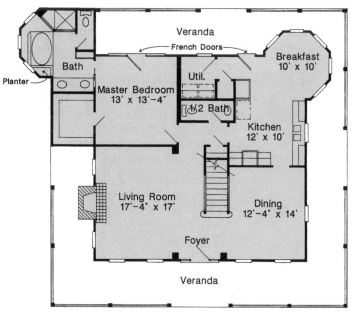

Veranda

French Doors

Bath

Breakfast
10' x 10'

Planter

Master Bedroom
13' x 13'-4"

Util.

1/2 Bath

Kitchen
12' x 10'

Living Room
17'-4" x 17'

Dining
12'-4" x 14'

Foyer

Veranda

Width 53'
Depth 45'-4"

DESIGN BY

Larry W. Garnett
& Associates, Inc.

Sitting Area
10' x 10'-4"

Bedroom 2
11'-4" x 15'-8"

Bedroom 3
12' x 14'-4"

Bath

A wraparound ve-randa and simple, uncluttered lines give this home an unassum-ing elegance that is characteristic of its farmhouse heritage.

## Design 9001

**First Floor:** 1,308 square feet
**Second Floor:** 751 square feet
**Total:** 2,059 square feet

The kitchen overlooks an octagon-shaped breakfast room with full-length windows and offers access to the veranda through a French door. The master bedroom features plenty of closet space and an elegant bath—a garden tub placed within an oversized bay window with adjoining glass-enclosed shower. Beautiful French doors lead to the rear veranda from the master bedroom. Upstairs, two bedrooms share a bath with a separate dressing area. The balcony sitting area is perfect as a playroom or study. Plans for a two-car garage are included.

**Quote One®**

Cost to build? See page 214 to order complete cost estimate to build this house in your area!

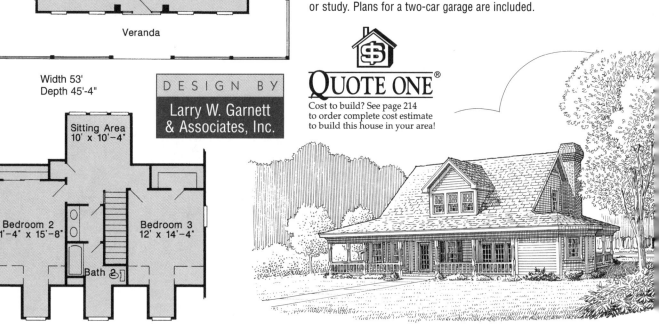

## Design 9779

**Square Footage:** 1,632

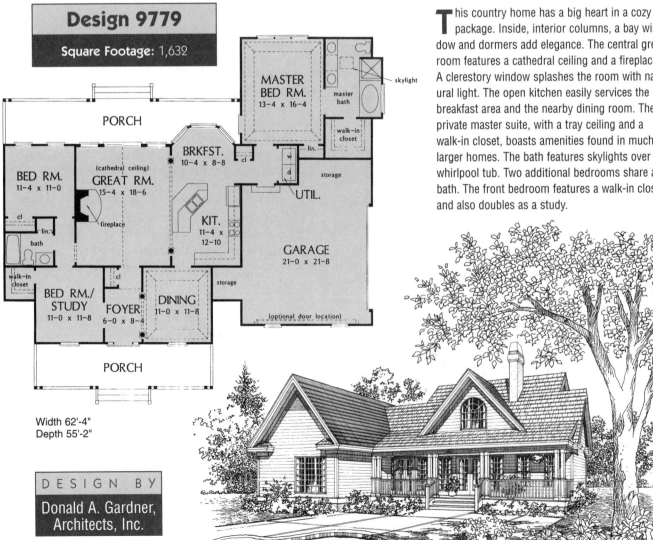

PORCH

**BED RM.**
11-4 x 11-0

cl

lin.

bath

walk-in closet

**BED RM./ STUDY**
11-0 x 11-8

**FOYER**
6-0 x 8-4

cl

**GREAT RM.**
15-4 x 18-6
(cathedral ceiling)

fireplace

**BRKFST.**
10-4 x 8-8

cl

**KIT.**
11-4 x 12-10

**DINING**
11-0 x 11-8

storage

PORCH

**MASTER BED RM.**
13-4 x 16-4

master bath

skylight

walk-in closet

lin.

w
d

**UTIL.**

storage

**GARAGE**
21-0 x 21-8

(optional door location)

Width 62'-4"
Depth 55'-2"

D E S I G N   B Y
Donald A. Gardner, Architects, Inc.

This country home has a big heart in a cozy package. Inside, interior columns, a bay window and dormers add elegance. The central great room features a cathedral ceiling and a fireplace. A clerestory window splashes the room with natural light. The open kitchen easily services the breakfast area and the nearby dining room. The private master suite, with a tray ceiling and a walk-in closet, boasts amenities found in much larger homes. The bath features skylights over the whirlpool tub. Two additional bedrooms share a bath. The front bedroom features a walk-in closet and also doubles as a study.

## Design 9747

**First Floor:** 1,335 square feet
**Second Floor:** 488 square feet
**Total:** 1,823 square feet

Elegant dormers and arch-topped windows offer a charming facade for this traditional design, with plenty of fabulous amenities to be found within. Lead guests leisurely through the foyer and central hall to a magnificent great room with vaulted ceiling and skylight, centered fireplace, decorative plant shelf and access to the rear deck. Attached to the nearby kitchen, a breakfast nook opens to a screened porch, perfect for informal dining alfresco. The well-appointed kitchen also serves the adjacent dining room for more formal occasions. A secluded main-floor master suite introduces high elegance with a cathedral ceiling and a Palladian-style window. A spacious walk-in closet, a whirlpool tub and a separate shower complete the comforts of this suite. Upstairs, a balcony hall connects two additional bedrooms which share a full bath.

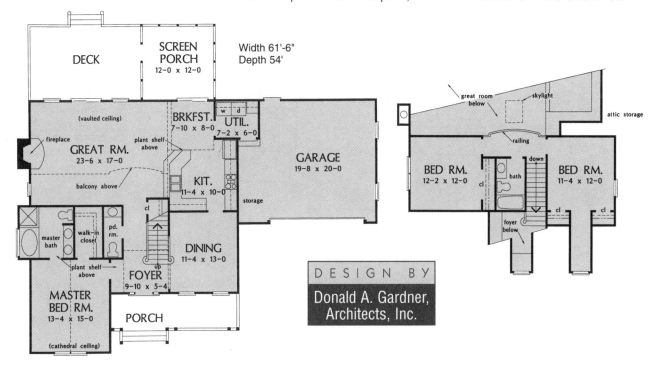

Width 61'-6"
Depth 54'

DESIGN BY

Donald A. Gardner,
Architects, Inc.

## Design 7607

**First Floor:** 1,512 square feet
**Second Floor:** 477 square feet
**Total:** 1,989 square feet

Decorative columns, multi-pane windows and a wraparound porch with a balustrade create an exceptional exterior with this country-style home, derived from a best-selling bungalow design. The planned-to-perfection interior offers many striking amenities. A grand, columned foyer opens to a spacious great room with cathedral ceiling and centered fireplace. A stylish, windowed bay fills the formal dining room with rich, natural light. The convenient island kitchen serves both formal dining area and breakfast room with access to the covered porch. A plush master suite is secluded on the first-floor, with a picture window, a walk-in closet and a windowed garden tub. The second floor offers two additional bedrooms and a full bath as well as a bonus room with skylights, perfect for hobbies and crafts.

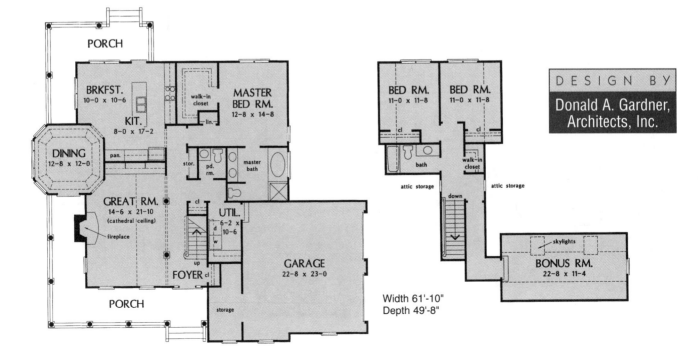

Width 61'-10"
Depth 49'-8"

DESIGN BY

Donald A. Gardner, Architects, Inc.

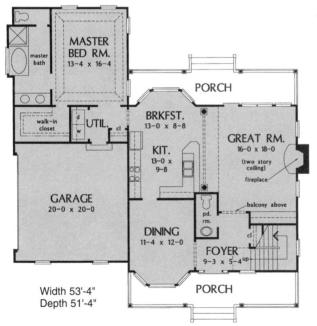

MASTER
BED RM.
13-4 x 16-4

master
bath

walk-in
closet

UTIL.

GARAGE
20-0 x 20-0

BRKFST.
13-0 x 8-8

KIT.
13-0 x
9-8

DINING
11-4 x 12-0

PORCH

GREAT RM.
16-0 x 18-0

(two story
ceiling)

fireplace

balcony above

pd.
rm.

FOYER
9-3 x 5-4 up

PORCH

Width 53'-4"
Depth 51'-4"

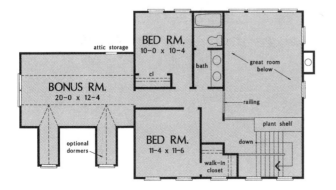

attic storage

BED RM.
10-0 x 10-4

cl

bath

great room
below

BONUS RM.
20-0 x 12-4

railing

optional
dormers

BED RM.
11-4 x 11-6

plant shelf

down

walk-in
closet

## Design 7611

**First Floor:** 1,395 square feet
**Second Floor:** 502 square feet
**Total:** 1,897 square feet

This traditional plan blends a country exterior with a stylish, entirely livable interior plan. The foyer opens to a U-shaped staircase on the right and a bay-windowed formal dining room on the left. Directly ahead is a stunning, two-story great room with centered fireplace and views to the rear property as well as access to a covered porch, perfect for warm summer evenings. A columned archway joins the great room to the kitchen and bay-windowed breakfast nook, creating an open, spacious living area. The secluded master suite enjoys a raised ceiling and a pampering bath with a windowed garden tub. Two family or guest bedrooms share a full bath on the second floor, which provides a balcony overlook to the family room below. A bonus room offers space for a hobby room or for additional storage.

DESIGN BY

Donald A. Gardner,
Architects, Inc.

Design 3600

# Design 3600

**Square Footage:** 2,258

**L**

## QUOTE ONE®

Cost to build? See page 214
to order complete cost estimate
to build this house in your area!

**DESIGN BY**
**Home Planners**

This unique one-story plan seems tailor-made for empty-nesters or for a small family. A grand, tiled foyer opens to formal and informal living areas: to the left, an elegant formal dining room with raised ceiling and bay window, and to the right, a living room with sloped ceiling and view to the front property through triple windows. Ahead, the foyer leads to an open living area: a family room with vaulted ceiling, centered fireplace with tiled hearth, and access to the rear deck. The morning room bay adjoins a roomy well-equipped kitchen with a food preparation island, and offers separate access to the wood deck. The master suite is secluded to the rear of the plan and offers a sumptuous bath with a whirlpool tub, dual lavatories, a separate shower and walk-in closet. An adjoining office/den boasts a private porch. One family bedroom or guest room with a private, full bath is positioned for privacy on the opposite side of the plan.

**MASTER SUITE** 13⁰ X 14⁴

**MORNING RM** 9² X 12⁶

**KIT** 13⁸ X 14²

**FAMILY RM** 15⁸ X 14²

**MASTER BATH**

**OFFICE/ DEN** 12⁰ X 10¹⁰

**BEDROOM** 11⁸ X 11⁰

**DINING RM** 12⁴ X 13⁰

**LIVING RM** 11¹⁰ X 14⁶

**FOYER**

**GARAGE** 26² X 19⁸

**STORAGE/ WORKSHOP**

**COVERED PORCH**

Width 68'
Depth 64'

## Quote One®

Cost to build? See page 214
to order complete cost estimate
to build this house in your area!

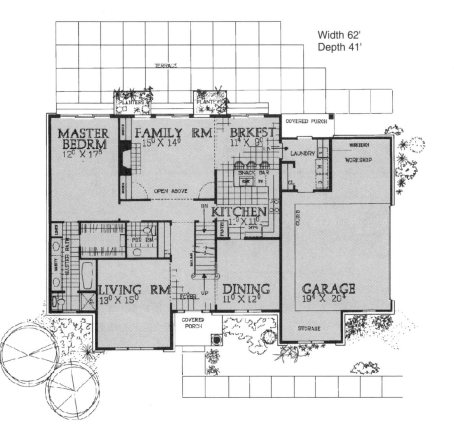

Width 62'
Depth 41'

## Design 3458

**First Floor:** 1,617 square feet
**Second Floor:** 725 square feet
**Total:** 2,342 square feet

**L** **D**

**B**rick veneer and horizontal siding blend beautifully with radial head windows and five gables to create this transitional exterior. The interior plan offers generous second-floor bedroom space for "visiting" family members and guests. Informal and formal living areas are perfectly blended in the first-floor plan, with living and dining rooms just off the foyer, and the two-story family room directly ahead, offering a dramatic view of the rear grounds. This is a comfortable area, open to the breakfast room, with built-in bookcases flanking the centered fireplace with tile hearth, and rear terrace access. In the U-shaped kitchen, a snack bar caters to on-the-run meals. The upstairs balcony hall offers an overlook to the family room below. Bonus space is available in the basement, should the development of a recreational or hobby area be desired.

**DESIGN BY**
**Home Planners**

This cozy English cottage might be found hidden away in a European garden. All the charm of gables, stonework and multi-level roof lines combine to create this home. To the left of the foyer you will see the sunlit dining room, highlighted by a dramatic tray ceiling and expansive windows with transoms. This room and the living room flow together to form one large entertainment area. In the gourmet kitchen are a work island, an oversized pantry and a bright adjoining octagonal breakfast room with a gazebo ceiling. The great room features a pass-through wet bar, a fireplace and bookcases or an entertainment center. The master suite enjoys privacy at the rear of the home. An open-rail loft above the foyer leads to additional bedrooms with walk-in closets, private vanities and a shared bath. This home is designed with a basement foundation.

## Quote One®

Cost to build? See page 214
to order complete cost estimate
to build this house in your area!

DESIGN BY
**Design Traditions**

DECK

BREAKFAST
10'-4" x 10'-4"

MASTER SITTING
10'-4" x 6'-0"

GREAT ROOM
17'-0" X 17'-0"

MASTER BEDROOM
15'-4" X 13'-0"

KITCHEN
13'-4" X 17'-0"

MASTER BATH
12'-2" X 12'-8"

DINING ROOM
12'-10" X 10'-6"

FOYER
5'-0" x 13'-6"

POWDER

LAUNDRY
6'-0" X 6'-10"

W.I.C.

LIVING ROOM
11'-4" X 10'-6"

STOOP

TWO CAR GARAGE
21'-4" X 21'-4"

Width 47'-10"
Depth 63'-10"

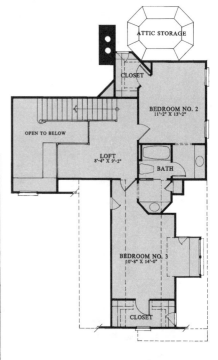

ATTIC STORAGE

CLOSET

BEDROOM NO. 2
11'-2" X 13'-2"

OPEN TO BELOW

LOFT
8'-4" X 9'-2"

BATH

BEDROOM NO. 3
10'-8" X 14'-0"

CLOSET

## Design 9813

**First Floor:** 1,724 square feet
**Second Floor:** 700 square feet
**Total:** 2,424 square feet

Copyright 1992 Stephen S. Fuller, Inc.

DECK

DN

BREAKFAST
11'-4" X 7'-4"

GREAT ROOM
14'-0" X 19'-6"

KITCHEN
11'-4" X 12'-0"

MASTER
BEDROOM
12'-6" X 16'-0"

W.I.C.

MASTER
BATH

W.I.C.

W.I.C.

UP

DN

DINING ROOM
11'-4" X 12'-6"

FOYER
5'-0" X 8'-8"

POWDER

LAUNDRY

BEDROOM NO. 3
12'-0" X 11'-0"

COAT

STOOP

BEDROOM NO. 2
12'-9" X 11'-9"

BATH

DESIGN BY
Design Traditions

Width 48'
Depth 47'-5"

## Design 9914

**Square Footage:** 1,770

**P**erfect for a sloping lot, this European one-story plan offers privacy for the sleeping quarters by placing them a few steps up from the living area. The master suite is secluded off the central hallway, partitioned by double doors which are echoed by lovely French doors to the rear deck and by doors leading to a sumptuous bath with a windowed garden tub. Secondary bedrooms or guest quarters share a full bath with a double-bowl vanity. A spacious great room with centered fireplace offers rear deck access and opens to the breakfast room with a boxed window. The well-appointed U-shaped kitchen easily serves both formal and casual eating areas. The lower level offers bonus space that may be developed for recreational use. This home is designed with a basement foundation.

QUOTE ONE®

Cost to build? See page 214
to order complete cost estimate
to build this house in your area!

## Design 2964

**First Floor:** 1,441 square feet
**Second Floor:** 621 square feet
**Total:** 2,062 square feet

Tudor houses offer their own unique exterior design features—gable roofs, simulated beam work, diamond-lite windows, muntins, panelled doors, varying roof planes and hefty cornices. This exquisite two-story home boasts a sensational first-floor master bedroom as well as generous guest quarters with a hallway balcony and lounge above. The master suite affords privacy in style with a whirlpool tub, knee-space vanity, walk-in closet and its own access to the rear terrace. The grand, two-story foyer leads to a spacious living room with sloped ceiling, warming fireplace and stunning views as well as access to the rear grounds. The formal dining area, breakfast room and U-shaped kitchen, conveniently clustered nearby, offer two additional glass doors to the rear terrace, which further enhance the bright, cheerful atmosphere of this area. Bonus space is available in the basement for development if desired.

DESIGN BY
Home Planners

Width 55'
Depth 59'-8"

QUOTE ONE®
Cost to build? See page 214
to order complete cost estimate
to build this house in your area!

Covered porches front and rear are the first signal that this is a fine example of Folk Victorian styling. Complementing the exterior is a grand plan for family living. A formal living room and attached dining room provide space for entertaining guests. The large family room with fireplace is a gathering room for everyday. Both areas have access to outdoor spaces. Four bedrooms occupy the second floor. The master suite features two lavatories, a window seat and three closets. One of the family bedrooms has its own private balcony and could be used as a study. Note the open staircase and linen storage.

DESIGN BY
Home Planners

Width 56'
Depth 44'

## Design 3385

**First Floor:** 1,096 square feet
**Second Floor:** 900 square feet
**Total:** 1,996 square feet

L D

QUOTE ONE®
Cost to build? See page 214
to order complete cost estimate
to build this house in your area!

This home, as shown in the photograph, may differ from the actual blueprints.
For more detailed information, please check the floor plans carefully.

*Photo by Bob Greenspan*

## Design 2711

**First Floor:** 975 square feet
**Second Floor:** 1,024 square feet
**Total:** 1,999 square feet

**L  D**

**QUOTE ONE®**

Cost to build? See page 214
to order complete cost estimate
to build this house in your area!

**S**leek, modern lines define this two-story
comtemporary home. Open planning in the
living areas create a spaciousness found in much
larger plans. The formal dining area and informal
eating counter, both easily served by the U-shaped
kitchen, share the cozy warmth of the centered
fireplace and generous views to the rear grounds
offered by the gathering room. Amenities abound
in the second-floor master suite with a private
balcony, walk-in closet, separate dressing area and knee-space vanity. Two
secondary bedrooms and a full bath
complete this floor, perfect for guests
or visiting relatives—or make one
room a study or hobby room.

Width 40'-4"
Depth 52'

DESIGN BY
**Home Planners**

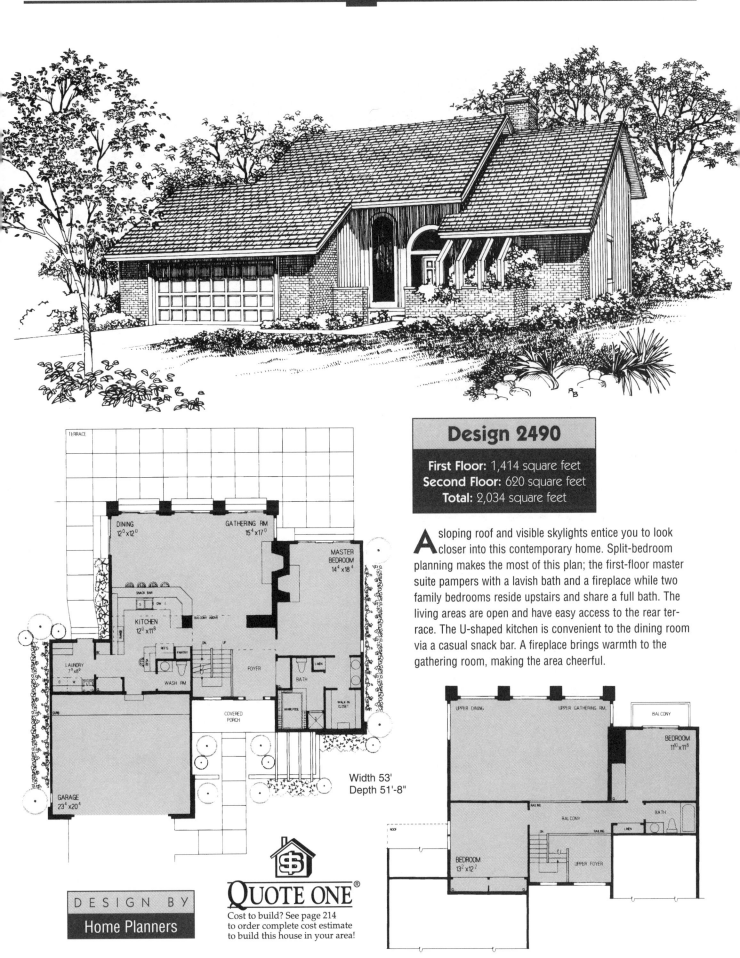

## Design 2490

**First Floor:** 1,414 square feet
**Second Floor:** 620 square feet
**Total:** 2,034 square feet

A sloping roof and visible skylights entice you to look closer into this contemporary home. Split-bedroom planning makes the most of this plan; the first-floor master suite pampers with a lavish bath and a fireplace while two family bedrooms reside upstairs and share a full bath. The living areas are open and have easy access to the rear terrace. The U-shaped kitchen is convenient to the dining room via a casual snack bar. A fireplace brings warmth to the gathering room, making the area cheerful.

Width 53'
Depth 51'-8"

DESIGN BY
Home Planners

**Quote One®**
Cost to build? See page 214
to order complete cost estimate
to build this house in your area!

Decorative columns, shutters and multi-pane windows create a cozy appeal with this traditional design. An elegant tiled entry, garnished with plant shelves, opens to a formal dining room with dropped perimeter ceiling and a bay window. Large window areas at the rear of the plan bathe the living areas in natural light, with picture windows flanking a centered fireplace in the expansive two-story great room. The nearby U-shaped kitchen, with a

snack bar, shares light from the adjoining bayed breakfast nook with views and access to the rear yard. The perfect marriage of style and comfort is created in this plush, secluded master suite with tiered 10-foot ceiling, corner whirlpool and spacious walk-in closet. Three second-floor bedrooms—or two and a study—plus a full bath and a balcony hall overlooking the great room, complete the plan.

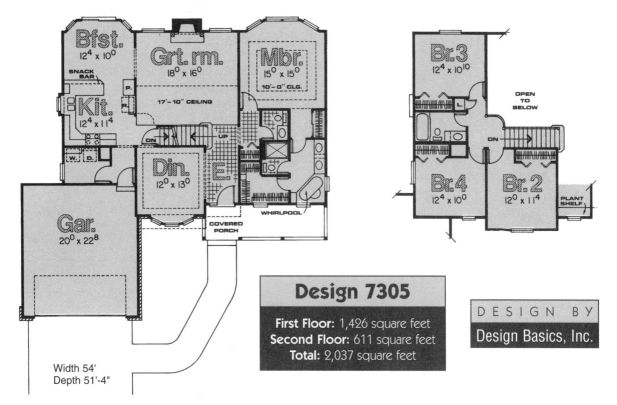

## Design 7305

**First Floor:** 1,426 square feet
**Second Floor:** 611 square feet
**Total:** 2,037 square feet

Width 54'
Depth 51'-4"

DESIGN BY
Design Basics, Inc.

# ESSENTIAL SPACE

## *Distinctive Designs For Modern Families*

Designs that offer an esthetic, even ascetic, treatment of space honor the homeowner's longing for repose and create rooms that work to make our lives easier and more pleasurable. An impromptu after-dinner gathering, a quiet evening of reading or catching up on correspondence all want space that feels cozy and private; open, but not overwhelming.

Professional couples and smaller families consider plans that offer style, versatility, and—because they usually command a broader discretionary budget—more than a hint of luxury. Whether hosting a Sunday afternoon football gathering or a formal dinner party, today's entertainers want a design that measures up to the occasion: formal dining rooms and casual breakfast nooks, private master suites and gourmet kitchens. Design 9661 (page 114) is filled with great ideas—casually elegant, this home offers plenty of natural light, good inside to outside flow, and a living area that loves a crowd as well as intimate gatherings. Our modern Prairie-style home, Design 2826 (page 117), blends traditional-style architecture with a high, wide and handsome look—it's worth a second glance.

These designs reflect simplicity in shape and space with elegance, drama and style in good measure. And though our up-to-date floor plans offer modern amenities—vaulted ceilings, lots of windows and spacious bathrooms—we know buyers don't want merely a contemporary home, they want a *timeless* home they'll love living in for years.

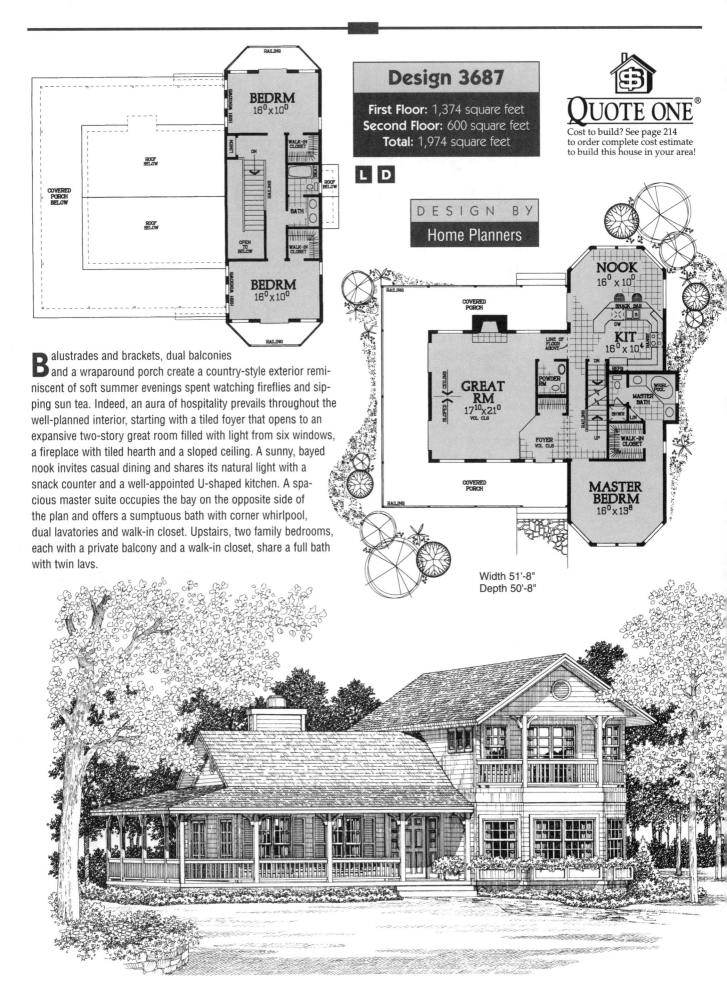

## Design 3687

**First Floor:** 1,374 square feet
**Second Floor:** 600 square feet
**Total:** 1,974 square feet

L D

DESIGN BY
**Home Planners**

### Quote One®

Cost to build? See page 214
to order complete cost estimate
to build this house in your area!

BEDRM
16⁰ x 10⁰

BEDRM
16⁰ x 10⁰

COVERED
PORCH
BELOW

ROOF
BELOW

ROOF
BELOW

WALK-IN
CLOSET

BATH

WALK-IN
CLOSET

OPEN
TO
BELOW

RAILING

NOOK
16⁰ x 10⁰

SNACK BAR

KIT
16⁰ x 10⁴

COVERED
PORCH

LINE OF
FLOOR
ABOVE

GREAT
RM
17¹⁰ x 21⁰
VOL. CLG.

POWDER
RM

MASTER
BATH

WHIRL
POOL

FOYER
VOL. CLG.

WALK-IN
CLOSET

COVERED
PORCH

MASTER
BEDRM
16⁰ x 13⁸

Width 51'-8"
Depth 50'-8"

**B**alustrades and brackets, dual balconies
and a wraparound porch create a country-style exterior reminiscent of soft summer evenings spent watching fireflies and sip-
ping sun tea. Indeed, an aura of hospitality prevails throughout the
well-planned interior, starting with a tiled foyer that opens to an
expansive two-story great room filled with light from six windows,
a fireplace with tiled hearth and a sloped ceiling. A sunny, bayed
nook invites casual dining and shares its natural light with a
snack counter and a well-appointed U-shaped kitchen. A spacious master suite occupies the bay on the opposite side of
the plan and offers a sumptuous bath with corner whirlpool,
dual lavatories and walk-in closet. Upstairs, two family bedrooms,
each with a private balcony and a walk-in closet, share a full bath
with twin lavs.

*This home, as shown in the photograph, may differ from the actual blueprints. For more detailed information, please check the floor plans carefully.*

Photo by Bob Greenspan

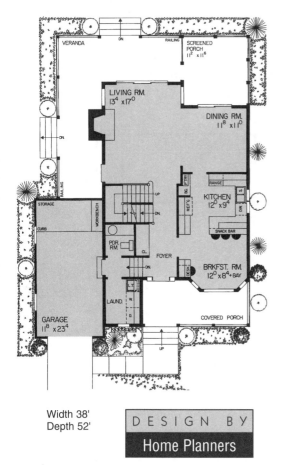

Width 38'
Depth 52'

DESIGN BY
**Home Planners**

ATTIC
26⁰ x 34⁰
(HEADROOM 21⁰ x 29⁰)

## Design 2974

**First Floor:** 911 square feet
**Second Floor:** 861 square feet
**Total:** 1,772 square feet
**Attic:** 1,131 square feet

**L**

**QUOTE ONE**®

Cost to build? See page 214 to order complete cost estimate to build this house in your area!

Victorian homes are well known for their orientation on narrow building sites. This house is 38' wide, but the livability is tremendous. From the front covered porch, the foyer directs traffic all the way to the back of the house with its open living and dining rooms. The U-shaped kitch-en conveniently services both the dining room and the front breakfast room. Both the veranda and the screened porch in the rear living area highlight the outdoor livability in this design. Three bedrooms account for the second floor; the third floor provides ample storage space.

## Design 9060

**First Floor:** 1,326 square feet
**Second Floor:** 1,086 square feet
**Total:** 2,412 square feet

The oval-glass front door of this elegant Queen Anne home opens into the foyer, which showcases the bannistered stairs. The spacious family room enjoys a bay-windowed alcove and a fireplace. French doors lead to the game room, which can easily become guest quarters with a private bath. The kitchen offers a walk-in pantry and abundant cabinet and counter space. Adjacent to the bay-windowed breakfast room is a utility area with room for a washer, a dryer, a freezer and a small counter top with cabinets above. A door from this area can provide access to the two-car, detached garage for which plans are included. Upstairs, Bedrooms 2 and 3 each feature walk-in closets, along with built-in bookcases. The master area, with its sitting alcove and special bath, is the perfect retreat.

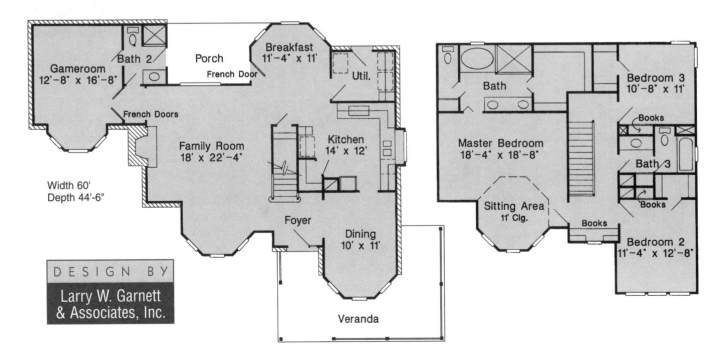

DESIGN BY
**Larry W. Garnett & Associates, Inc.**

## Design 9063

**First Floor:** 1,236 square feet
**Second Floor:** 835 square feet
**Total:** 2,071 square feet

Bedroom 3
10' x 12'-4"
10' Ceiling

Slope Ceiling

Bath

Linen

French Doors

Books

Gameroom
10' x 12'-8"

10' Ceiling

Bedroom 2
14'-4" x 12'-10"

10' Vaulted Ceiling

Leaded Glass
Transom Windows

11' Ceiling

Bath

Linen

Veranda

French Doors

Master Bedroom
14' x 15'

Dining
10' x 12'

French Door

Pantry

42" Bar

Screened
Porch
10'-8" x 15'

Cathedral Ceiling

Kitchen
10' x 10'

Living Room
14'-4" x 17'

Veranda

Width 40'-4"
Depth 62'-10"

The living area of this spectacular Queen Anne Style home features a fireplace and a bay-windowed alcove. The centrally located kitchen overlooks a dining area with full-length windows and a French door. The master bedroom features a large walk-in closet and French doors opening to the rear veranda. The master bath provides additional closet space, along with a glass-enclosed shower and an oval tub in an octagon-shaped alcove. Upstairs, French doors open into a game room with octagonal bay, which offers views of the front property. Family bedrooms include walk-in closets and raised ceilings, with a raised octagon-shaped ceiling in Bedroom 3. Plans are included for a detached two-car garage and an optional screen porch.

DESIGN BY
### Larry W. Garnett & Associates, Inc.

## QUOTE ONE®

Cost to build? See page 214
to order complete cost estimate
to build this house in your area!

## Design 3620

**First Floor:** 1,295 square feet
**Second Floor:** 600 square feet
**Total:** 1,895 square feet

DESIGN BY
**Home Planners**

This Southern country farmhouse seems to reach right out and greet you, extending a warm welcome. The octagonal entry hall is balanced by two bay windows—one belonging to the master bedroom, the other to the formal dining room. Inside, Colonial columns and pilasters provide a charming entrance to a two-story family/great room enhanced by a fireplace and three sets of French doors opening onto the rear wraparound porch. An arched opening leads to

the L-shaped country kitchen highlighted by a bay-windowed eating area with a window seat. The spacious first-floor master suite is complemented by French doors opening onto the porch and a wealth of closet space. A bay window in the master bath effectively surrounds an old fashioned claw-foot tub. The second floor holds two secondary bedrooms and a full bath. Plans for an optional indoor swimming pool/spa and detached garage are included.

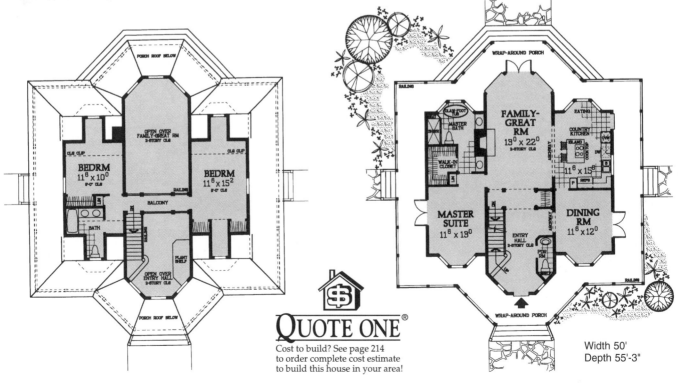

Width 50'
Depth 55'-3"

## Design 3681

**First Floor:** 1,093 square feet
**Second Floor:** 576 square feet
**Total:** 1,669 square feet

**L** **D**

Here's a great country farmhouse with a lot of contemporary appeal—Palladian and arch-topped windows make a sweet complement to the fine details of this classic wraparound porch. The generous use of windows—including two sets of triple muntin windows in the front—adds exciting visual elements to the exterior as well as plenty of natural light to the interior. An impressive tiled entry opens to a two-story great room with a raised hearth and views to the front and side grounds. The U-shaped kitchen conveniently combines with this area and offers a snack counter in addition to a casual dining nook with rear porch access. The family bedrooms reside on the main floor, while an expansive master suite with adjacent study creates a resplendent retreat upstairs, complete with a private balcony, walk-in closet and pampering bath.

Width 52'
Depth 46'

**Quote One®**

Cost to build? See page 214
to order complete cost estimate
to build this house in your area!

DESIGN BY
**Home Planners**

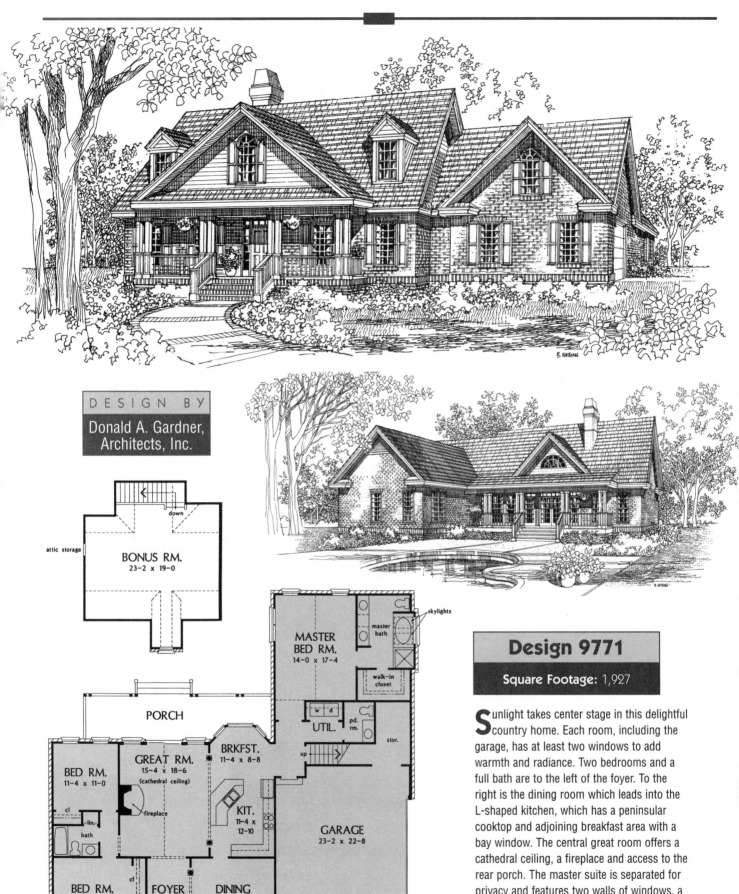

**attic storage**

**BONUS RM.**
23-2 x 19-0

down

**PORCH**

**MASTER BED RM.**
14-0 x 17-4

master bath

skylights

walk-in closet

w | d

**UTIL.**

pd. rm.

stor.

up

**BED RM.**
11-4 x 11-0

**GREAT RM.**
15-4 x 18-6
(cathedral ceiling)

fireplace

cl

lin.

bath

**BRKFST.**
11-4 x 8-8

**KIT.**
11-4 x 12-10

**GARAGE**
23-2 x 22-8

**BED RM.**
13-8 x 11-8

cl

**FOYER**
7-4 x 11-8

cl

**DINING**
14-8 x 11-8

© 1994 Donald A. Gardner Architects, Inc.

**PORCH**

Width 64'-7"
Depth 64'-2"

## Design 9771

**Square Footage:** 1,927

Sunlight takes center stage in this delightful country home. Each room, including the garage, has at least two windows to add warmth and radiance. Two bedrooms and a full bath are to the left of the foyer. To the right is the dining room which leads into the L-shaped kitchen, which has a peninsular cooktop and adjoining breakfast area with a bay window. The central great room offers a cathedral ceiling, a fireplace and access to the rear porch. The master suite is separated for privacy and features two walls of windows, a large walk-in closet and a luxurious whirlpool bath with skylights. Additional storage space is available in the garage and in the attic.

B. NATHAN

Width 70'-4"
Depth 56'-4"

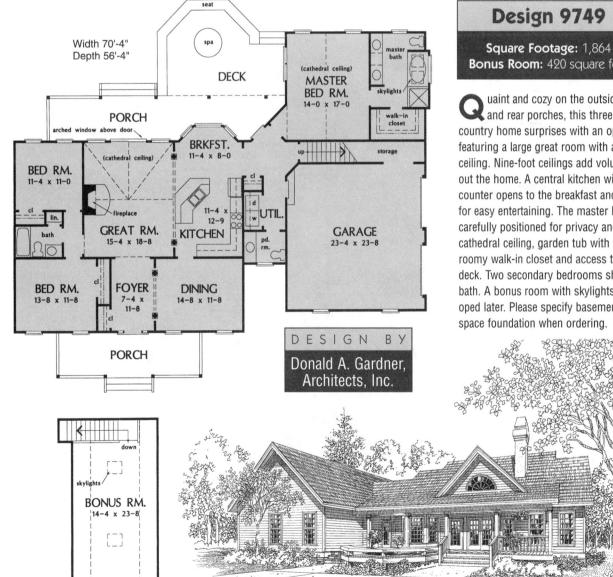

## Design 9749

**Square Footage:** 1,864
**Bonus Room:** 420 square feet

Quaint and cozy on the outside with front and rear porches, this three-bedroom country home surprises with an open floor plan featuring a large great room with a cathedral ceiling. Nine-foot ceilings add volume throughout the home. A central kitchen with an angled counter opens to the breakfast and great rooms for easy entertaining. The master bedroom is carefully positioned for privacy and offers a cathedral ceiling, garden tub with skylights, roomy walk-in closet and access to the rear deck. Two secondary bedrooms share a full hall bath. A bonus room with skylights may be developed later. Please specify basement or crawl-space foundation when ordering.

DESIGN BY
Donald A. Gardner, Architects, Inc.

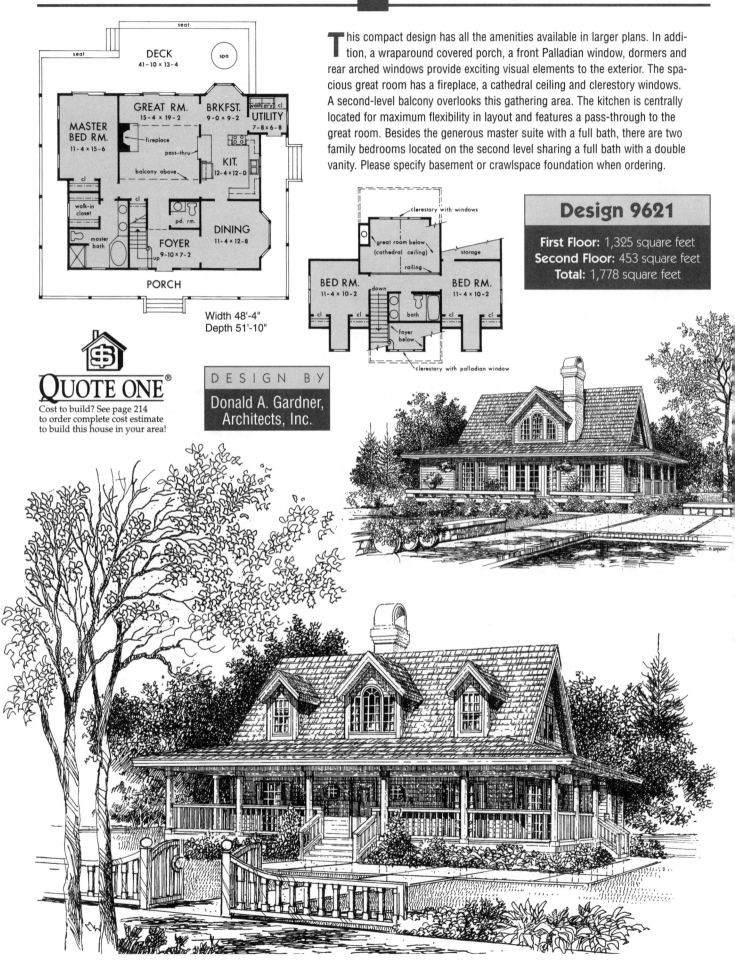

DECK
41 – 10 x 13 – 4

spa

seat

seat

GREAT RM.
15 – 4 x 19 – 2

BRKFST.
9 – 0 x 9 – 2

wash dry cl

UTILITY
7 – 8 x 6 – 8

MASTER
BED RM.
11 – 4 x 15 – 6

fireplace

pass-thru

balcony above

KIT.
12 – 4 x 12 – 0

cl

walk-in
closet

cl

pd. rm.

DINING
11 – 4 x 12 – 8

master
bath

FOYER
9 – 10 x 7 – 2

up

PORCH

Width 48'-4"
Depth 51'-10"

This compact design has all the amenities available in larger plans. In addition, a wraparound covered porch, a front Palladian window, dormers and rear arched windows provide exciting visual elements to the exterior. The spacious great room has a fireplace, a cathedral ceiling and clerestory windows. A second-level balcony overlooks this gathering area. The kitchen is centrally located for maximum flexibility in layout and features a pass-through to the great room. Besides the generous master suite with a full bath, there are two family bedrooms located on the second level sharing a full bath with a double vanity. Please specify basement or crawlspace foundation when ordering.

clerestory with windows

great room below
(cathedral ceiling)

storage

railing

BED RM.
11 – 4 x 10 – 2

down

BED RM.
11 – 4 x 10 – 2

cl

cl

bath

cl

cl

foyer
below

clerestory with palladian window

## Design 9621

**First Floor:** 1,325 square feet
**Second Floor:** 453 square feet
**Total:** 1,778 square feet

QUOTE ONE®

Cost to build? See page 214
to order complete cost estimate
to build this house in your area!

DESIGN BY
Donald A. Gardner,
Architects, Inc.

*This home, as shown in the photograph, may differ from the actual blueprints. For more detailed information, please check the floor plans carefully.*

Photo by Jon Riley

## Design 9645

**First Floor:** 1,356 square feet
**Second Floor:** 542 square feet
**Total:** 1,898 square feet
**Bonus Room:** 393 square feet

The welcoming charm of this country farmhouse is expressed by its many windows and its covered, wraparound porch. A two-story entrance foyer is enhanced by a Palladian window in a clerestory dormer above to allow natural lighting. A first-floor master suite allows privacy and accessibility. The master bath includes a whirlpool tub, a shower and double-bowl vanity along with a walk-in closet. The first floor features nine-foot ceilings throughout with the exception of the kitchen area, which features an eight-foot ceiling. The second floor provides two additional bedrooms, a full bath and plenty of storage space. An unfinished basement and bonus room provide room to grow. Please specify basement or crawlspace foundation when ordering.

**BONUS RM.**
23-8 × 14-4
© 1991 Donald A. Gardner Architects, Inc.

**QUOTE ONE®**
Cost to build? See page 214
to order complete cost estimate
to build this house in your area!

Width 59'
Depth 64'

**DINING** 13-0 × 12-0
**KIT.** 10-4 × 12-0
**BRKFST.** 10-8 × 9-8
**UTIL.**
**GARAGE** 20-4 × 21-8
**DECK** 34-8 × 12-0
**GREAT RM.** 13-4 × 19-4
fireplace
**MASTER BED RM.** 13-4 × 13-0
**FOYER**
walk-in closet
master bath
pd. rm.
dry wash
storage
seat
**PORCH**

© 1991 Donald A. Gardner Architects, Inc.

**BED RM.** 13-4 × 10-8
**BED RM.** 17-0 × 10-8
attic storage
attic storage
bath
down
foyer below
clerestory with palladian window

**DESIGN BY**
**Donald A. Gardner, Architects, Inc.**

75

*Photo by Andrew D. Lautman*

*This home, as shown in the photograph, may differ from the actual blueprints. For more detailed information, please check the floor plans carefully.*

## Design 3316

**First Floor:** 1,111 square feet
**Second Floor:** 886 square feet
**Total:** 1,997 square feet

**L**

**D**on't be fooled by a small-looking exterior. This plan offers three bedrooms and plenty of living space. Notice that the screened porch leads to a rear terrace with access to the breakfast room. A living room/dining room combination adds spaciousness to the floor plan. Other welcome amenities include: boxed-bay windows in the breakfast room and dining room, fireplace in the living room, planning desk and pass-through snack bar in the kitchen, whirlpool tub in the master bath and an open two-story foyer. The thoughtfully placed flower box, outside the kitchen window above the sink, adds a homespun touch to this already comfortable design.

DESIGN BY
**Home Planners**

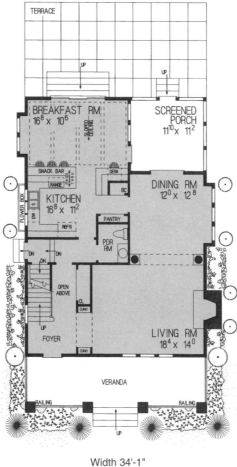

Width 34'-1"
Depth 50'

# QUOTE ONE®

Cost to build? See page 214 to order complete cost estimate to build this house in your area!

## Design 3678

**First Floor:** 1,393 square feet
**Second Floor:** 487 square feet
**Total:** 1,880 square feet

**L**

Country living is at its best with this charming Farmhouse exterior—arched windows, shutters and columned front and rear porches all say "welcome!" A classy, tiled foyer opens to the two-story dining room through columned archways. This spacious, well-lit area leads through a decorative archway to a well-appointed U-shaped kitchen. To the rear of the plan, a voluminous great room with sloped ceiling offers views of the rear grounds as well as covered patio access. A centered fireplace with a raised hearth lends a warm glow to this area, making it a comfortable place for family and friends to gather. Two family bedrooms share a private full bath, with an entrance from each room, while the central hallway offers a powder room for guests. A scrupulously designed second floor master suite provides a windowed garden tub, compartmented toilet, walk-in closet and decorative plant shelves—then adds a little more with a sloped ceiling and access to attic storage.

### Quote One®

Cost to build? See page 214 to order complete cost estimate to build this house in your area!

Width 52'
Depth 49'

DESIGN BY
**Home Planners**

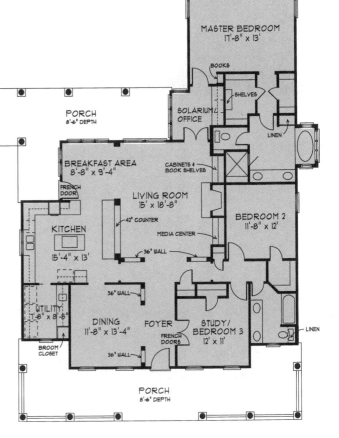

This is not just an average farmhouse plan. It was designed to delight and cater to those looking for special details. The full front porch greets all comers and leads to a center-hall foyer. On the left is a formal dining room accented by half-walls. On the right is a study or bedroom that is accessed through French doors. The main living area has a fireplace, built in bookshelves and cabinets and a media center. It is open to the breakfast area and island kitchen. The master suite features a small solarium/office. A pampering bath containing two large walk-in closets, a bumped-out tub, a shower and dual vanities enhance the master suite. An additional family bedroom also has a walk-in closet. The two-car garage can be reached via the rear covered porch.

**Design 8997**

**Square Footage:** 2,077

Width 50'-4"
Depth 69'-10"

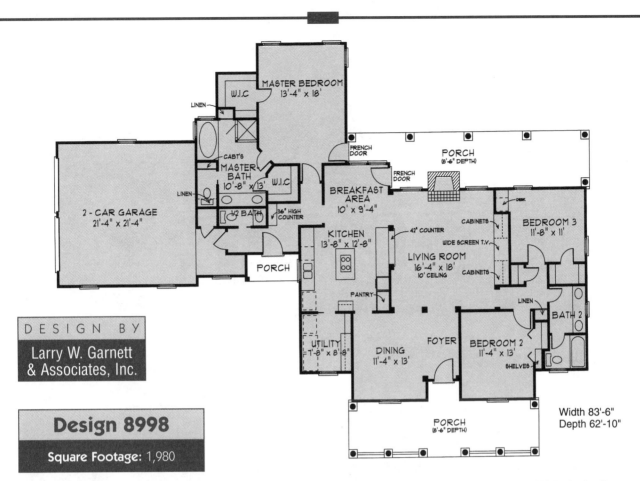

MASTER BEDROOM
13'-4" x 18'

W.I.C

LINEN

MASTER
BATH
10'-8" x 13'

CABT'S

W.I.C

2 - CAR GARAGE
21'-4" x 21'-4"

LINEN

1/2 BATH

36" HIGH
COUNTER

PORCH

FRENCH
DOOR

PORCH
(8'-6" DEPTH)

FRENCH
DOOR

BREAKFAST
AREA
10' x 9'-4"

KITCHEN
13'-8" x 12'-8"

42" COUNTER

DESK

CABINETS

BEDROOM 3
11'-8" x 11'

WIDE SCREEN T.V.

LIVING ROOM
16'-4" x 18'
10' CEILING

CABINETS

PANTRY

LINEN

BATH 2

UTILITY
7'-8" x 8'-8"

DINING
11'-4" x 13'

FOYER

BEDROOM 2
11'-4" x 13'

SHELVES

PORCH
(8'-6" DEPTH)

Width 83'-6"
Depth 62'-10"

## DESIGN BY
### Larry W. Garnett & Associates, Inc.

## Design 8998

**Square Footage:** 1,980

Encompassing just one floor, this farmhouse plan provides excellent livability. From the large covered porch, the foyer opens to a dining room on the left and a center living room with space for a wide-screen TV flanked by cabinets and a fireplace with a scenic view on each side. The large kitchen sports an island cooktop and easy accessibility to the rear breakfast area, the utility room, and the dining room. While the family bedrooms reside on the right side of the plan and share a full bath with twin vanities, the master bedroom takes advantage of its secluded rear location. It features twin walk-in closets and vanities, a windowed corner tub, a separate shower and private access to the rear covered porch.

## Design 3461

**First Floor:** 1,391 square feet
**Second Floor:** 611 square feet
**Total:** 2,002 square feet

**L**

**M**untin windows, shutters and flower boxes add exterior appeal to this well-designed family farmhouse. The high ceiling, open staircase and wide, columned opening to the living room all lend themselves to an impressive entry foyer. In the living room, a long expanse of windows and two, long blank walls for effective furniture placement set the pace. Informal living takes off in the open kitchen and family room. An island cooktop will be a favorite feature, as will the fireplace. On the way to the garage, with its workshop area, is the laundry room and its handy closet. Sleeping accommodations are defined by the master bedroom where a bay window provides a perfect sitting nook. The master bath has a large, walk-in closet, a vanity, twin lavatories, a stall shower and a whirlpool tub. Three family bedrooms reside upstairs.

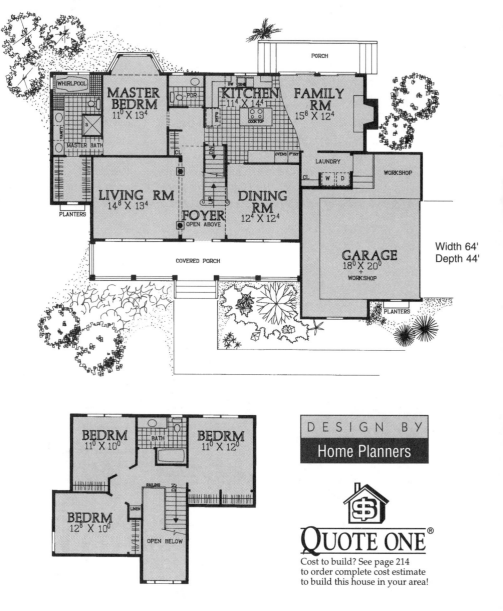

Width 64'
Depth 44'

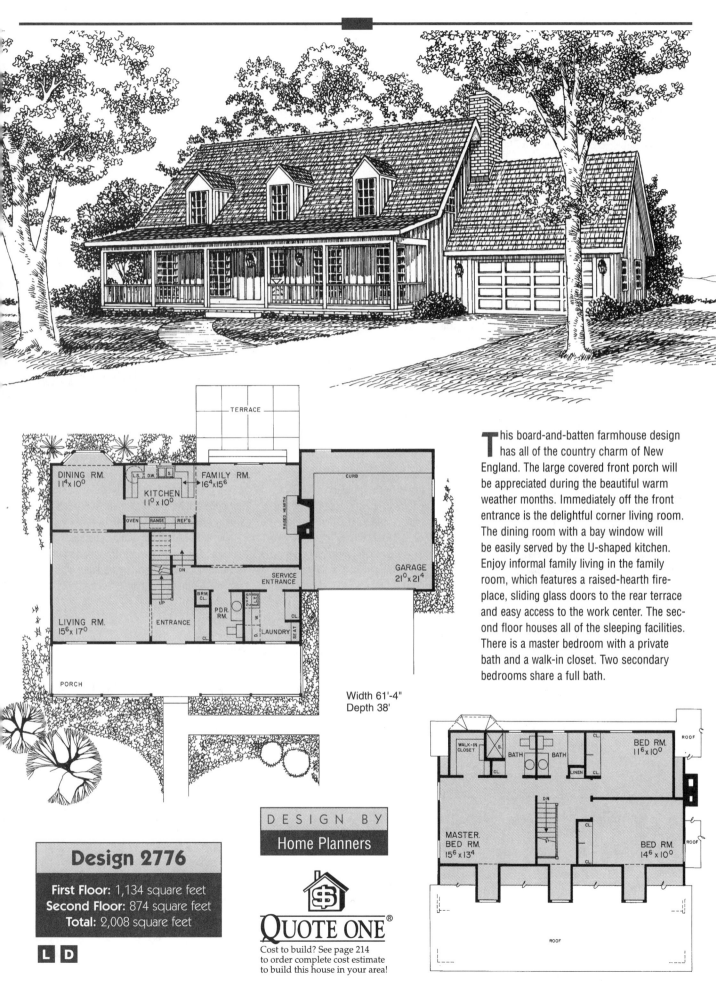

TERRACE

DINING RM.
11⁴x10⁰

KITCHEN
11⁰x10⁰

FAMILY RM.
16⁴x15⁶

OVEN  RANGE  REF'G

CURB

GARAGE
21⁰x21⁴

LIVING RM.
15⁶x17⁰

ENTRANCE

SERVICE
ENTRANCE

BRM. CL.

PDR. RM.

LAUNDRY

PORCH

Width 61'-4"
Depth 38'

This board-and-batten farmhouse design has all of the country charm of New England. The large covered front porch will be appreciated during the beautiful warm weather months. Immediately off the front entrance is the delightful corner living room. The dining room with a bay window will be easily served by the U-shaped kitchen. Enjoy informal family living in the family room, which features a raised-hearth fireplace, sliding glass doors to the rear terrace and easy access to the work center. The second floor houses all of the sleeping facilities. There is a master bedroom with a private bath and a walk-in closet. Two secondary bedrooms share a full bath.

WALK-IN CLOSET

BATH  BATH

LINEN

BED RM.
11⁶x10⁰

ROOF

MASTER.
BED RM.
15⁶x13⁴

BED RM.
14⁶x10⁰

ROOF

ROOF

**Design 2776**

**First Floor:** 1,134 square feet
**Second Floor:** 874 square feet
**Total:** 2,008 square feet

L  D

DESIGN BY
Home Planners

QUOTE ONE®
Cost to build? See page 214
to order complete cost estimate
to build this house in your area!

## Design/8993

**First Floor:** 1,731 square feet
**Second Floor:** 758 square feet
**Total:** 2,489 square feet

For the country-home enthusiast that prefers split-bedroom planning, this farmhouse dominates its class. A large Palladian window on the front lights up the central foyer. A formal dining room, defined by columns, is just to the right and connects to an island kitchen. The living room with its fireplace, and a breakfast room with porch access complete the livability. Located on the first floor for privacy, the master suite provides the ultimate in relaxation. The master bath contains an oversize walk-in closet, a skylit bath and a separate shower. Family bedrooms are found on the second floor. One features a private bath while the other two share a full bath.

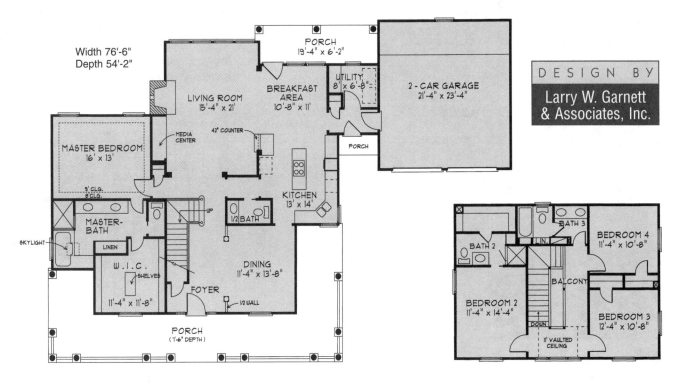

Width 76'-6"
Depth 54'-2"

PORCH
19'-4" x 6'-2"

LIVING ROOM
15'-4" x 21'

BREAKFAST AREA
10'-8" x 11'

UTILITY
8' x 6'-8"

2 - CAR GARAGE
21'-4" x 23'-4"

MEDIA CENTER

42" COUNTER

PORCH

MASTER BEDROOM
16' x 13'

9' CLG.
8' CLG.

KITCHEN
13' x 14'

DESIGN BY
Larry W. Garnett
& Associates, Inc.

SKYLIGHT

MASTER-BATH

LINEN

1/2 BATH

W. I. C.
11'-4" x 11'-8"

SHELVES

FOYER

1/2 WALL

DINING
11'-4" x 13'-8"

PORCH
(7'-6" DEPTH)

BATH 3

BATH 2

BEDROOM 4
11'-4" x 10'-8"

LIN.

BALCONY

BEDROOM 2
11'-4" x 14'-4"

DOWN

11' VAULTED CEILING

BEDROOM 3
12'-4" x 10'-8"

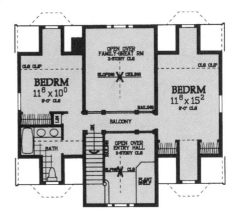

**T**here's nothing that tops gracious Southern hospitality—unless it's offered Southern farmhouse style! The entry hall opens through an archway on the right to a formal dining room. Nearby, the efficient country kitchen shares space with a bay-windowed eating area. The two-story family/great room is warmed by a fireplace in the winter and open to outdoor country comfort in the summer via double French doors. The first floor master suite offers room to kick off your shoes and curl up with a good book by the bay window or access the porch through French doors. An abundance of closet space precedes the amenity-filled master bath. The second floor holds two family bedrooms that share a full bath. Plans for an optional indoor swimming pool/spa and detached garage are included.

## Design 3619

**First Floor:** 1,171 square feet
**Second Floor:** 600 square feet
**Total:** 1,771 square feet

**L** **D**

Width 50'
Depth 44'

The exterior of this three-bedroom country-style home is enhanced by its many gables, arched windows and wrap-around porch. A large great room with an impressive fireplace leads to both the dining room and screened porch. Sized for entertaining, the deck wraps to provide room for a spa and outdoor dining space adjacent to the dining room and the informal breakfast area. An open kitchen offers a country-kitchen atmosphere. The second-level master suite has two walk-in closets and an impressive bath enhanced with a bumped-out tub. Two family bedrooms share a full bath and plenty of storage. Bonus space over the garage can be developed for future use.

DESIGN BY

**Donald A. Gardner,
Architects, Inc.**

SCREENED PORCH
13-0 × 11-0

DECK

spa

DINING
12-0 × 12-4

KITCHEN
11-4 × 11-4

DECK

fireplace

storage

BRKFST.
11-4 × 8-4

up

balcony above

GREAT RM.
13-0 × 22-4

FOYER

UTILITY
9-0 × 7-4

cl

pd. rm.

PORCH

storage

GARAGE
20-8 × 24-0

Width 53'-8"
Depth 67'-8"

master bath

BED RM.
11-0 × 12-4

BED RM.
10-0 × 12-4

closet

closet

cl

walk-in closet

MASTER BED RM.
13-0 × 14-4

down

sto.

storage

balcony

foyer below

bath

sto.

BONUS RM.
12-4 × 24-0

**Design 9662**

**First Floor:** 1,025 square feet
**Second Floor:** 911 square feet
**Total:** 1,936 square feet

QUOTE ONE®

Cost to build? See page 214
to order complete cost estimate
to build this house in your area!

84

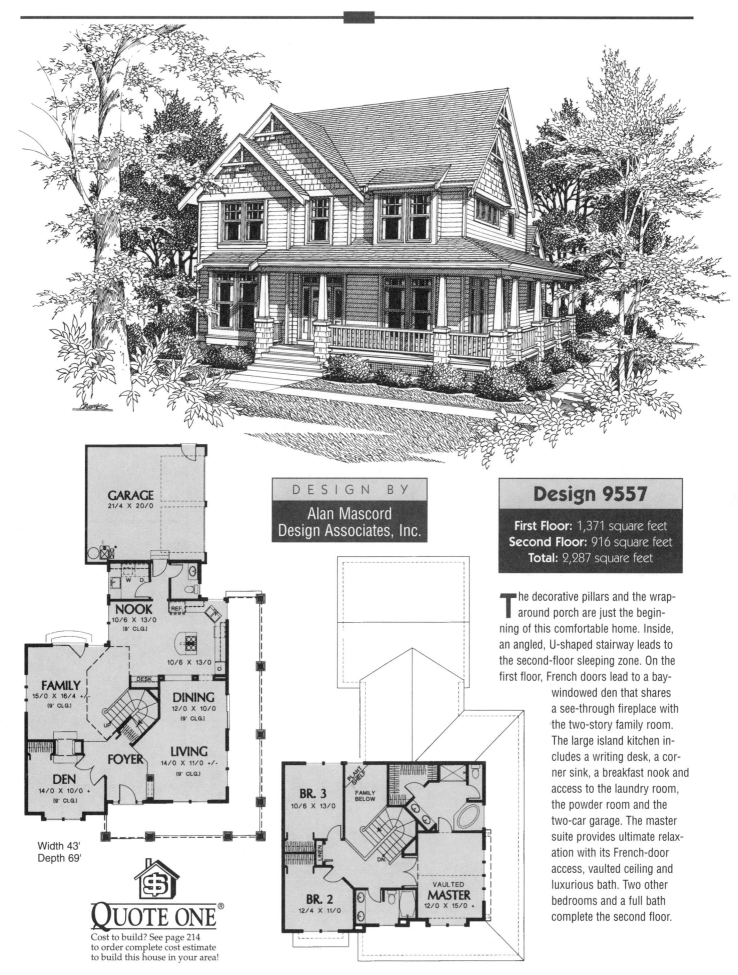

**GARAGE**
21/4 X 20/0

W. D.

**NOOK**
10/6 X 13/0
[9' CLG.]

REF.

10/6 X 13/0

DESK

**FAMILY**
15/0 X 16/4 +/-
[9' CLG.]

**DINING**
12/0 X 10/0
[9' CLG.]

UP

**FOYER**

**LIVING**
14/0 X 11/0 +/-
[9' CLG.]

**DEN**
14/0 X 10/0 +
[9' CLG.]

Width 43'
Depth 69'

**QUOTE ONE®**

Cost to build? See page 214
to order complete cost estimate
to build this house in your area!

PLANT SHELF

**BR. 3**
10/6 X 13/0

FAMILY BELOW

LINEN

DN

**BR. 2**
12/4 X 11/0

**VAULTED MASTER**
12/0 X 15/0 +

D E S I G N   B Y

**Alan Mascord
Design Associates, Inc.**

## Design 9557

**First Floor:** 1,371 square feet
**Second Floor:** 916 square feet
**Total:** 2,287 square feet

The decorative pillars and the wrap-around porch are just the beginning of this comfortable home. Inside, an angled, U-shaped stairway leads to the second-floor sleeping zone. On the first floor, French doors lead to a bay-windowed den that shares a see-through fireplace with the two-story family room. The large island kitchen includes a writing desk, a corner sink, a breakfast nook and access to the laundry room, the powder room and the two-car garage. The master suite provides ultimate relaxation with its French-door access, vaulted ceiling and luxurious bath. Two other bedrooms and a full bath complete the second floor.

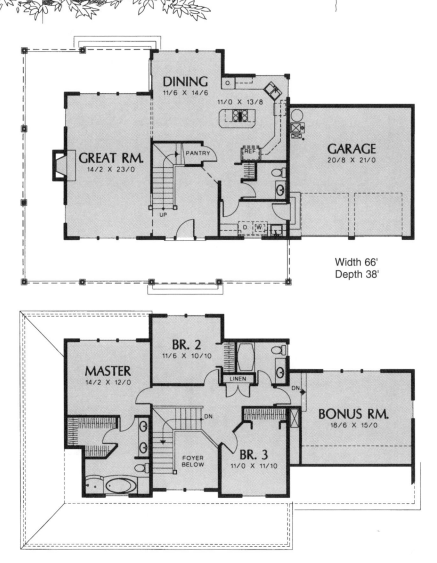

## Design 9588

**First Floor:** 1,032 square feet
**Second Floor:** 870 square feet
**Total:** 1,902 square feet
**Bonus Room:** 306 square feet

**A** wraparound covered porch and symmetrical dormers produce an inviting appearance to this farmhouse. Inside, the two-story foyer leads directly to the large great room graced by a fireplace and an abundance of windows. The U-shaped island kitchen is convenient to the sunny dining room and has a powder room nearby. The utility room offers access to the two-car garage. Upstairs, two family bedrooms share a full hall bath and have convenient access to a large bonus room. The master suite is full of amenities including a walk-in closet and a pampering bath.

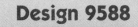

DESIGN BY

Alan Mascord
Design Associates, Inc.

Width 66'
Depth 38'

## Design 7494

**First Floor:** 1,072 square feet
**Second Floor:** 1,108 square feet
**Total:** 2,180 square feet

Three pillars support a gabled porch roof on this fine two-story Craftsman home. The foyer opens directly into a vaulted living room, which is defined from the formal dining room by graceful columns. A unique kitchen features a nearby nook and has easy access to the family room. Three bedrooms on the second floor share a full hall bath with a cozy den, while the master suite is designed to pamper. Complete with a walk-in closet, a separate shower and tub and a dual-bowled vanity, this suite is sure to please.

DESIGN BY
**Alan Mascord
Design Associates, Inc.**

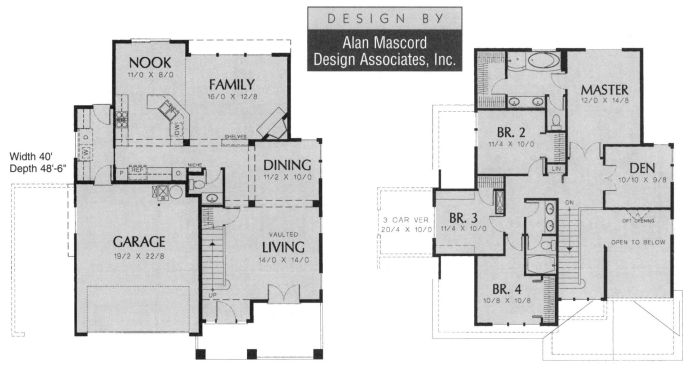

Width 40'
Depth 48'-6"

NOOK
11/0 X 8/0

FAMILY
16/0 X 12/8

DINING
11/2 X 10/0

GARAGE
19/2 X 22/8

VAULTED
LIVING
14/0 X 14/0

SHELVES

DW

NICHE

REF.

P

W D

UP

3 CAR VER.
20/4 X 10/0

MASTER
12/0 X 14/8

BR. 2
11/4 X 10/0

DEN
10/10 X 9/8

BR. 3
11/4 X 10/0

BR. 4
10/8 X 10/8

LIN

DN

OPT OPENING

OPEN TO BELOW

## Design Q220

**First Floor:** 976 square feet
**Second Floor:** 977 square feet
**Total:** 1,953 square feet

**B**ay windows accent both the dining room and living room, which are separated by a dominating masonry fireplace. The family room, which opens to the rear patio, and the breakfast area flank the galley-style kitchen. A powder room completes the first floor. An open, railed staircase ascends to the gallery, which has a window seat in the dormer window. The laundry alcove is on this floor to ease household chores. Three family bedrooms share a bath, while the master bedroom has a private bath. The bonus room over the garage provides an additional 228 square feet of space and can be a game room or a media center.

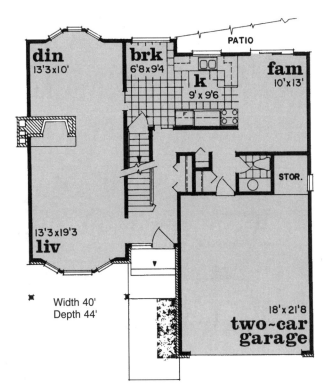

**din** 13'3x10'

**brk** 6'8x9'4

PATIO

**fam** 10'x13'

**k** 9' x 9'6

STOR.

13'3x19'3
**liv**

Width 40'
Depth 44'

18'x21'8

**two~car garage**

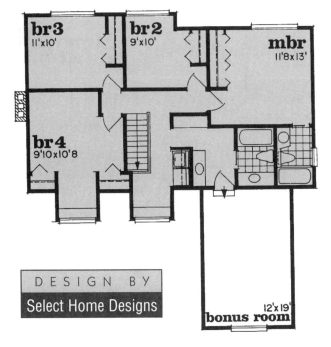

**br3** 11'x10'

**br2** 9'x10'

**mbr** 11'8x13'

**br4** 9'10x10'8

DESIGN BY
**Select Home Designs**

12'x19'
**bonus room**

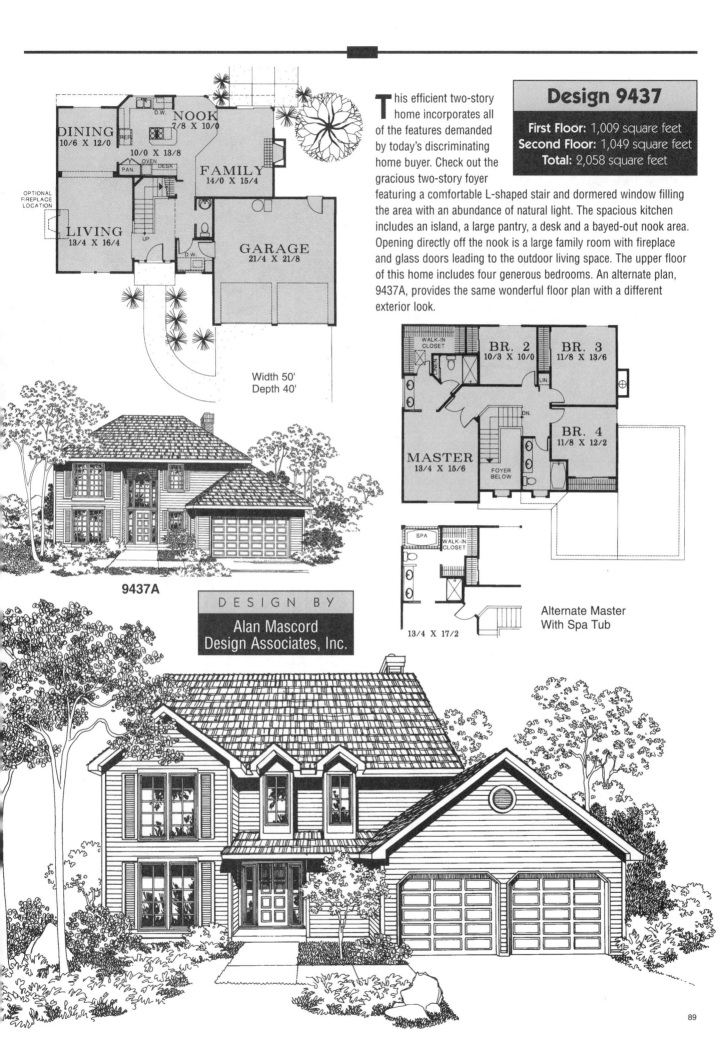

DINING
10/6 X 12/0

NOOK
7/8 X 10/0

D.W.

10/0 X 13/8

FAMILY
14/0 X 15/4

OVEN

DESK

PAN.

OPTIONAL
FIREPLACE
LOCATION

LIVING
13/4 X 16/4

UP

GARAGE
21/4 X 21/8

D.W.

Width 50'
Depth 40'

9437A

**This** efficient two-story home incorporates all of the features demanded by today's discriminating home buyer. Check out the gracious two-story foyer featuring a comfortable L-shaped stair and dormered window filling the area with an abundance of natural light. The spacious kitchen includes an island, a large pantry, a desk and a bayed-out nook area. Opening directly off the nook is a large family room with fireplace and glass doors leading to the outdoor living space. The upper floor of this home includes four generous bedrooms. An alternate plan, 9437A, provides the same wonderful floor plan with a different exterior look.

## Design 9437

**First Floor:** 1,009 square feet
**Second Floor:** 1,049 square feet
**Total:** 2,058 square feet

WALK-IN
CLOSET

LINEN

BR. 2
10/3 X 10/0

LIN.

BR. 3
11/8 X 13/6

BR. 4
11/8 X 12/2

MASTER
13/4 X 15/6

DN.

FOYER
BELOW

SPA

WALK-IN
CLOSET

13/4 X 17/2

Alternate Master
With Spa Tub

DESIGN BY
Alan Mascord
Design Associates, Inc.

## Design 3340

**Square Footage:** 1,689

**L**

A skylit covered porch extends an invitation to enjoy all seasons in comfort. The interior provides its own special appeal. Bedrooms are effectively arranged to the front of the plan, out of the traffic flow of the house. One bedroom could double nicely as a TV room or study. The adjacent master bedroom provides the ultimate in relaxation and features a large walk-in closet and a private bath. The living room/dining area features a fireplace, sliding glass doors to the skylit porch, and an open staircase with a built-in planter. The breakfast room provides a built-in desk—making it a breeze to get organized—and also accesses the rear covered porch for extended outdoor dining. An efficient U-shaped kitchen and a laundry room complete the plan.

### QUOTE ONE®

Cost to build? See page 214 to order complete cost estimate to build this house in your area!

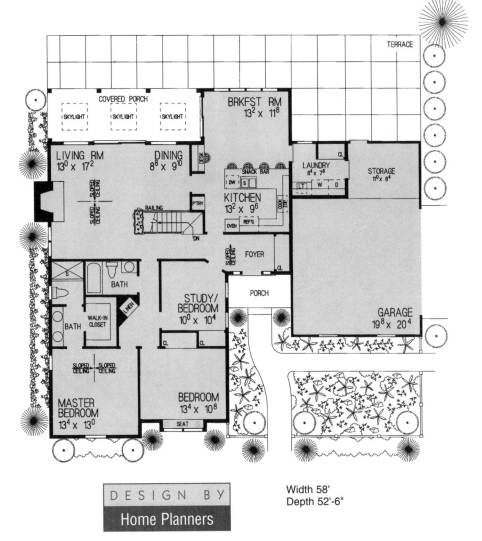

DESIGN BY

Home Planners

Width 58'
Depth 52'-6"

## Design 9619

### Square Footage: 2,021

DESIGN BY
**Donald A. Gardner, Architects, Inc.**

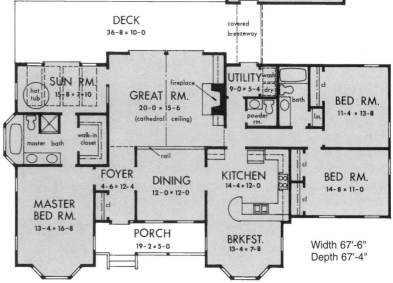

**M**ulti-pane windows, dormers, bay windows and a delightful covered porch provide a neighborly welcome into this delightful country cottage. The great room contains a fireplace, a cathedral ceiling and sliding glass doors with an arched window above to allow for natural illumination. A sunroom with a hot tub leads to an adjacent deck. This space can also be reached from the master bath. The generous master suite is filled with amenities that include a walk-in closet and a spacious bath with a double-bowl vanity, a shower and a garden tub. Two additional bedrooms are located at the other end of the house for privacy. The garage is connected to the house by a breezeway. Please specify basement or crawlspace foundation when ordering.

GARAGE
20-4 × 20-4

DECK
36-8 × 10-0

covered breezeway

SUN RM.
15-8 × 7-10

hot tub

GREAT RM.
20-0 × 15-6
(cathedral ceiling)

fireplace

UTILITY
9-0 × 5-4

wash
dry

bath

BED RM.
11-4 × 13-8

lin.

cl

powder rm.

master bath

walk-in closet

rail

FOYER
4-6 × 12-4

DINING
12-0 × 12-0

KITCHEN
14-4 × 12-0

cl

cl

BED RM.
14-8 × 11-0

cl

MASTER BED RM.
13-4 × 16-8

PORCH
19-2 × 5-0

BRKFST.
13-4 × 7-8

Width 67'-6"
Depth 67'-4"

## Design 9950

**Square Footage:** 2,095

This smart cottage offers a thoroughly modern interior design. Make a grand entrance, from the foyer through decorative archways into formal and informal living areas. A glowing fireplace with flanking built-in bookcases highlight the family room which also offers a sloped ceiling and rear deck access, and opens to a sunny bayed breakfast nook. The adjacent kitchen shares light from this area and easily serves the formal dining room to the front of the plan. A split bedroom plan affords the master suite privacy, and amenities abound here: a tiered ceiling, a view to the rear grounds, and a sumptuous bath with twin lavatories, garden tub, separate shower and large walk-in closet. Two opposing family bedrooms and a full bath complete the plan. This home is designed with a basement foundation.

DESIGN BY
**Design Traditions**

Width 65'
Depth 55'-6"

QUOTE ONE®

Cost to build? See page 214
to order complete cost estimate
to build this house in your area!

PORCH

BEDROOM/
OFFICE
10'-4" X 11'-0"

BREAKFAST
13'-4" X 9'-0"

KITCHEN
13'-4" X 10'-6"

GREAT ROOM
17'-0" X 17'-8"

BATH

LAUNDRY

DN.

TWO CAR GARAGE
20'-6" X 19'-6"

DINING ROOM
11'-4" X 12'-10"

FOYER
5'-4" X
12'-10"

PORCH

MASTER
BATH

MASTER BEDROOM
16'-4" X 13'-6"

BEDROOM NO. 2
10'-4" X 12'-0"

BATH

BEDROOM/
STUDY
11'-2" X 12'-0"

Width 61'
Depth 70'-6"

## Design 9853

**Square Footage:** 2,090

This traditional home features board-and-batten and cedar shingles in an attractively proportioned exterior. Finishing touches include a covered entrance and porch with column detailing and an arched transom, flower boxes and shuttered windows. The foyer opens to both the dining room and the great room, with French doors opening onto the porch. Through the double doors to the right of the foyer is the combination bedroom/study. A short hallway leads to a full bath and a secondary bedroom with ample closet space. The master bedroom is spacious, with walk-in closets on both sides of the entrance to the master bath. With separate vanities, a shower and a toilet, the master bath forms a private retreat at the rear of the home. Convenient to both the great room and dining room, the kitchen opens to an attractive breakfast area featuring a bay window. An additional room is remotely located off the kitchen, providing a retreat for today's at-home office or for guests. This home is designed with a basement foundation.

## Design 9088

**Square Footage:** 1,994

**T**his design offers an abundance of space and style at a budget-conscious price. A well-lit formal dining area with a ten-foot ceiling is just off the decorative foyer, which opens ahead to a grand living room designed for formal as well as informal entertaining. This area offers a centered fireplace with flanking French doors and leads to a sunny bayed nook for casual dining. An angled, peninsular counter leaves the kitchen open to the living area. Sleeping quarters define the left side of the plan. The master suite features a corner tub and a glass-enclosed shower with seat. A large utility room and storage area occupy space in the garage.

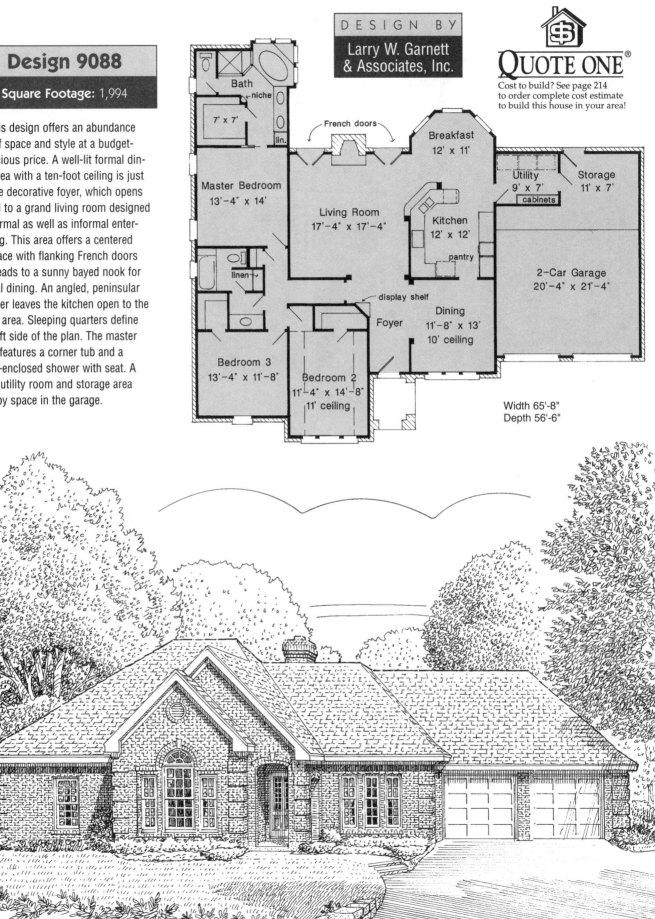

DESIGN BY
**Larry W. Garnett & Associates, Inc.**

**QUOTE ONE®**
Cost to build? See page 214 to order complete cost estimate to build this house in your area!

Bath
7' x 7'
niche
lin.

French doors

Breakfast
12' x 11'

Utility
9' x 7'
cabinets

Storage
11' x 7'

Master Bedroom
13'-4" x 14'

Living Room
17'-4" x 17'-4"

Kitchen
12' x 12'

pantry

2-Car Garage
20'-4" x 21'-4"

linen

display shelf

Foyer

Dining
11'-8" x 13'
10' ceiling

Bedroom 3
13'-4" x 11'-8"

Bedroom 2
11'-4" x 14'-8"
11' ceiling

Width 65'-8"
Depth 56'-6"

## Design 9161

**Square Footage:** 1,923

Cost to build? See page 214 to order complete cost estimate to build this house in your area!

Width 62'
Depth 57'-4"

DESIGN BY
**Larry W. Garnett & Associates, Inc.**

**A**rch-topped windows, triple gables, charming shutters and graceful rooflines lend a timeless beauty to this traditional design. A foyer and gallery with ten-foot ceilings are open to an expansive living room that includes a centered fireplace with flanking double doors to the rear covered patio. This area is open to a well-lit breakfast room with separate access to the patio. The kitchen offers a snack counter and a walk-in pantry. Entertaining couldn't be easier with the spacious formal dining room with ten-foot vaulted ceiling just a step away. The secluded master bedroom offers magnificent amenities with raised ceiling, generous views of the rear grounds and a pleasurable bath with a glass enclosed shower, spa tub, double-bowl vanity and dressing table. On the opposite side of the plan, two family bedrooms—one with a vaulted ceiling—share a full bath.

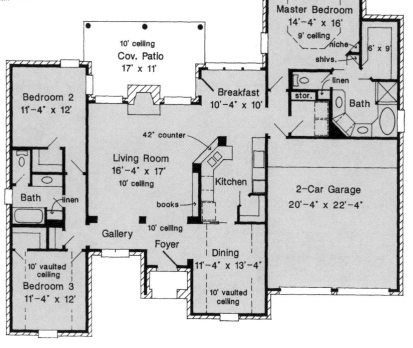

Copyright 1992 Stephen S. Fuller, Inc.

## Design 9894

**Square Footage:** 1,650

Delightfully different, this brick one-story home has everything for the active family. The foyer opens to a formal dining room accented with decorative columns, and to a great room with a warming fireplace and lovely French doors to the rear deck. The efficient kitchen has an attached, light-filled breakfast nook. A split bedroom plan offers a secluded master suite with coffered ceiling, His and Hers walk-in closets, double vanity and garden tub. Two family bedrooms, or one and a study, have separate access to a full bath on the left side of the plan. This home is designed with a basement foundation.

DESIGN BY
**Design Traditions**

DECK

BREAKFAST
11'-4" X 8'-6"

BEDROOM NO. 3
11'-6" X 11'-0"

GREAT ROOM
14'-0" X 17'-6"

KITCHEN
11'-4" X 10'-0"

MASTER BEDROOM
12'-4" X 15'-6"

BATH

HIS

FOYER
6'-6" X 6'-6"

DN.

PWDR.

MASTER BATH

BEDROOM NO. 2
11'-0" X 14'-8"

DINING ROOM
11'-4" X 10'-6"

LAUNDRY

HERS

Width 55'-6"
Depth 57'-6"

TWO-CAR GARAGE
20'-4" X 19'-4"

**Quote One®**

Cost to build? See page 214
to order complete cost estimate
to build this house in your area!

Copyright 1992 Stephen S. Fuller, Inc.

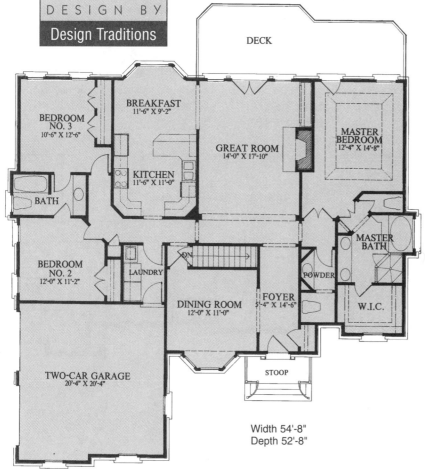

DECK

BEDROOM
NO. 3
10'-6" X 12'-6"

BREAKFAST
11'-6" X 9'-2"

GREAT ROOM
14'-0" X 17'-10"

MASTER
BEDROOM
12'-4" X 14'-8"

KITCHEN
11'-6" X 11'-0"

BATH

MASTER
BATH

BEDROOM
NO. 2
12'-0" X 11'-2"

LAUNDRY

DN

POWDER

W.I.C.

DINING ROOM
12'-0" X 11'-0"

FOYER
5'-4" X 14'-6"

TWO-CAR GARAGE
20'-4" X 20'-4"

STOOP

Width 54'-8"
Depth 52'-8"

## Design 9895

**Square Footage:** 1,850

This stately brick one-story home features a side-loading garage, which helps to maintain a beautiful facade. The elegant entry leads to a central hallway, connecting living areas and sleeping quarters, and opens to a formal dining room on the left. Plenty of natural light and views of the rear yard show off the great room, which includes a handsome fireplace and built-in bookcases. The spacious kitchen shares sunlight from the bayed breakfast nook, which opens to the great room. A splendid master suite with coffered ceiling offers private access to the rear deck as well as a pleasant bath with garden tub, glass-enclosed shower, dressing area and walk-in closet. Two secondary bedrooms to the left of the plan share a full bath. This home is designed with a basement foundation.

## Design 9840

**Square Footage:** 1,650
(without basement)

Charmingly compact, this one-story home is as beautiful as it is practical. The grace of an impressive arch over the double front door is echoed by an arched window in the formal dining room. The theme continues with columned archways that open the dining area to the great room, where lovely double doors lead to the rear deck. A handsome fireplace with extended hearth warms this area in the winter. Nearby a well-appointed kitchen with adjoining bayed breakfast nook with its own access to the rear deck offers an informal gathering space. Split bedrooms create privacy for the master suite with a splendid bath and His and Hers walk-in closets. Additional space in the basement may be developed later.

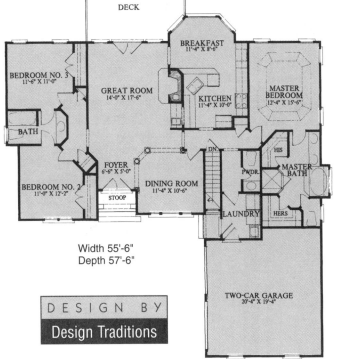

Width 55'-6"
Depth 57'-6"

DESIGN BY
**Design Traditions**

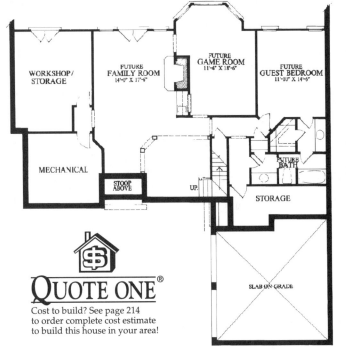

**QUOTE ONE**®
Cost to build? See page 214
to order complete cost estimate
to build this house in your area!

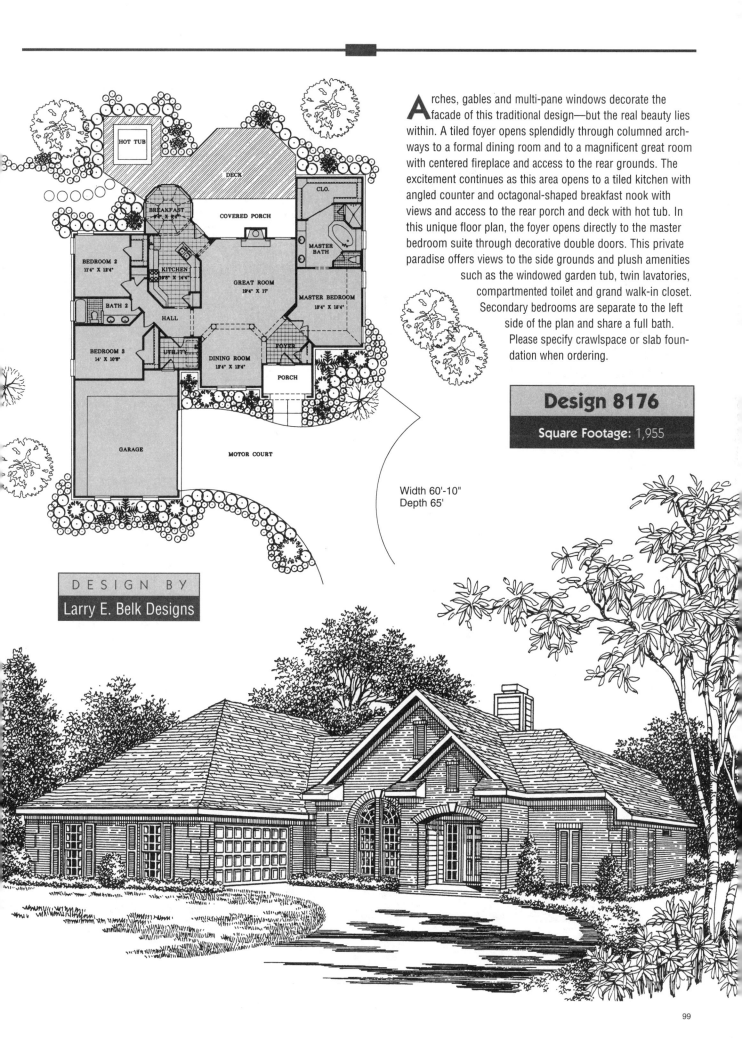

**A**rches, gables and multi-pane windows decorate the facade of this traditional design—but the real beauty lies within. A tiled foyer opens splendidly through columned archways to a formal dining room and to a magnificent great room with centered fireplace and access to the rear grounds. The excitement continues as this area opens to a tiled kitchen with angled counter and octagonal-shaped breakfast nook with views and access to the rear porch and deck with hot tub. In this unique floor plan, the foyer opens directly to the master bedroom suite through decorative double doors. This private paradise offers views to the side grounds and plush amenities such as the windowed garden tub, twin lavatories, compartmented toilet and grand walk-in closet. Secondary bedrooms are separate to the left side of the plan and share a full bath. Please specify crawlspace or slab foundation when ordering.

## Design 8176

**Square Footage:** 1,955

Width 60'-10"
Depth 65'

DESIGN BY
Larry E. Belk Designs

### Floor Plan Labels

- HOT TUB
- DECK
- BREAKFAST
- COVERED PORCH
- CLO.
- MASTER BATH
- BEDROOM 2 11'4" X 12'4"
- KITCHEN
- GREAT ROOM 18'4" X 17'
- BATH 2
- HALL
- MASTER BEDROOM 15'4" X 15'4"
- BEDROOM 3 14' X 10'8"
- UTILITY
- DINING ROOM 12'4" X 13'4"
- FOYER
- PORCH
- GARAGE
- MOTOR COURT

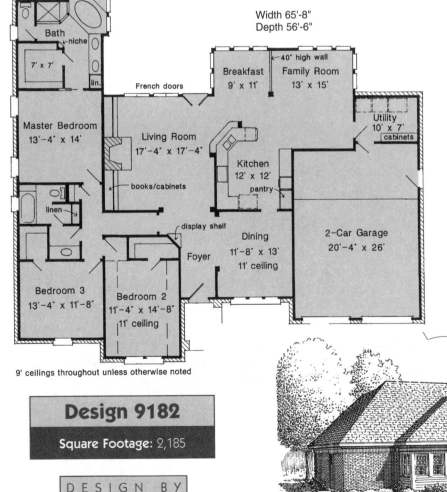

**Width 65'-8"**
**Depth 56'-6"**

Bath
7' x 7'
niche
lin.

40" high wall

Breakfast
9' x 11'

Family Room
13' x 15'

French doors

Master Bedroom
13'-4" x 14'

Living Room
17'-4" x 17'-4"

Utility
10' x 7'
cabinets

books/cabinets

Kitchen
12' x 12'

pantry

linen

display shelf

Dining
11'-8" x 13'
11' ceiling

2-Car Garage
20'-4" x 26'

Foyer

Bedroom 3
13'-4" x 11'-8"

Bedroom 2
11'-4" x 14'-8"
11' ceiling

9' ceilings throughout unless otherwise noted

## Design 9182

**Square Footage:** 2,185

### DESIGN BY

**Larry W. Garnett & Associates, Inc.**

In just over 2,000 square feet, this three-bedroom family plan offers livability to spare. The centered kitchen overlooks the living room which features built-in bookshelves and a warming fireplace for winter evenings. French doors provide natural light to the interior and access to outdoor areas. A windowed breakfast nook further brightens the living area and opens to the kitchen and to the family room over a decorative 40"-high wall. A utility room off this area offers additional storage space and direct access to the two-car garage. Clustered sleeping quarters off a central hallway include a roomy master suite with an expansive walk-in closet, a corner whirlpool spa, a glass-enclosed shower and a double-bowl vanity. Two family bedrooms each enjoy a walk-in closet.

**QUOTE ONE**®

Cost to build? See page 214
to order complete cost estimate
to build this house in your area!

## Design 8923

**Square Footage:** 2,361

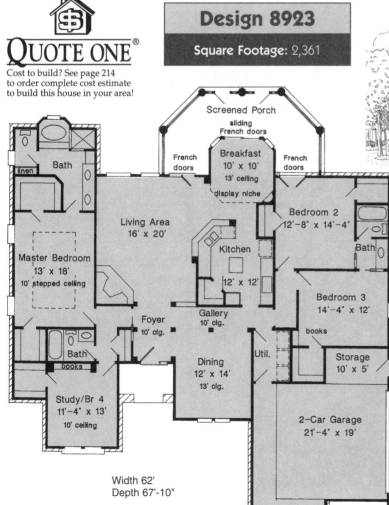

The combination of finely detailed brick and shingle siding recalls some of the distinctive architecture of the East Coast during the early part of this century. A dramatic columned foyer opens to a central gallery and to the formal dining room. The expansive living area offers a corner fireplace and access to the rear porch through lovely French doors. The bayed breakfast nook, though, is going to be the family's favorite area of the home—in the summer, fling wide open the French doors leading to the screened porch and take in the sunshine and the sounds of birds. A master suite with coffered ceiling and windowed garden tub adjoins a study or guest room with its own bath. Family bedrooms are to the right of the plan—Bedroom 2 offers private access to the screened porch through French doors.

**DESIGN BY**

**Larry W. Garnett & Associates, Inc.**

Width 62'
Depth 67'-10"

## Design 9201

**Square Footage:** 1,996

This stately brick facade conceals an interior that offers all of the essential amenities, plus a few surprises—it's a perfect plan for small, active families. The tiled entry extends to a central hallway that connects living areas and sleeping quarters. The formal living room can become a third bedroom if you choose. A magnificent great room with a fireplace and views to the rear grounds serves nicely as the main living area. A coffered ceiling, His and Hers walk-in closets and a sumptuous bath with skylights and corner whirlpool tub highlight the luxurious master suite. One family bedroom and a hall bath complete this side of the plan. The sunny, bayed breakfast nook with triple transomed windows, the convenient U-shaped kitchen and the formal dining room with built-in hutch and coffered ceiling are nicely clustered to the left of the plan. A tandem drive-through garage offers room for a third car, bicycles or even a hobby area.

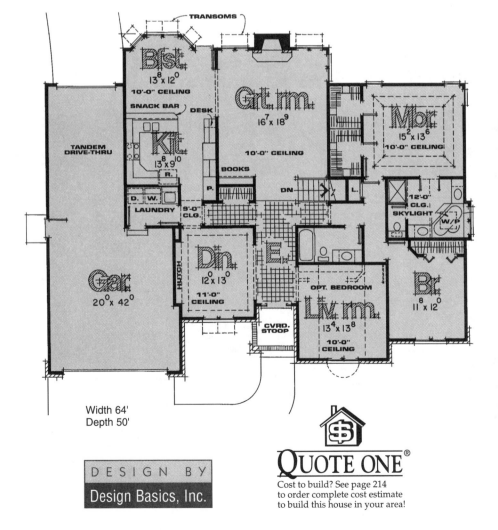

Width 64'
Depth 50'

**DESIGN BY**

**Design Basics, Inc.**

**QUOTE ONE**®

Cost to build? See page 214
to order complete cost estimate
to build this house in your area!

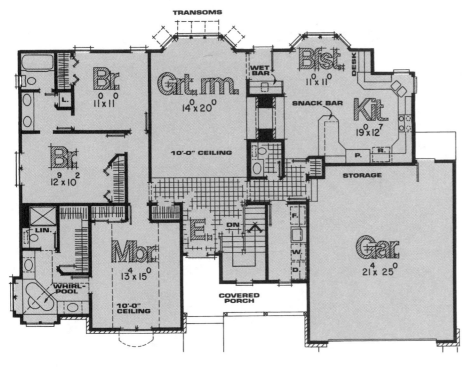

TRANSOMS

Br.
11 x 11

Grt. m.
14⁰ x 20⁰

10'-0" CEILING

WET BAR

SNACK BAR

Bfst.
11' x 11'

DESK

Kit.
19⁰ x 12⁷

P.    R.

STORAGE

Br.
12 x 10

LIN.

WHIRL-POOL

Mbr
13 x 15

10'-0" CEILING

DN

F.

W.

D.

Gar.
21⁴ x 25⁰

COVERED PORCH

Width 64'
Depth 44'

## Design 9202

**Square Footage:** 1,808

**D**iscriminating buyers will love the refined yet inviting look of this three-bedroom ranch plan. A tiled entry with ten-foot ceilings leads into the spacious great room with large bay window. An open-hearth fireplace warms both the great room and kitchen. The sleeping area features a large master suite with a dramatic arched window and a bath with whirlpool, His and Hers vanities and walk-in closet. Don't miss the storage space in the oversized garage.

DESIGN BY

Design Basics, Inc.

## Design 9884

### Square Footage: 2,120

**G**raceful arches accent this traditional facade and announce a floor plan that's just a little different than the rest. The foyer, formal dining room and an expansive family room with centered fireplace flanked by picture windows, are open to one another through columned archways. To the right of this central living area are the master suite with coffered ceiling and plush bath with dressing area, as well as a private den. On the opposite side of the living area, a superb arrangement of the island kitchen, the breakfast room with views of the side courtyard and a spectacular sun room create a casual place for family and guests to gather. Two family bedrooms and a full bath are to the rear of the plan, connected by a hall just off the sun room. This home is designed with a basement foundation.

**QUOTE ONE®**

Cost to build? See page 214
to order complete cost estimate
to build this house in your area!

DESIGN BY
**Design Traditions**

BATH

BEDROOM NO. 3
11'-6" X 11'-0"

BEDROOM NO. 2
11'-4" X 11'-0"

SUN ROOM
12'-0" X 13'-9"

MASTER BATH

W.I.C.

PORCH

MASTER BEDROOM
13'-4" X 15'-8"

BREAKFAST
10'-0" X 9'-0"

FAMILY ROOM
18'-0" X 14'-0"

LAUNDRY

KITCHEN
12'-0" X 13'-9"

BATH

DN.

TWO CAR GARAGE
20'-4" X 20'-8"

DINING ROOM
10'-6" X 13'-6"

FOYER

DEN
11'-4" X 12'-6"

STOOP

Width 62'
Depth 62'-6"

Copyright 1992 Stephen S. Fuller, Inc.

**Design 9874**

**Square Footage:** 2,095

DECK

BREAKFAST
11'-4" X 9'-4"

BATH

BEDROOM NO. 2
11'-0" X 12'-0"

KITCHEN
10'-8" X 12'-2"

FAMILY ROOM
17'-8" X 15'-4"

MASTER BEDROOM
13'-8" X 15'-4"

DN.

POWDER

BEDROOM NO. 3
11'-0" X 12'-0"

LAUNDRY

MASTER BATH

FOYER
6'-0" X 12'-0"

LIVING ROOM
11'-4" X 14'-0"

W.I.C.

DINING ROOM
11'-8" X 15'-0"

STOOP

TWO CAR GARAGE
20'-4" X 19'-10"

Width 65'
Depth 55'-11"

**Quote One**

Cost to build? See page 214
to order complete cost estimate
to build this house in your area!

Flared eaves, multi-pane windows and graceful arches decorate the outside of this spectacular home and introduce a theme for an interior that offers just a little more. An elegant foyer opens to both the living room and the formal dining room—which features dramatic window detail—and leads through a central hallway to an expansive family room. This versatile area is great for formal as well as informal gatherings, offering a sloped ceiling, fireplace with extended hearth, built-in bookcases and rear deck access. A beautiful, bayed breakfast nook with views to the rear grounds opens to a spacious kitchen with a peninsula cooktop counter. A butler's pantry is strategically located just off the kitchen for easy access when entertaining. The secluded master suite with coffered ceiling, dual vanities, jacuzzi tub and separate shower is complete with a roomy walk-in closet. To the rear of the plan are two family bedrooms; each have private access to a full bath which offers each room its own vanity area. This home is designed with a basement foundation.

Width 48'-6"
Depth 70'-11"

## Design 9812

**First Floor:** 1,580 square feet
**Second Floor:** 595 square feet
**Total:** 2,175 square feet
**Bonus Room:** 290 square feet

**T**his home features a front porch which warmly welcomes family and visitors, as well as protecting them from the weather— a true Southern original. Inside, the spacious foyer leads directly to a large vaulted great room with a massive fireplace. A grand kitchen offers both storage and large work areas opening up to the breakfast area. In the privacy and quiet of the rear of the home is the master suite with its garden bath, His and Hers vanities and oversized closet. The second floor provides two additional bedrooms with a shared bath along with a balcony overlook to the foyer below. Ample amounts of storage space or an additional bedroom can be created in space over the garage. This home is designed with a basement foundation.

QUOTE ONE®

Cost to build? See page 214
to order complete cost estimate
to build this house in your area!

**B**rick takes a bold stand in grand style in this traditional design. From the front entry to rear deck, the floor plan serves family needs in just over 2,000 square feet. The front study has a nearby full bath, making it a handy guest bedroom. The family room with fireplace opens to a cozy breakfast area. For more formal entertaining there's a dining room just off the entry. The kitchen features a preparation island and a walk-in pantry. Upstairs, a luxurious master suite opens from a balcony hall and features a coffered ceiling, windowed sitting area and a spacious bath with garden tub, twin lavatories and walk-in closet. Two family bedrooms share a full bath. This home is designed with a basement foundation.

Width 52'
Depth 34'

## Design 9842

**First Floor:** 1,053 square feet
**Second Floor:** 1,053 square feet
**Total:** 2,106 square feet
**Bonus Room:** 212 square feet

DESIGN BY
**Design Traditions**

**Quote One®**

Cost to build? See page 214
to order complete cost estimate
to build this house in your area!

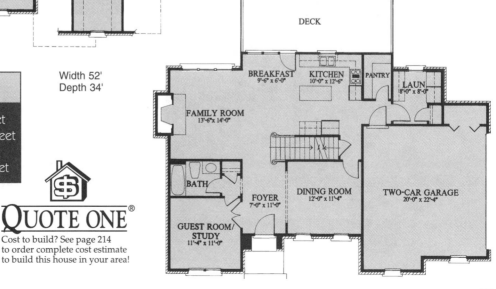

This stately two-story Georgian home echoes tradition with the use of brick and jack-arch detailing. Once inside, the foyer is flanked by a spacious dining room to the right and living room on the left; with the addition of French doors this room can also function as a guest room, if needed. Beyond the foyer lies a two-story family room accented by a warming fireplace and open railing staircase. This room flows casually into the spacious breakfast room and well-planned kitchen with access to the laundry room and garage. The secluded master bedroom with a tray ceiling and master bath including His and Hers vanities, a garden tub and walk-in closet completes the main level of this home. Upstairs, two additional bedrooms with roomy closets and two baths combine to finish this traditional country home. A future bedroom can be finished later if desired. This home is designed with a basement foundation.

## Design 9877

**First Floor:** 1,660 square feet
**Second Floor:** 665 square feet
**Total:** 2,325 square feet
**Bonus Room:** 240 square feet

Width 64'
Depth 48'-6"

W.I.C.

COVERED PORCH

MASTER BATH

TWO STORY
FAMILY ROOM
15'-0" X 19'-0"

BREAKFAST
11'-4" X 10'-8"

MASTER BEDROOM
14'-4" X 13'-0"

UP

DN.

KITCHEN
11'-4" X 12'-4"

TWO CAR GARAGE
21'-8" X 21'-4"

POWDER

LAUNDRY

LIVING ROOM
14'-4" X 11'-8"

TWO STORY
FOYER
7'-0" X 11'-4"

DINING ROOM
11'-4" X 14'-0"

STOOP

QUOTE ONE®

Cost to build? See page 214 to order complete cost estimate to build this house in your area!

DESIGN BY
Design Traditions

OPEN TO BELOW

BEDROOM
NO. 3
11'-4" X 14'-0"

BATH

FUTURE
BEDROOM
NO. 4
10'-6" X 14'-0"

DN.

W.I.C.

W.I.C.

FUTURE
W.I.C.

OPEN TO
BELOW

BEDROOM
NO. 2
11'-4" X 14'-0"

BATH

Copyright 1992 Stephen S. Fuller, Inc.

**T**his European design offers ample space for formal and informal occasions. An impressive foyer opens to a fabulous two-story family room with fireplace and views to the rear yard. The adjacent windowed breakfast room with access to the rear covered porch is easily served by the kitchen with angled counter. Formal rooms flank the foyer—each enjoys a stunning bay window and opens to the foyer through decorative archways. An expansive master suite is secluded to the rear of the first-floor plan and offers a coffered ceiling, corner vanity, garden tub and roomy walk-in closet. Upstairs, Bedroom 2 features a bay window and has its own bath. Bedroom 3 offers a walk-in closet and full bath which leads to future bedroom space. This home is designed with a basement foundation.

Width 64'
Depth 48'-6"

## Design 9893

**First Floor:** 1,660 square feet
**Second Floor:** 665 square feet
**Total:** 2,325 square feet

DESIGN BY
**Design Traditions**

## Design 9907

**First Floor:** 1,720 square feet
**Second Floor:** 545 square feet
**Total:** 2,265 square feet

This French country cottage is a charming example of European architecture. Stucco and stone blend with multiple gables and hipped rooflines to establish the character of the design. A two-story foyer opens to an even more impressive two-story family room with fireplace. To the right, a formal living area opens to a dining room through decorative columns.

This room is easily served by a gener-ous kitchen with island cooktop counter. The master suite is also located on the first floor and is well appointed with a coffered ceiling, a walk-in closet and a double-bowl vanity in the bath. The second floor holds two family bedrooms, a full bath, space for an additional bedroom and future bath, and bonus storage space. This home is designed with a basement foundation.

DESIGN BY
**Design Traditions**

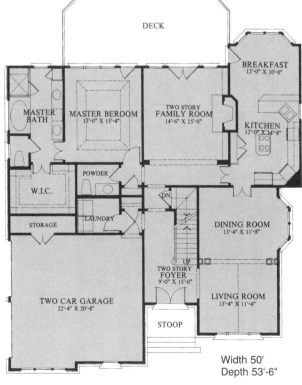

DECK

BREAKFAST
12'-0" X 10'-0"

MASTER
BATH

MASTER BEROOM
13'-0" X 15'-4"

TWO STORY
FAMILY ROOM
14'-6" X 15'-0"

KITCHEN
12'-0" X 14'-8"

POWDER

W.I.C.

DN.

LAUNDRY

STORAGE

DINING ROOM
13'-4" X 11'-8"

UP

TWO STORY
FOYER
9'-0" X 15'-0"

TWO CAR GARAGE
22'-4" X 20'-8"

LIVING ROOM
13'-4" X 11'-4"

STOOP

Width 50'
Depth 53'-6"

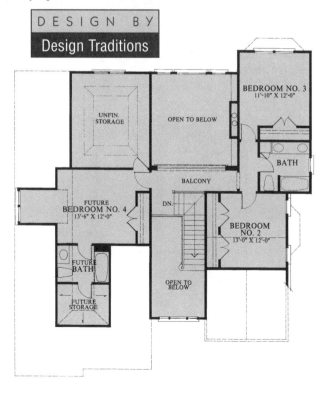

BEDROOM NO. 3
11'-10" X 12'-0"

UNFIN.
STORAGE

OPEN TO BELOW

BATH

BALCONY

FUTURE
BEDROOM NO. 4
13'-6" X 12'-0"

DN.

BEDROOM
NO. 2
13'-0" X 12'-0"

FUTURE
BATH

OPEN TO
BELOW

FUTURE
STORAGE

Width 52'-6"
Depth 43'-6"

DECK

BREAKFAST
11'-8" X 9'-0"

FAMILY ROOM
19'-2" X 15'-2"

KITCHEN
11'-8" X 11'-0"

STORAGE  LAUNDRY

POWDER

VERANDA

TWO CAR GARAGE
20'-4" X 21'-10"

DN.  UP

LIVING ROOM
11'-4" X 13'-0"

DINING ROOM
11'-8" X 13'-0"

FOYER
7'-6" X 13'-0"

STOOP

**T**his charming exterior conceals a perfect family plan. The formal dining and living rooms are located to either side of the foyer. At the rear of the home is a family room with a fireplace and access to a deck and a side veranda. The modern kitchen features a sunlit breakfast area. The second floor provides room for four bedrooms, one of which may be finished at a later date and used as a guest suite. The master bedroom includes a pampering bath and a walk-in closet. Note the extra storage space in the garage. This home is designed with a basement foundation.

MASTER
BATH

MASTER BEDROOM
19'-2" X 13'-8"

W.I.C.

W.I.C.  BATH

UNFIN.
BEDROOM NO. 4
13'-0" X 13'-0"

DN.

W.I.C.  W.I.C.

BEDROOM NO. 3
11'-8" X 13'-0"

OPEN TO
BELOW

BEDROOM NO. 2
11'-4" X 13'-0"

BATH

## Design 9892

**First Floor:** 1,205 square feet
**Second Floor:** 1,160 square feet
**Total:** 2,365 square feet

## Design 8155

**Square Footage:** 1,973

### DESIGN BY
### Larry E. Belk Designs

An angled entry is defined by arches and columns, giving this traditional home an elegant flavor. This split bedroom plan offers privacy for the master suite, which opens just off the foyer through double doors and offers a sumptuous bath with angled garden tub, knee-space vanity, twin lavatories and a walk-in closet with dressing area. Family bedrooms are clus-

tered to the left of the plan and share a hall bath. Decorative archways grace entrances to the great room, which offers an impressive fireplace flanked by windows, giving views to the rear grounds. The nearby kitchen with angled counter and walk-in pantry opens to a bright breakfast room with triple windows. Please specify crawlspace or slab foundation when ordering.

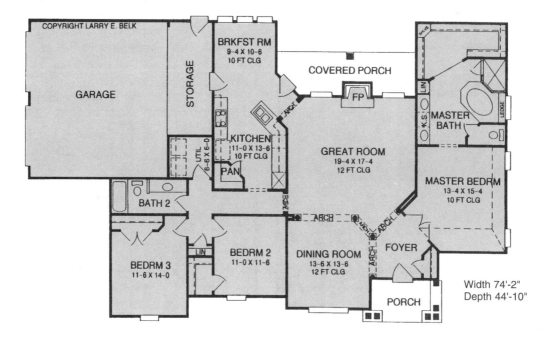

COPYRIGHT LARRY E. BELK

GARAGE

STORAGE

BRKFST RM
9-4 X 10-6
10 FT CLG

COVERED PORCH

FP

MASTER BATH

KITCHEN
11-0 X 13-6
10 FT CLG

GREAT ROOM
19-4 X 17-4
12 FT CLG

UTIL
6-6 X 6-0

PAN

MASTER BEDRM
13-4 X 15-4
10 FT CLG

BATH 2

ARCH

BEDRM 3
11-6 X 14-0

BEDRM 2
11-0 X 11-6

DINING ROOM
13-6 X 13-6
12 FT CLG

ARCH

FOYER

Width 74'-2"
Depth 44'-10"

PORCH

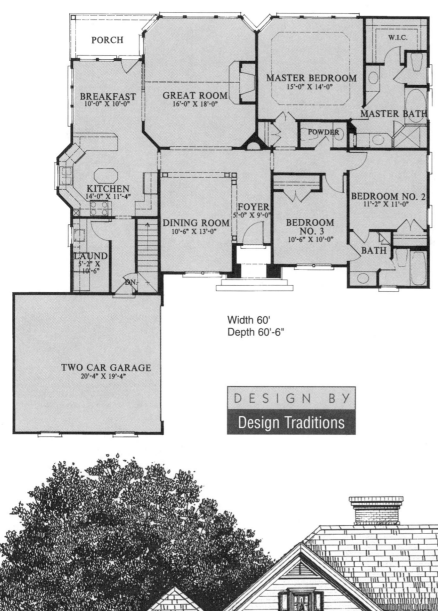

PORCH

BREAKFAST
10'-0" X 10'-0"

GREAT ROOM
16'-0" X 18'-0"

MASTER BEDROOM
15'-0" X 14'-0"

W.I.C.

MASTER BATH

POWDER

KITCHEN
14'-0" X 11'-4"

FOYER
5'-0" X 9'-0"

DINING ROOM
10'-6" X 13'-0"

BEDROOM
NO. 3
10'-6" X 10'-0"

BEDROOM NO. 2
11'-2" X 11'-0"

BATH

LAUND
5'-2" X
10'-6"

DN.

TWO CAR GARAGE
20'-4" X 19'-4"

Width 60'
Depth 60'-6"

DESIGN BY
Design Traditions

## Design 9915

**Square Footage:** 1,815

**W**ith zoned living at the core of this floor plan, livability takes a convenient turn. Living areas are to the left of the plan; sleeping areas to the right. The formal dining room is open to the central hallway and foyer, and features graceful columned archways to define its space. The great room has angled corners and a magnificent central fireplace and offers ample views to the rear grounds. Steps away is a well-lit breakfast room with private rear-porch access and an adjoining U-shaped kitchen with unique angled counter space and sink. Sleeping quarters are clustered around a private hallway which offers a guest bath. The master suite includes a resplendent bath with garden tub, dual lavatories and walk-in closet. Two family bedrooms share a full bath with compartmented toilet and tub. This home is designed with a basement foundation.

Photo by Jon Riley

This home, as shown in the photograph, may differ from the actual blueprints. For more detailed information, please check the floor plans carefully.

## Design 9661

**First Floor:** 1,416 square feet
**Second Floor:** 445 square feet
**Total:** 1,861 square feet
**Bonus Room:** 284 square feet

An arched entrance and windows provide a touch of class to the exterior of this plan. The foyer leads to all areas of the house, minimizing corridor space. The dining room displays round columns at the entrance while the great room boasts a cathedral ceiling, fireplace and arched window over exterior doors to the deck. The large kitchen is open to the breakfast nook, and sliding glass doors present a second access to the deck. In the master suite are two walk-in closets and a lavish bath. On the second level are two bedrooms and a full bath. Bonus space over the garage can be developed later. Please specify basement or crawlspace foundation when ordering.

Width 58'-3"
Depth 68'-9"

### DESIGN BY
Donald A. Gardner, Architects, Inc.

*This home, as shown in the photograph, may differ from the actual blueprints.*
*For more detailed information, please check the floor plans carefully.*

Photo by Andrew D. Lautman

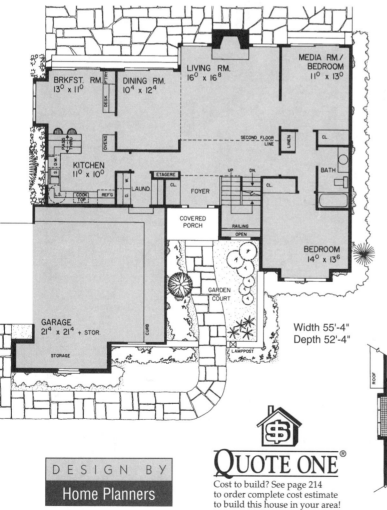

Width 55'-4"
Depth 52'-4"

## Design 2927

**First Floor:** 1,425 square feet
**Second Floor:** 704 square feet
**Total:** 2,129 square feet

**D**

This charming Early American adaptation offers a warm welcome—inside and out. The first floor features a convenient kitchen with a pass-through to the breakfast room. There's also a formal dining room just steps away in the rear of the house. An adjacent rear living room enjoys its own fireplace. Other features include a rear media room (or optional third bedroom) and a complete second-floor master suite. A downstairs bedroom enjoys an excellent front view. Other features include a garden court, a covered porch and a two-car garage with extra storage.

*This home, as shown in the photograph, may differ from the actual blueprints.*
*For more detailed information, please check the floor plans carefully.*

Photos by Andrew D. Lautman

## Design 2822

**First Floor:** 1,363 square feet
**Second Floor:** 351 square feet
**Total:** 1,714 square feet

**L**

Tailor-made for small families, this is a one-level design with second floor possibilities. The bonus room upstairs (please see alternate layout) can be nearly anything you want it to be: lounge, guest room, playroom for the kids—partitioned or open. Downstairs, a little space goes a long way: an extensive great room with extended hearth, a formal dining room with private covered porch, and a master wing which includes a study, spacious bath with dressing area, walk-in closet and access to a hot tub/spa.

### DESIGN BY
**Home Planners**

Width 54'-8"
Depth 54'

**QUOTE ONE®**
Cost to build? See page 214
to order complete cost estimate
to build this house in your area!

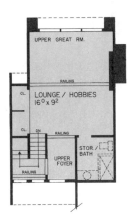

Alternate Second Floor

Photos by Andrew D. Lautman

This home, as shown in the photograph, may differ from the actual blueprints.
For more detailed information, please check the floor plans carefully.

Cost to build? See page 214

## DESIGN BY
### Home Planners

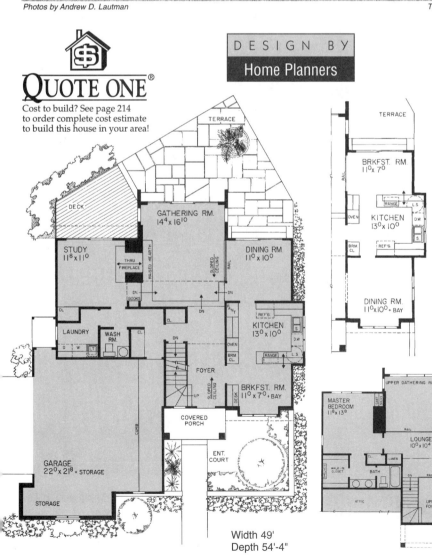

Width 49'
Depth 54'-4"

This is an outstanding example of the type of informal, traditional-style architecture that has captured the modern imagination. Notice the spacious sunken gathering room with sliding glass doors to the rear terrace, which shares a through-fireplace with the quiet study that offers access to a rear deck. Formal and informal dining areas are nicely separated by a roomy U-shaped kitchen.

Upstairs, the master bedroom suite is sure to please, while two family bedrooms and a lounge fulfill the family's needs.

## Design 2826

**First Floor:** 1,112 square feet
**Second Floor:** 881 square feet
**Total:** 1,993 square feet

**D**

## Design 3569

**Square Footage:** 1,981

**L** **D**

**A**n impressive arched entry graces this Transitional one-story design. An elegant foyer introduces an open gathering room/dining room combination. A front-facing study with sloped ceiling could easily be converted to a guest room with a full bath accessible from the rear of the room. In the kitchen, such features as an island cooktop and a built-in desk add style and convenience. A corner bedroom offers front and side views, and the nearby master suite sports a whirlpool bath and walk-in closet, and offers access to the rear terrace. Other special features of the plan include multi-pane windows, a warming fireplace, a cozy covered dining porch and a two-car garage. Note the handy storage closet in the laundry area.

**QUOTE ONE®**

Cost to build? See page 214
to order complete cost estimate
to build this house in your area!

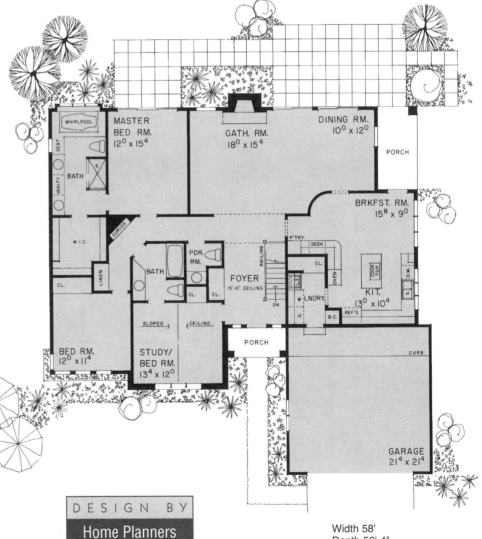

MASTER
BED RM.
12⁰ x 15⁴

GATH. RM.
18⁰ x 15⁴

DINING RM.
10⁰ x 12⁰

PORCH

BRKFST. RM.
15⁸ x 9⁰

BATH

W.I.C.

LINEN

CL.

BATH

PDR. RM.

FOYER
13'-0" CEILING

P'TRY.

DESK

CL.

OVEN

COOK TOP

KIT.
13⁰ x 10⁴

LNDRY.

REF'G

B.C.

BED RM.
12⁰ x 11⁴

STUDY/
BED RM.
13⁴ x 12⁰

SLOPED

CEILING

PORCH

CURB

GARAGE
21⁴ x 21⁴

DESIGN BY
Home Planners

Width 58'
Depth 56'-4"

**Covered Patio**

**Breakfast**
volume ceiling

**Master Bedroom**
volume ceiling
16⁸ • 12⁰

opt. summer kitchen

**Bath**

w.i.c.

**Great Room**
15⁸ • 14⁰

opt. media center

volume ceiling
wall to 8'

**Kitchen**

**Bedroom 2**
volume ceiling
13⁴ • 10⁰

**Utility**

**Dining**
12⁰ • 10¹⁰

**Bath**

**Bedroom 3**
volume ceiling
13⁴ • 11⁴

**Foyer**

ac

wh  ac

**Double Garage**

w.i.c.

**Entry**

**Study/ Bedroom 4**
volume ceiling
14⁰ • 11⁰

Width 45'
Depth 66'

wh  ac

**Foyer**

**Bedroom 3**

**Opt. 3 Car Garage**

**Entry**

**T**his innovative plan features an angled entry into the home, lending visual impact to the facade and giving the interior floor plan space for a fourth bedroom. A fabulous central living area with volume ceiling includes a dining area with kitchen access, a great room with built-in media center and access to the rear covered patio. The tiled kitchen shares natural light from the bayed breakfast area with volume ceiling. The kitchen and breakfast nook overlook the outdoor living space which even offers an optional summer kitchen—great for entertaining. A plush master suite opens from the great room through a privacy door and offers vistas onto the rear and side grounds. The traditional feel of the exterior and the up-to-date interior make this home a perfect design for the 90s.

## Design 8633

**Square Footage:** 1,865

DESIGN BY
**Home Design Services, Inc.**

## Design 2948

**Square Footage:** 1,830

Styled for Southwest living, this home is a good choice in many areas. Among its many highlights are a gathering room/dining room combination that includes a fireplace, a snack bar pass-through and sliding glass doors to the rear terrace. The kitchen is uniquely shaped and sports a walk-in pantry plus a breakfast room with windows to the front covered porch. Bedrooms include a master suite with a sloped ceiling, access to the rear terrace, a whirlpool spa and a double vanity. Two additional bedrooms share a full bath. One of these bedrooms makes a fine study and features built-in shelves for books as well as a built-in cabinet.

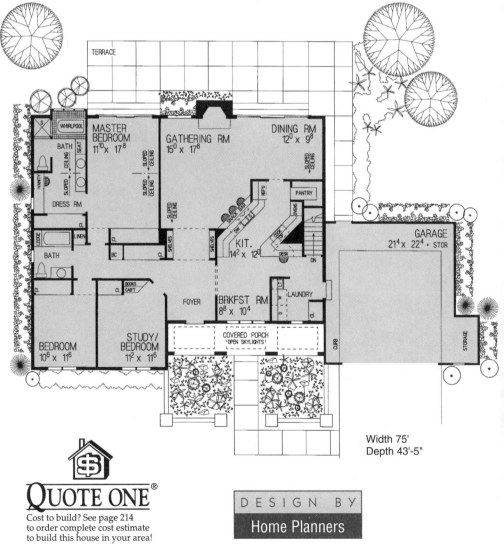

Width 75'
Depth 43'-5"

DESIGN BY

**Home Planners**

## Design 2875

**Square Footage:** 1,913

L D

This elegant Spanish design incorporates excellent indoor/outdoor living relationships for modern families who enjoy the sun and the comforts of a well-planned new home. Note the overhead openings for rain and sun to fall upon a front garden, while a twin arched entry leads to the front porch and foyer. Inside, the floor plan features a modern kitchen with pass-through to a large gathering room with fireplace. Other features include a dining room, laundry room, a study off the foyer, plus three bedrooms including a master suite with its own whirlpool.

DESIGN BY
**Home Planners**

QUOTE ONE®

Cost to build? See page 214 to order complete cost estimate to build this house in your area!

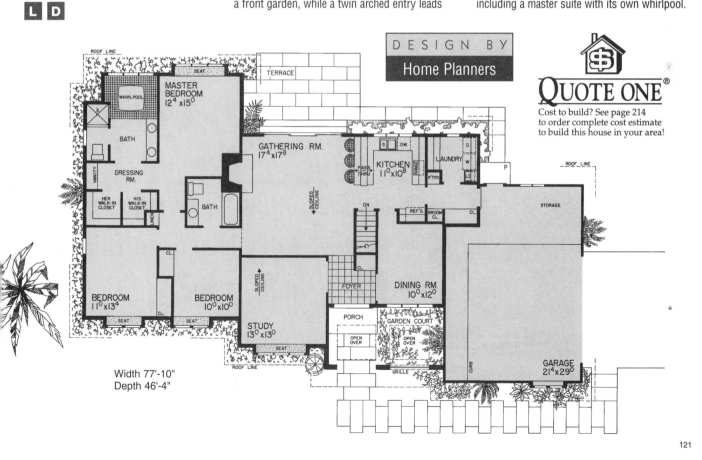

Width 77'-10"
Depth 46'-4"

## Design 3431

**Square Footage:** 1,907

Graceful curves welcome you into the courtyard of this Santa Fe home. Inside, a gallery directs traffic to the work zone on the left or the sleeping zone on the right. Straight ahead lies a sunken gathering room with a beamed ceiling and a raised-hearth fireplace. A large pantry offers extra storage space for kitchen items. The covered rear porch is accessible from the dining room, gathering room and secluded master bedroom. Luxury describes the feeling in the master bath with a whirlpool tub, a separate shower, a double vanity and closet space. Two family bedrooms share a compartmented bath. The study could serve as a guest room, a media room or a home office.

## QUOTE ONE®

Cost to build? See page 214
to order complete cost estimate
to build this house in your area!

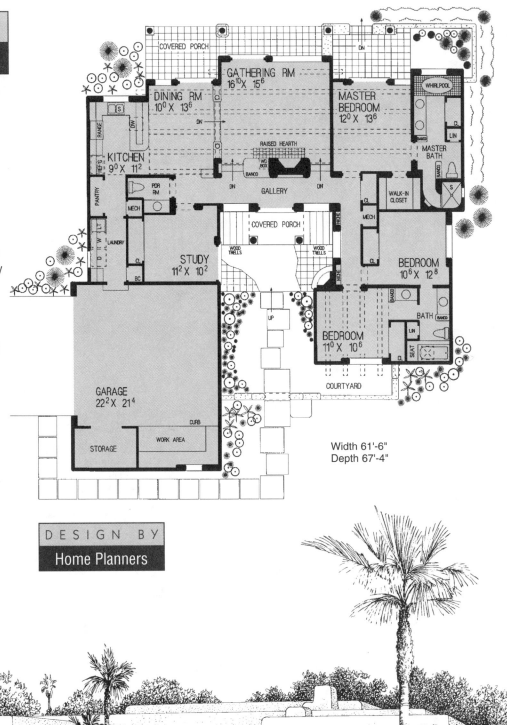

Width 61'-6"
Depth 67'-4"

DESIGN BY
**Home Planners**

MASTER BEDRM
15⁸ x 12⁴
10'-0" CLG

COVERED PATIO

NOOK
9⁶ x 9⁸
10'-0" CLG

KIT
9⁰ x 16²

FAMILY RM
15⁴ x 15⁴
15'-0" CLG

WHIRL-POOL

MASTER BATH

LIN

SEAT

SHWR

NICHE

WALK-IN CLOSET

SHLVS

LIVING RM
14² x 14²
VIGA CLG AT 13'-0"

BANCO

RAISED HEARTH

BOOKSHELVES

PANTRY

REFG

BEDRM
10⁴ x 12⁰
9'-4" CLG

BEDRM
11⁸ x 13⁴
8'-8" CLG

LINEN

BATH

DINING RM
10⁴ x 13⁰
10'-0" CLG W/ 11'-0" TRAY

HALF WALL

FOYER
10'-0" CLG

POWDER

STOR

HVAC

COVERED PORCH

LAUNDRY ROOM

GARAGE
26⁴ x 22⁸

Width 85'-9"
Depth 67'-10"

### Design 3643

**Square Footage:** 2,092

**L**

**S**tucco exterior walls highlighted by simple window treatment and effective glass-block patterns introduce a fine, western-style home. High ceilings and open planning contribute to the spaciousness of the interior. The large foyer effectively routes traffic to the main living areas. To the left is the angular formal dining room with its half walls and tray ceiling. Straight ahead from the double front doors is the formal living room. It has a high *viga*, or beamed ceiling and a commanding corner fireplace with a raised hearth and *banco*, or bench. French doors open to the covered rear patio. Past the built-in bookshelves of the family room is the hallway to the sleeping zone.

DESIGN BY
Home Planners

123

## Design 3376

**Square Footage:** 1,999

**L D**

Small families will appreciate the layout of this traditional ranch. The foyer opens to the gathering room with fireplace and sloped ceiling. The dining room opens to the gathering room for entertaining ease and offers sliding glass doors to a rear terrace. The breakfast room also provides access to a covered porch for dining outdoors. The media room to the left of the home offers a bay window and a wet bar, or it can double as a third bedroom.

## QUOTE ONE®

Cost to build? See page 214 to order complete cost estimate to build this house in your area!

DESIGN BY

**Home Planners**

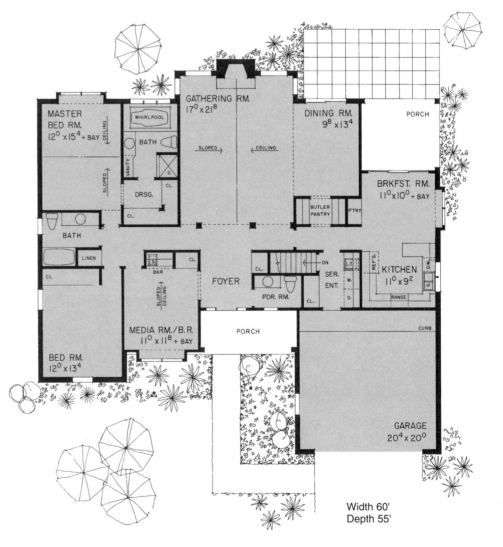

MASTER BED RM.
12⁰ x 15⁴ + BAY

WHIRLPOOL

BATH

VANITY

DRSG.

CL.

S.

CL.

BATH

LINEN

CL.

BAR

CL.

SLOPED CEILING

MEDIA RM./B.R.
11⁰ x 11⁸ + BAY

BED RM.
12⁰ x 13⁴

GATHERING RM.
17⁰ x 21⁸

SLOPED        CEILING

DINING RM.
9⁸ x 13⁴

PORCH

BRKFST. RM.
11⁰ x 10⁰ + BAY

BUTLER PANTRY

P'TRY

FOYER

CL.

PDR. RM.

SER. ENT.

DN

W.

D.

REF'G.

KITCHEN
11⁰ x 9²

RANGE

S.

DW.

PORCH

CURB

GARAGE
20⁴ x 20⁰

Width 60'
Depth 55'

# ON THE GROW
## *Chic Plans For Moving Up*

**W**hat will the 21st-Century home look like? The trend in home design is toward traditional values, but the discriminating demands of today's savvy home-builder will easily carry over to the next millennium—and that throws new light on the home of the future.

Trendsetting Baby Boomers are stoking the American dream with a sophisticated *savoir-vivre*. With incomes climbing and families growing, this generation wants a home plan that fits their hard-earned success as well as their lifestyles. And household arrangements today come in new flavors, so flexibility is key. Live-in grandparents, double-income parents and breadwinners who work at home entreat bright ideas for interior space.

Ergonomics and aesthetics can work together to take home design beyond style and into a comfortable, personalized way of life. Design 2973, a popular Victorian featured on page 126, offers places to kick off your shoes or put on a bash. And Design 3662 (page 152) combines traditional and *avant-garde* elements that succeed in giving it a contemporary spirit that's right at home with a rustic leitmotif.

New trends in building want well-heeled, intelligent designs that simmer with individuality and don't scrimp on style. Elegance partnered with restraint and simplicity creates homes that are impressive but not imposing, refined but not stuffy—tomorrow's home, the one you've been waiting for.

Photo by Andrew D. Lautman

This home, as shown in the photograph, may differ from the actual blueprints. For more detailed information, please check the floor plans carefully.

## Design 2973

**First Floor:** 1,269 square feet
**Second Floor:** 1,227 square feet
**Total:** 2,496 square feet

**L**

A most popular feature of the Victorian house has always been its covered porches. The two finely detailed outdoor living spaces found on this home add much to formal and informal entertaining options. However, in addition to its wonderful Victorian facade, this home provides a myriad of interior features that cater to the active, growing family. Living and dining areas include a formal living room and dining room, a family room with a fireplace, a study and a kitchen with an attached breakfast nook. The second floor has three family bedrooms and a luxurious master bedroom with whirlpool spa and His and Hers walk-in closets.

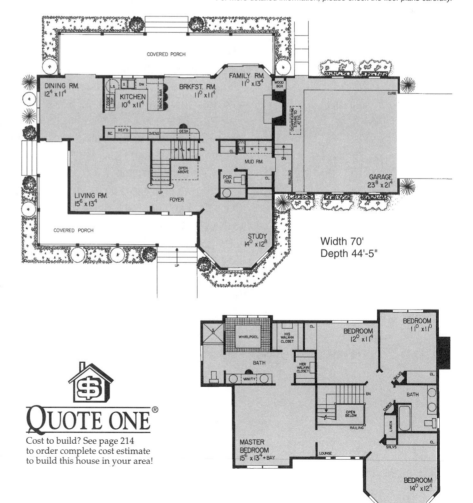

**Quote One** ®

Cost to build? See page 214 to order complete cost estimate to build this house in your area!

DESIGN BY
Home Planners

Width 70'
Depth 44'-5"

This home, as shown in the photograph, may differ from the actual blueprints.
For more detailed information, please check the floor plans carefully.

Photo by Bob Greenspan

## Design 3309

**First Floor:** 1,375 square feet
**Second Floor:** 1,016 square feet
**Total** 2,391 square feet

Covered porches, front and back, are a fine preview to the livable nature of this Victorian. Living areas are defined in a family room with a fireplace, formal living and dining rooms and a kitchen with a breakfast room. Note the sliding glass doors from the breakfast room to the rear veranda. An ample laundry room, a garage with storage area and a powder room round out the first floor. Three second-floor bedrooms are joined by a study and two full baths. The master suite on this floor has two closets (one a convenient walk-in), a double vanity, a whirlpool tub and a separate shower.

**L**

Width 62'-7"
Depth 54'

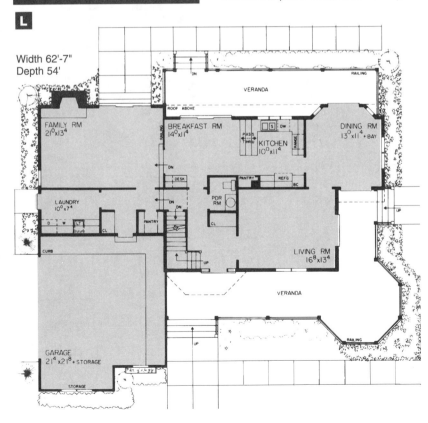

DESIGN BY
**Home Planners**

**QUOTE ONE**®

Cost to build? See page 214
to order complete cost estimate
to build this house in your area!

Photo by Andrew D. Lautman

This home, as shown in the photograph, may differ from the actual blueprints. For more detailed information, please check the floor plans carefully.

With its exceptional detail and proportions, this home is reminiscent of the Queen Anne Style. The foyer opens to a living area with a bay windowed alcove and a fireplace with flanking bookshelves. Natural light fills the breakfast area with a full-length bay window and a French door. Upstairs, the master bedroom offers unsurpassed elegance and convenience. The sitting area has an eleven-foot ceiling with arch-top windows. The bath area features a large walk-in closet, His and Hers lavatories and plenty of linen storage. Plans for a two-car detached garage are included.

## Design 9055

**First Floor:** 997 square feet
**Second Floor:** 1,069 square feet
**Total:** 2,066 square feet

DESIGN BY

**Larry W. Garnett & Associates, Inc.**

QUOTE ONE®

Cost to build? See page 214 to order complete cost estimate to build this house in your area!

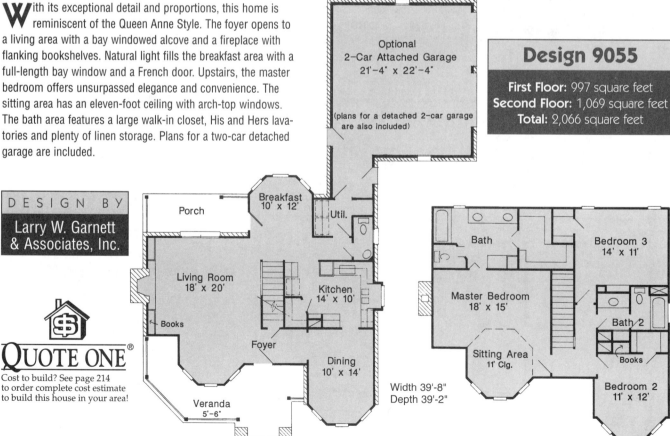

Optional
2-Car Attached Garage
21'-4" x 22'-4"

(plans for a detached 2-car garage are also included)

Breakfast
10' x 12'

Porch

Util.

Living Room
18' x 20'

Books

Foyer

Kitchen
14' x 10'

Dining
10' x 14'

Veranda
5'-6"

Width 39'-8"
Depth 39'-2"

Bath

Master Bedroom
18' x 15'

Bedroom 3
14' x 11'

Bath 2

Sitting Area
11' Clg.

Books

Bedroom 2
11' x 12'

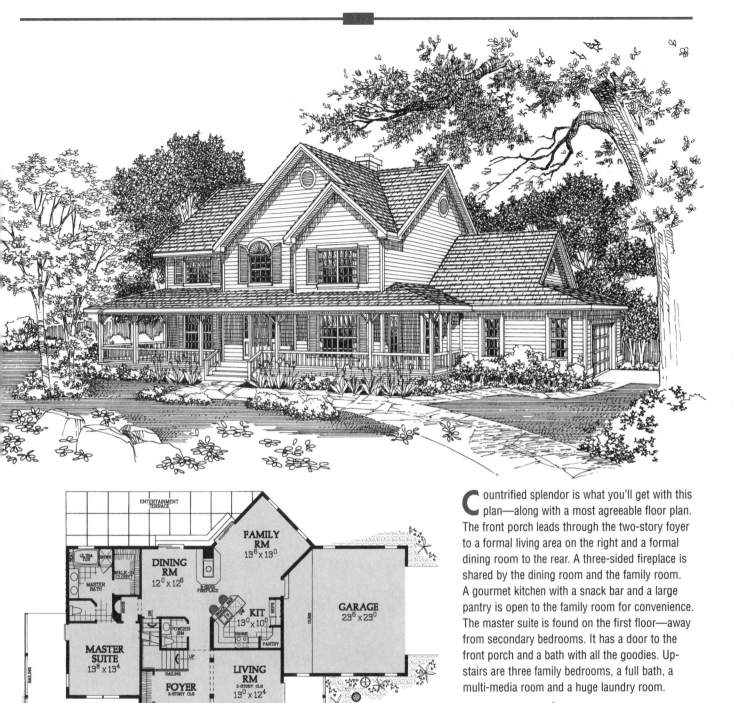

**Countrified** splendor is what you'll get with this plan—along with a most agreeable floor plan. The front porch leads through the two-story foyer to a formal living area on the right and a formal dining room to the rear. A three-sided fireplace is shared by the dining room and the family room. A gourmet kitchen with a snack bar and a large pantry is open to the family room for convenience. The master suite is found on the first floor—away from secondary bedrooms. It has a door to the front porch and a bath with all the goodies. Up-stairs are three family bedrooms, a full bath, a multi-media room and a huge laundry room.

ENTERTAINMENT TERRACE

ULTRA TUB · SHWR

WALK-IN CLOSET

MASTER BATH

DINING RM
12⁰ x 12⁶

3-SIDED FIREPLACE

FAMILY RM
13⁶ x 13⁰

GARAGE
29⁶ x 29⁰

DK

POWDER RM

SNACK BAR

KIT
13⁰ x 10⁰

REF

CLOS

MASTER SUITE
13⁸ x 13⁴

UP

RANGE

PANTRY

FOYER
2-STORY CLG

RAILING

LIVING RM
2-STORY CLG
13⁰ x 12⁴

COVERED PORCH

RAILING

RAILING

RAILING

Width 74'
Depth 46'

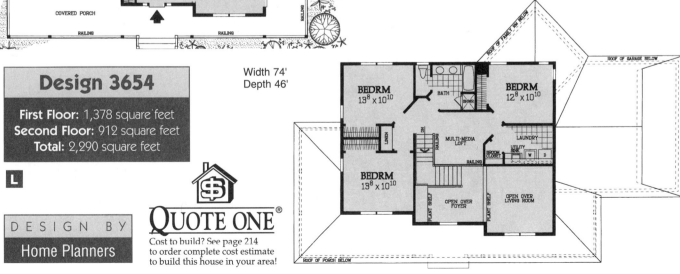

BEDRM
13⁸ x 10¹⁰

BATH

SHWR

BEDRM
12⁸ x 10¹⁰

LINEN

DN

MULTI-MEDIA LOFT

LAUNDRY

BROOM CLOSET

UTILITY SINK

W    D

RAILING

ROOF OF FAMILY RM BELOW

ROOF OF GARAGE BELOW

BEDRM
13⁸ x 10¹⁰

PLANT SHELF

OPEN OVER FOYER

PLANT SHELF

OPEN OVER LIVING ROOM

ROOF OF PORCH BELOW

## Design 3654

**First Floor:** 1,378 square feet
**Second Floor:** 912 square feet
**Total:** 2,290 square feet

**L**

DESIGN BY

**Home Planners**

**QUOTE ONE®**

Cost to build? See page 214
to order complete cost estimate
to build this house in your area!

A wraparound veranda with delicate spindlework and a raised turret with leaded-glass windows recall the Queen Anne-style Victorians of the late 1880s. Double doors open from the two-story foyer to a study with built-in bookcases and a bay window. A fireplace adds warmth to the breakfast area and the island kitchen. Above the two-car garage is an optional area that is perfect for a home office or guest quarters. Upstairs, the balcony overlooks the foyer below. An octagon-shaped ceiling and leaded-glass windows define a cozy sitting area in the master suite. A raised alcove in the master bath contains a garden tub and glass-enclosed shower. An optional exercise loft and plant shelves complete this elegant master bath. Two additional bedrooms, one with a private deck, and the other with a cathedral ceiling share a dressing area and bath.

## Design 9012

**First Floor:** 1,357 square feet
**Second Floor:** 1,079 square feet
**Total:** 2,436 square feet

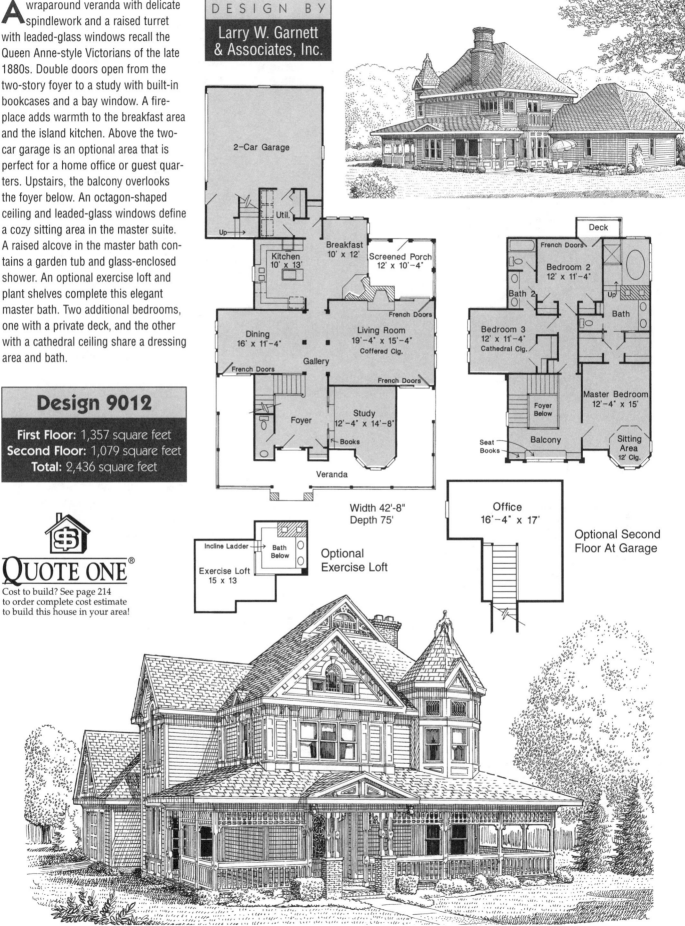

DESIGN BY
Larry W. Garnett & Associates, Inc.

2-Car Garage

Up

Util.

Kitchen
10' x 13'

Breakfast
10' x 12'

Screened Porch
12' x 10'-4"

French Doors

Dining
16' x 11'-4"

Living Room
19'-4" x 15'-4"
Coffered Clg.

French Doors

Gallery

French Doors

French Doors

Foyer

Study
12'-4" x 14'-8"

Books

Veranda

Width 42'-8"
Depth 75'

Deck

French Doors

Bedroom 2
12' x 11'-4"

Bath 2

Up

Bath

Bedroom 3
12' x 11'-4"
Cathedral Clg.

Foyer
Below

Master Bedroom
12'-4" x 15'

Seat
Books

Balcony

Sitting
Area
12' Clg.

Incline Ladder

Bath
Below

Exercise Loft
15 x 13

Optional
Exercise Loft

Office
16'-4" x 17'

Optional Second
Floor At Garage

## Design 9585

**First Floor:** 1,337 square feet
**Second Floor:** 1,025 square feet
**Total:** 2,362 square feet

An octagonal tower, a wraparound porch and a wealth of amenities combine to give this house its charming Victorian appeal. The tower furnishes more than a pretty face, containing a sunny den on the first floor and a delightful bedroom on the second floor. To the right of the foyer, the formal living room and dining room unite to provide a wonderful place to celebrate special occasions and holidays. A large kitchen featuring an island cooktop easily serves both the formal dining room and the adjoining nook. Here, family members will appreciate the built-in desk for use in meal planning or paying bills. The spacious family room completes the casual living area and supplies easy access to the rear porch. Upstairs, two bedrooms share a full hall bath while the master bedroom revels in its own luxurious private bath. A two-car garage accommodates the family vehicles.

Width 50'-6"
Depth 72'-6"

DESIGN BY
**Alan Mascord Design Associates, Inc.**

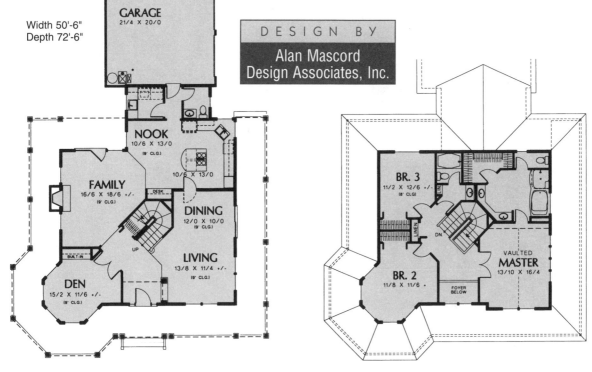

## Design 9252

**First Floor:** 1,113 square feet
**Second Floor:** 965 square feet
**Total:** 2,078 square feet

Elegant detail, a charming veranda and a tall brick chimney make a pleasing facade on this four-bedroom, two-story Victorian home. Yesterday's simpler lifestyle is reflected throughout this plan. From the large bayed parlor with sloped ceiling to the sunken gathering room with fireplace, there's plenty to appreciate about the floor plan. The formal dining room opens to the parlor for convenient entertaining. An L-shaped kitchen with attached breakfast room is nearby. Upstairs quarters include a master suite with private dressing area and whirlpool, and three family bedrooms.

DESIGN BY
**Design Basics, Inc.**

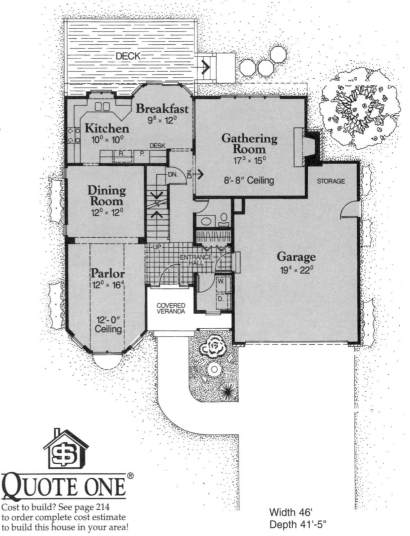

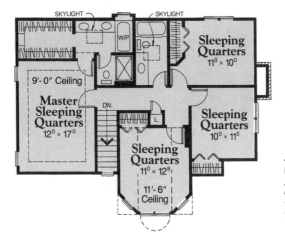

Quote One®

Cost to build? See page 214 to order complete cost estimate to build this house in your area!

Width 46'
Depth 41'-5"

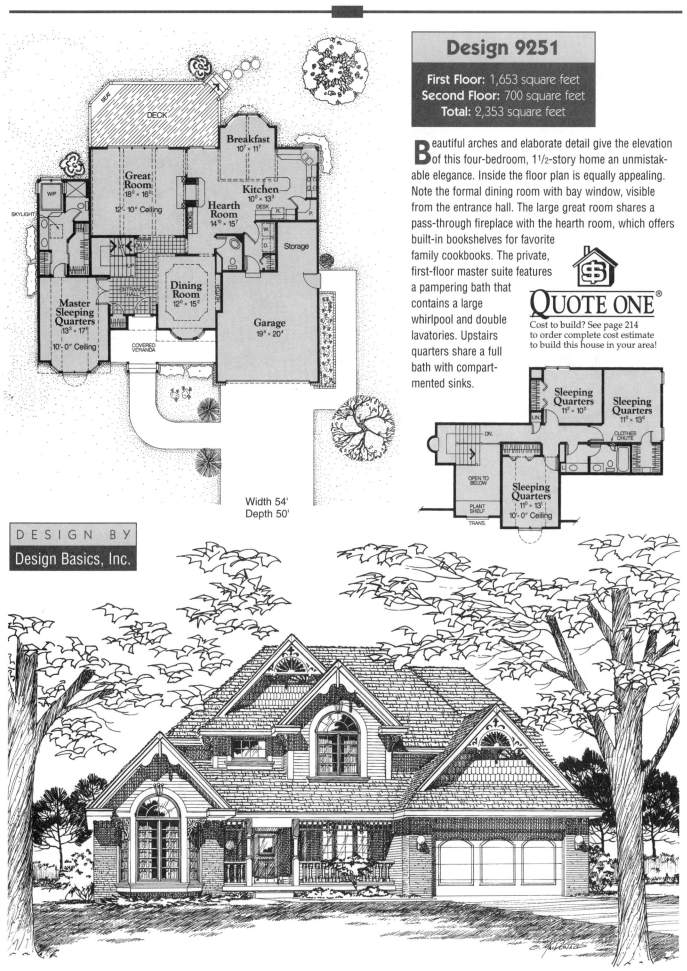

## Design 9251

**First Floor:** 1,653 square feet
**Second Floor:** 700 square feet
**Total:** 2,353 square feet

**B**eautiful arches and elaborate detail give the elevation of this four-bedroom, 1¹/₂-story home an unmistakable elegance. Inside the floor plan is equally appealing. Note the formal dining room with bay window, visible from the entrance hall. The large great room shares a pass-through fireplace with the hearth room, which offers built-in bookshelves for favorite family cookbooks. The private, first-floor master suite features a pampering bath that contains a large whirlpool and double lavatories. Upstairs quarters share a full bath with compartmented sinks.

**QUOTE ONE®**
Cost to build? See page 214 to order complete cost estimate to build this house in your area!

DECK

**Great Room**
18⁰ × 16⁰
12'-10" Ceiling

SEAT

W/P

SKYLIGHT

**Breakfast**
10⁷ × 11⁷

**Kitchen**
10⁰ × 13³

**Hearth Room**
14¹⁰ × 15⁷

BOOKS

DESK

UP

DN.

W.

D.

Storage

**Master Sleeping Quarters**
13³ × 17⁶
10'-0" Ceiling

**ENTRANCE HALL**

**Dining Room**
12⁰ × 15²

**Garage**
19⁴ × 20⁴

**COVERED VERANDA**

Width 54'
Depth 50'

**Sleeping Quarters**
11² × 10⁰

**Sleeping Quarters**
11⁰ × 13⁶

LIN.

CLOTHES CHUTE

DN.

OPEN TO BELOW

PLANT SHELF

TRANS.

**Sleeping Quarters**
11⁰ × 13¹
10'-0" Ceiling

DESIGN BY
**Design Basics, Inc.**

133

## Design 9206

**First Floor:** 1,421 square feet
**Second Floor:** 578 square feet
**Total:** 1,999 square feet

Growing families will love this unique plan which combines all the essentials with an abundance of stylish touches. Start with the living areas—a spacious great room with high ceilings, windows overlooking the back yard, a through-fireplace to the kitchen and access to the rear yard. A dining room with hutch space accommodates formal occasions. The hearth kitchen features a well-planned work area and a bay-windowed breakfast area. The master suite with whirlpool and a walk-in closet is found downstairs while three family bedrooms are upstairs.

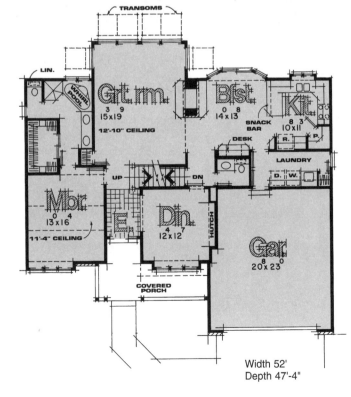

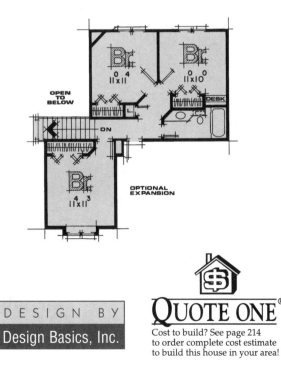

Width 52'
Depth 47'-4"

DESIGN BY
**Design Basics, Inc.**

**QUOTE ONE®**
Cost to build? See page 214 to order complete cost estimate to build this house in your area!

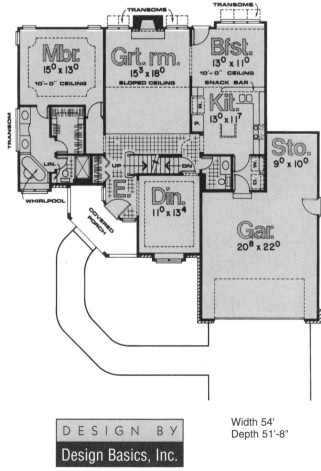

## Design 7236

**First Floor:** 1,413 square feet
**Second Floor:** 563 square feet
**Total:** 1,976 square feet

Charming shutter treatments and an angled porch with balustrade inspire a country mood with this traditional design. An extended tiled entry opens to a majestic great room, where an aura of spaciousness beckons with a high ceiling and sunny, transomed windows which frame the centered fireplace. Nearby, a well-designed kitchen offers daily cooking ease and shares a snack counter with a bright breakfast room with triple transoms. The spacious master bath features an angled whirlpool, dual lavatories, separate shower and spacious walk-in closet. Upstairs, three family bedrooms and a hall bath complete the livable floor plan. An additional storage area in the garage helps maximize full usage of the home.

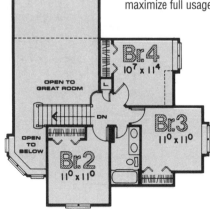

Width 54'
Depth 51'-8"

DESIGN BY

**Design Basics, Inc.**

## Design 9310

**First Floor:** 1,505 square feet
**Second Floor:** 610 square feet
**Total:** 2,115 square feet

**M**any windows, lap siding and a covered porch give this elevation a welcoming country flair. The formal dining room with hutch space is conveniently located near the island kitchen. A main floor laundry room with a sink is discreetly located next to the bright breakfast area with desk and pantry. Highlighting the spacious great room are a raised-hearth fireplace, a cathedral ceiling and trapezoid windows. Special features in the master suite include a large dressing area with a double vanity, a skylight, a step-up corner whirlpool and a generous walk-in closet. Upstairs, the three secondary bedrooms are well separated from the master bedroom and share a hall bath.

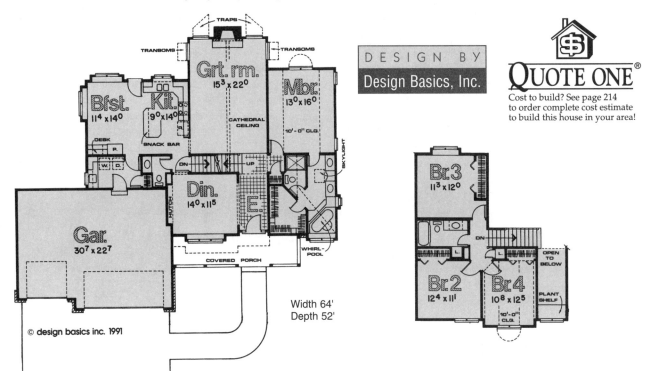

DESIGN BY
**Design Basics, Inc.**

**QUOTE ONE®**

Cost to build? See page 214
to order complete cost estimate
to build this house in your area!

Width 64'
Depth 52'

© design basics inc. 1991

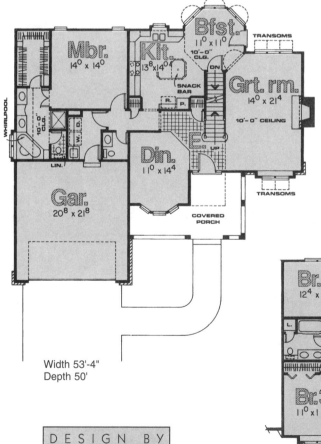

Width 53'-4"
Depth 50'

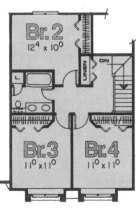

**N**ot all the bright lights are in the big city! Although the sunshine-filled breakfast bay in this traditional design would show off any lot, there's nothing like brightly lit windows filled with country scenery. Muntin windows, double dormers, decorative columns and a detailed balustrade accent the exterior. The entry opens to a voluminous great room with centered fireplace and high ceiling as well as to the formal dining room. A step away, the roomy island kitchen features a snack counter, a lazy Susan and "miles" of counter space. A secluded master suite offers blue-ribbon amenities including a spacious walk-in closet, dual lavatories, corner whirlpool bath, and separate shower. Three second-level bedrooms share a hall bath with twin lavs. The laundry room offers access from the garage and the kitchen.

## Design 7306

**First Floor:** 1,414 square feet
**Second Floor:** 641 square feet
**Total:** 2,055 square feet

## Design 8064

**Square Footage:** 1,742

**DESIGN BY**
**Larry E. Belk Designs**

This traditional design warmly welcomes both family and visitors with a delightful bay window, a Palladian window and shutters. The entry introduces a beautiful interior plan, starting with the formal dining room and the central great room with fireplace, and views and access to outdoor spaces. Ten-foot ceilings in the major living areas give the home an open, spacious feel. The kitchen features an angled eating bar, a pantry and lots of cabinet and counter space. Comfort and style abound in the distinctive master suite, offering a high ceiling, corner whirlpool tub, knee-space vanity and compartmented toilet. An ample walk-in closet with a window for natural light completes this owner's retreat. Bedrooms 2 and 3 are nearby and share a hall bath, and bedroom 3 offers a raised ceiling. Please specify basement or crawlspace foundation when ordering.

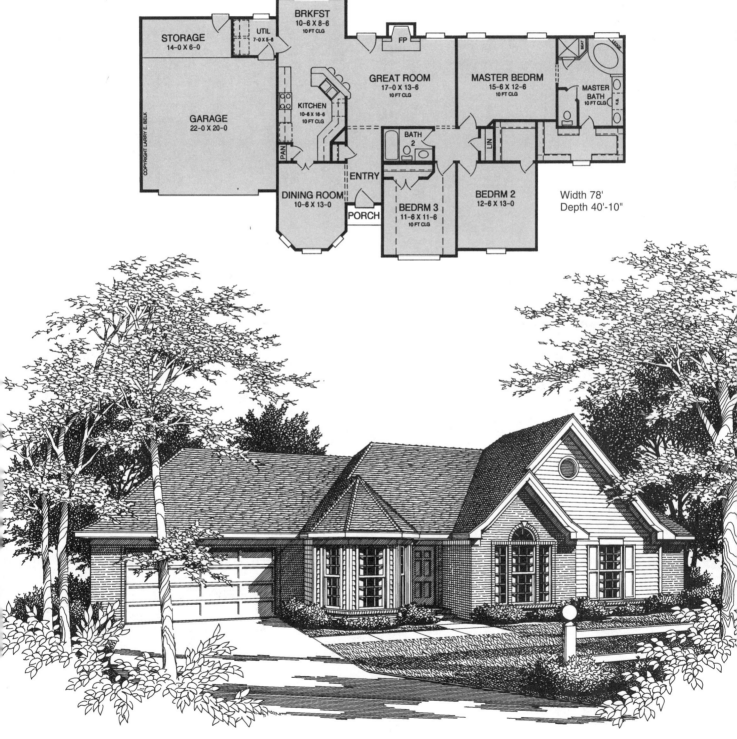

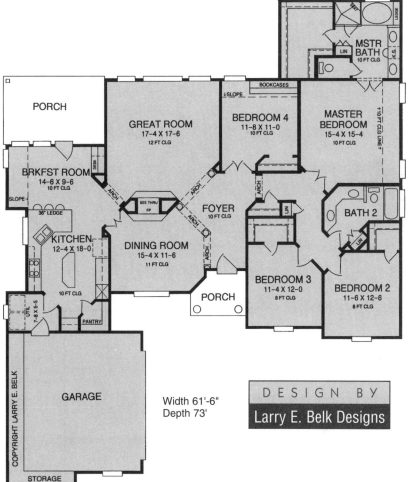

PORCH

BRKFST ROOM
14-6 X 9-6
10 FT CLG

SLOPE

36" LEDGE

KITCHEN
12-4 X 18-0

10 FT CLG

UTIL
7-8 X 5-5

PANTRY

GARAGE

STORAGE

COPYRIGHT LARRY E. BELK

GREAT ROOM
17-4 X 17-6
12 FT CLG

SEE THRU
FP

ARCH

ARCH

FOYER
10 FT CLG

DINING ROOM
15-4 X 11-6
11 FT CLG

ARCH

PORCH

SLOPE

BOOKCASES

BEDROOM 4
11-8 X 11-0
10 FT CLG

ARCH

BEDROOM 3
11-4 X 12-0
8 FT CLG

MSTR
BATH
10 FT CLG

LIN

LEDGE

M.K.S.

MASTER
BEDROOM
15-4 X 15-4
10 FT CLG

10 FT CLG LINE

LIN

BATH 2

LIN

BEDROOM 2
11-6 X 12-6
8 FT CLG

Width 61'-6"
Depth 73'

DESIGN BY
Larry E. Belk Designs

## Design 8136

**Square Footage:** 2,247

The combination of stucco and brick gives this one-story home a European feel. The dining room and great room are showcased by the dramatic entry, decorated by classic columns and graceful arches. A see-through fireplace warms both the dining room and great room, blending an abundance of natural light with the glow of a fire. Nearby, a brightly lit breakfast room with sloped ceiling shares its light and a snack counter with a roomy island kitchen with walk-in pantry. Four bedrooms are clustered to the right of the plan, including a plush master suite with 10-foot ceiling, an amenity-laden bath and a corner walk-in closet. Bedroom 4 could be made a study—or even a library—with built-in bookshelves, sloped ceiling and views to the rear grounds. Please specify crawlspace or slab foundation when ordering.

## Design 9742

**Square Footage:** 1,954
**Bonus Room:** 436 square feet

This beautiful brick country home has all the amenities needed for today's active family. Covered front and back porches along with a rear deck provide plenty of room for outdoor enjoyment. Inside, the focus is on the large great room with its cathedral ceiling and welcoming fireplace. To the right, columns separate the kitchen and breakfast area while keeping this area open. Resident gourmets will certainly appreciate the convenience of the kitchen with its center island and additional eating space. The master bedroom provides a splendid private retreat, featuring a cathedral ceiling and a large walk-in closet. A double-bowl vanity, a separate shower and a skylit whirlpool tub enhance the luxurious master bath. At the opposite end of the plan, two additional bedrooms share a full bath. A skylit bonus room above the garage allows for additional living space.

DESIGN BY
**Donald A. Gardner,
Architects, Inc.**

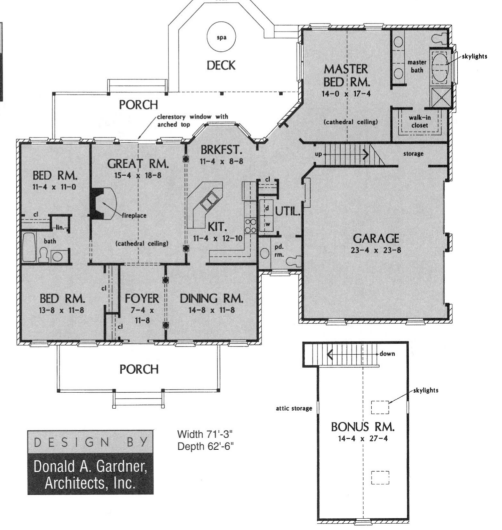

Width 71'-3"
Depth 62'-6"

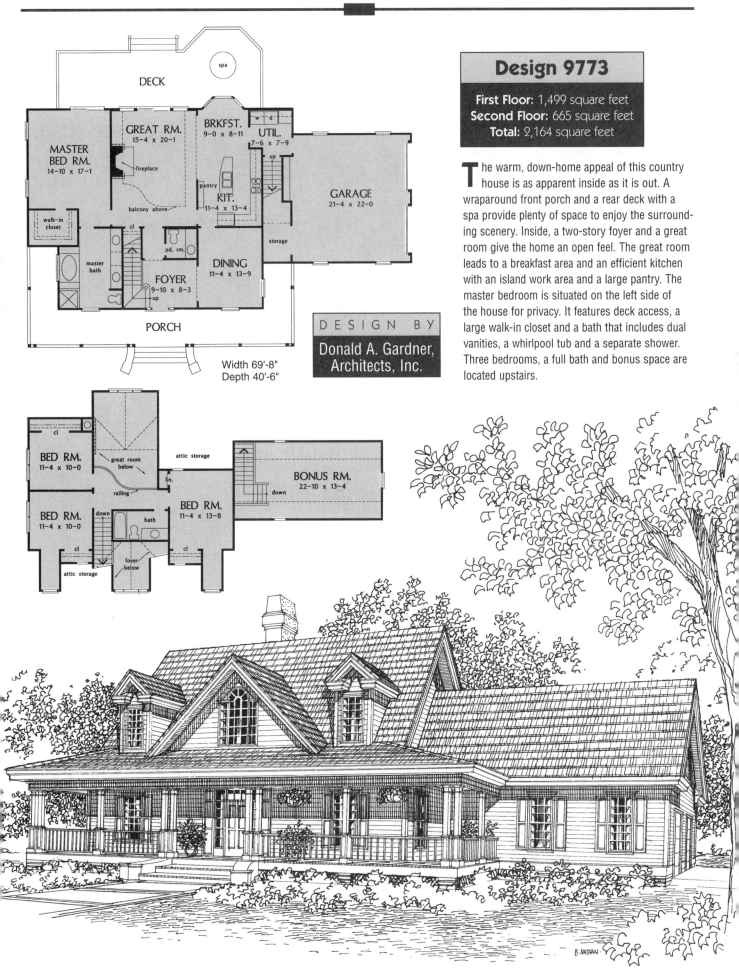

DECK

spa

GREAT RM.
15-4 x 20-1

BRKFST.
9-0 x 8-11

w | d

UTIL.
7-6 x 7-9

up

MASTER
BED RM.
14-10 x 17-1

fireplace

pantry

GARAGE
21-4 x 22-0

balcony above

KIT.
11-4 x 13-4

walk-in
closet

storage

cl

master
bath

pd. rm.

DINING
11-4 x 13-9

FOYER
9-10 x 8-3

up

PORCH

Width 69'-8"
Depth 40'-6"

DESIGN BY

Donald A. Gardner,
Architects, Inc.

# Design 9773

**First Floor:** 1,499 square feet
**Second Floor:** 665 square feet
**Total:** 2,164 square feet

The warm, down-home appeal of this country house is as apparent inside as it is out. A wraparound front porch and a rear deck with a spa provide plenty of space to enjoy the surrounding scenery. Inside, a two-story foyer and a great room give the home an open feel. The great room leads to a breakfast area and an efficient kitchen with an island work area and a large pantry. The master bedroom is situated on the left side of the house for privacy. It features deck access, a large walk-in closet and a bath that includes dual vanities, a whirlpool tub and a separate shower. Three bedrooms, a full bath and bonus space are located upstairs.

cl

BED RM.
11-4 x 10-0

great room
below

attic storage

lin.

BONUS RM.
22-10 x 13-4

railing

down

BED RM.
11-4 x 10-0

down

bath

BED RM.
11-4 x 13-8

cl

attic storage

foyer
below

cl

B. NATHAN

**G**abled dormers accent the facade of this classic farmhouse. The covered front porch is a perfect spot for enjoying cool evening breezes. Inside, this home's layout provides privacy for both the homeowner and the family. The children's bedrooms are found on the left of the foyer and share a full bath with dual vanities. To the right of the foyer is the formal dining room. The great room offers an angled, raised-hearth fireplace with an accommodating media shelf. The central, U-shaped kitchen is easily accessible from any room and opens to a sun-drenched morning room. The private master suite is impressive with its access to the sun patio, large walk-in closet and luxurious bath.

DESIGN BY
**Home Planners**

### Design 3677

**Square Footage:** 2,090

L D

Width 76'
Depth 64'

**QUOTE ONE**®
Cost to build? See page 214
to order complete cost estimate
to build this house in your area!

MASTER SUITE 20⁰ x 11⁶
SITTING
SEAT
SPA
SUN TERRACE
SLPNG · CLG
MASTER BATH
WALK-IN CLOSET
LOW SHELF
SHWR
GARDEN TUB
POWDER RM
MORNING ROOM 11⁶ x 13⁶ 9'-0" CLG
HVAC
WH
BROOM CLOSET
UTILITY SINK
GARAGE 21⁸ x 20⁰
COVERED PATIO
RAILING
BEDRM 11⁶ x 10⁰ SLOPED CLG
GREAT RM 19⁰ x 13⁰ SLOPED CLG
HOME CENTER
KIT 11⁶ x 18⁰ 9'-0" CLG
PANTRY
REF'R
W D
LAUNDRY ROOM
CURB
SHWR
BATH
MEDIA SHELF
BEDRM 11⁶ x 10⁶ SLOPED CLG
LOW WALL
FOYER
DINING RM 11⁴ x 11⁶ SLOPED CLG
COVERED PORCH
RAILING

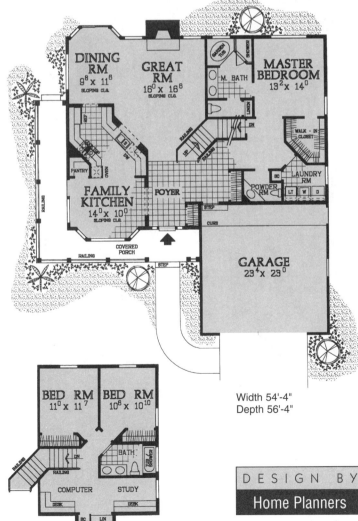

DINING RM
9⁸ x 11⁶
SLOPING CLG.

GREAT RM
18⁰ x 18⁶
SLOPING CLG.

MASTER BEDROOM
13² x 14⁰

M. BATH

WALK-IN CLOSET

DN

PANTRY

LAUNDRY RM

FAMILY KITCHEN
14⁰ x 10⁰
SLOPING CLG.

FOYER

POWDER RM

COVERED PORCH

RAILING

RAILING

UP

STEP

CURB

GARAGE
23⁴ x 29⁰

BED RM
11⁰ x 11⁷

BED RM
10⁶ x 10¹⁰

BATH

TUB SHOWER

COMPUTER

STUDY

DESK

DESK

DN

RAILING

LIN

Width 54'-4"
Depth 56'-4"

## Design 3609

**First Floor:** 1,624 square feet
**Second Floor:** 596 square feet
**Total:** 2,220 square feet

**L** **D**

This home's front-projecting garage allows utilization of a narrow, less expensive building site. The wrap-around porch provides sheltered entrances and outdoor living access from the family kitchen. Open planning, sloping ceilings and an abundance of windows highlight the formal dining room/great room area. Notice the second bay window in the dining room. The great room has a centered fireplace as its focal point. The master bedroom has a big walk-in closet and the master bath has twin lavatories, a garden tub, a stall shower and a compartmented toilet with a linen closet. Upstairs are two bedrooms, a bath with twin lavatories, plus an outstanding computer/study area.

DESIGN BY
**Home Planners**

QUOTE ONE®

Cost to build? See page 214
to order complete cost estimate
to build this house in your area!

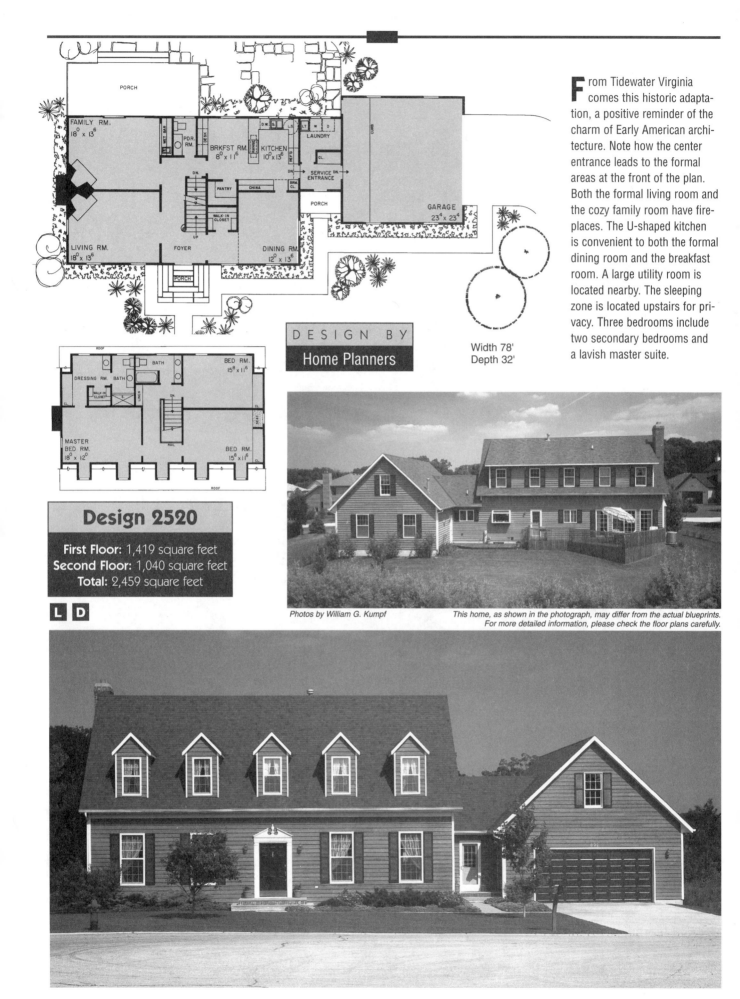

From Tidewater Virginia comes this historic adaptation, a positive reminder of the charm of Early American architecture. Note how the center entrance leads to the formal areas at the front of the plan. Both the formal living room and the cozy family room have fireplaces. The U-shaped kitchen is convenient to both the formal dining room and the breakfast room. A large utility room is located nearby. The sleeping zone is located upstairs for privacy. Three bedrooms include two secondary bedrooms and a lavish master suite.

**Width 78'**
**Depth 32'**

DESIGN BY
**Home Planners**

## Design 2520

**First Floor:** 1,419 square feet
**Second Floor:** 1,040 square feet
**Total:** 2,459 square feet

**L** **D**

Photos by William G. Kumpf

*This home, as shown in the photograph, may differ from the actual blueprints. For more detailed information, please check the floor plans carefully.*

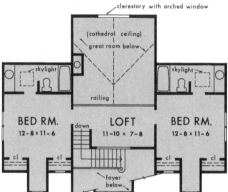

clerestory with arched window

(cathedral ceiling)
great room below

skylight                              skylight

railing

BED RM.          LOFT          BED RM.
12-8 x 11-6      11-10 x 7-8      12-8 x 11-6

down

cl          cl          cl          cl

foyer
below

clerestory with palladian window

**W**ith an elegant but casual exterior, this four-bedroom farmhouse celebrates sunlight with a Palladian window and triple dormers, a skylit screened porch and a rear arched window. The clerestory window in the two-story foyer throws natural light across the loft to the great room, with a fireplace and a cathedral ceiling. The center island kitchen and the breakfast area open to the great room through an elegant colonnade. The first-floor master suite is a calm retreat with its own access to the screened porch through a bay area—and a luxurious bath awaits with a garden tub, dual lavatories and a separate shower. Upstairs, two family bedrooms offer plush amenities: a skylight, a private bath, and a dormer window in each room. A hall loft overlooks the great room below.

D E S I G N   B Y
**Donald A. Gardner, Architects, Inc.**

**QUOTE ONE**®
Cost to build? See page 214
to order complete cost estimate
to build this house in your area!

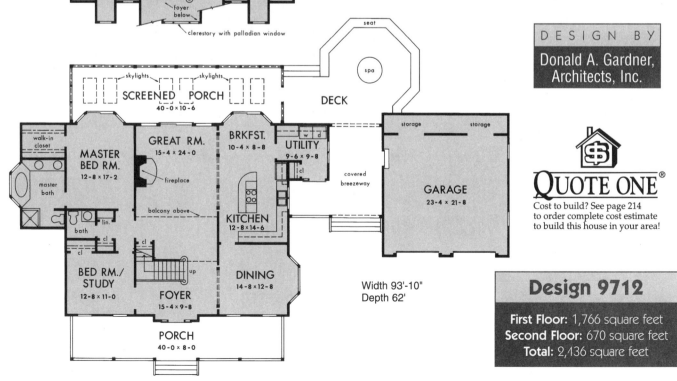

seat

spa

skylights        skylights

SCREENED   PORCH
40-0 x 10-6

DECK

walk-in
closet

MASTER
BED RM.
12-8 x 17-2

master
bath

GREAT RM.
15-4 x 24-0

fireplace

balcony above

bath          lin.

cl

BED RM./
STUDY
12-8 x 11-0

FOYER
15-4 x 9-8

up

BRKFST.
10-4 x 8-8

UTILITY
9-6 x 9-8

w   d

cl

covered
breezeway

storage          storage

GARAGE
23-4 x 21-8

KITCHEN
12-8 x 14-6

DINING
14-8 x 12-8

PORCH
40-0 x 8-0

Width 93'-10"
Depth 62'

**Design 9712**

**First Floor:** 1,766 square feet
**Second Floor:** 670 square feet
**Total:** 2,136 square feet

## Design 9196

**First Floor:** 1,525 square feet
**Second Floor:** 795 square feet
**Total:** 2,320 square feet

An L-shaped covered porch provides a happy marriage of indoor/outdoor relationships. The foyer opens onto a living room that presents opportunities to curl up in front of the fire with a good book, enjoy state-of-the art electronics housed in the built-in media center, or access the porch through a French door. A kitchen designed for efficiency combines with the breakfast area for informal meals and serves the nearby dining room for formal occasions. Located on the first floor for privacy, the master suite provides a relaxing retreat. A built-in bookcase stores your favorite novels and a spacious master bath features a whirlpool tub and a separate shower. Three bedrooms and a full bath complete the second floor.

DESIGN BY
**Larry W. Garnett & Associates, Inc.**

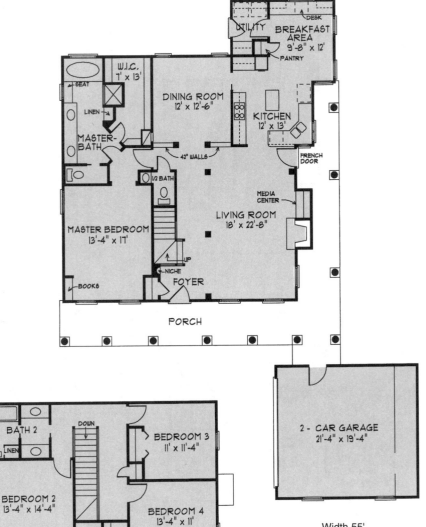

UTILITY

BREAKFAST AREA
9'-8" x 12'

DESK

PANTRY

W.I.C.
7' x 13'

SEAT

LINEN

DINING ROOM
12' x 12'-6"

KITCHEN
12' x 13'

MASTER BATH

42" WALLS

FRENCH DOOR

1/2 BATH

MEDIA CENTER

LIVING ROOM
18' x 22'-8"

MASTER BEDROOM
13'-4" x 17'

UP

NICHE

BOOKS

FOYER

PORCH

BATH 2

LINEN

DOWN

BEDROOM 3
11' x 11'-4"

BEDROOM 2
13'-4" x 14'-4"

BEDROOM 4
13'-4" x 11'

2 - CAR GARAGE
21'-4" x 19'-4"

Width 55'
Depth 74'-6"

This home, as shown in the photograph, may differ from the actual blueprints. For more detailed information, please check the floor plans carefully.

Photo by Carl Socolow

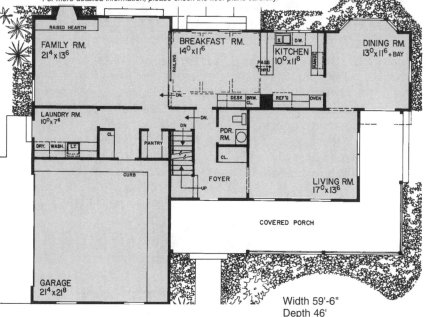

FAMILY RM.
21⁴x13⁶

RAISED HEARTH

BREAKFAST RM.
14⁰x11⁶

KITCHEN
10⁰x11⁸

DINING RM.
13⁰x11⁶ + BAY

LAUNDRY RM.
10⁰x7⁶

DRY. WASH.

CL.

PANTRY

DESK

BRM.
CL.

REF'G

OVEN

PDR.
RM.

CL.

CURB

FOYER

LIVING RM.
17⁰x13⁶

GARAGE
21⁴x21⁸

COVERED PORCH

Width 59'-6"
Depth 46'

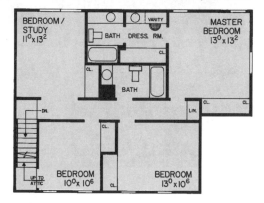

BEDROOM /
STUDY
11⁰x13²

BATH

DRESS. RM.

VANITY

MASTER
BEDROOM
13⁰x13²

CL.

BATH

LIN.

CL.

CL.

DN.

UP TO
ATTIC

BEDROOM
10⁰x10⁶

CL.

BEDROOM
13⁰x10⁶

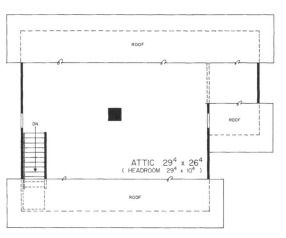

ROOF

ROOF

ROOF

DN

ATTIC 29⁴ x 26⁴
( HEADROOM 29⁴ x 10⁴ )

## Design 2774

**First Floor:** 1,366 square feet
**Second Floor:** 969 square feet
**Total:** 2,335 square feet

L  D

## Quote One®

Cost to build? See page 214
to order complete cost estimate
to build this house in your area!

Here's a great farmhouse adaptation with many of the most up-to-date features. There is the quiet corner living room which opens to the sizable dining room. This room enjoys plenty of natural light from the delightful bay window overlooking the rear yard and is conveniently located near the efficient U-shaped kitchen. The kitchen features many built-ins and a pass-through to the beam-ceilinged nook. Sliding glass doors to the terrace are found in both the family room and nook. The service entrance to the garage is flanked by a clothes closet and a large, walk-in pantry. Recreational activities and hobbies can be pursued in the basement area. Four bedrooms and two baths are located on the second floor. The master bedroom has a dressing room and double vanity.

DESIGN BY
Home Planners

## Design 9497

**First Floor:** 1,037 square feet
**Second Floor:** 1,090 square feet
**Total:** 2,127 square feet

Cedar siding makes a beautiful difference in this two-story country plan. Its symmetrical floor plan serves the needs of family living. Main living areas radiate from the entry hall: the formal living room is to the left and connects directly to the dining room; the family room is to the right and behind the garage. An L-shaped kitchen includes an island cooktop and a casual eating area that contains sliding glass doors to a rear terrace. The bedrooms are on the second floor and center around the open-railed staircase. The master suite enjoys a whirlpool spa, twin lavatories and a generous walk-in closet. Family bedrooms share a full bath with double-sink vanity.

DESIGN BY
**Alan Mascord Design Associates, Inc.**

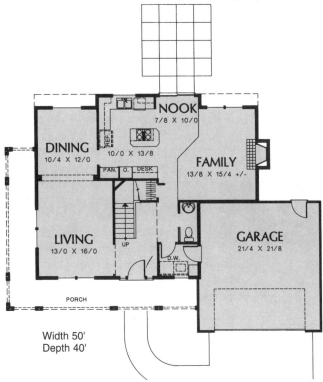

DINING 10/4 X 12/0

NOOK 7/8 X 10/0

10/0 X 13/8

FAMILY 13/8 X 15/4 +/-

LIVING 13/0 X 16/0

GARAGE 21/4 X 21/8

PORCH

Width 50'
Depth 40'

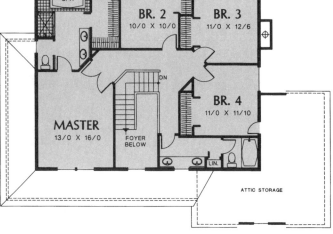

SPA

BR. 2 10/0 X 10/0

BR. 3 11/0 X 12/6

MASTER 13/0 X 16/0

FOYER BELOW

BR. 4 11/0 X 11/10

LIN.

ATTIC STORAGE

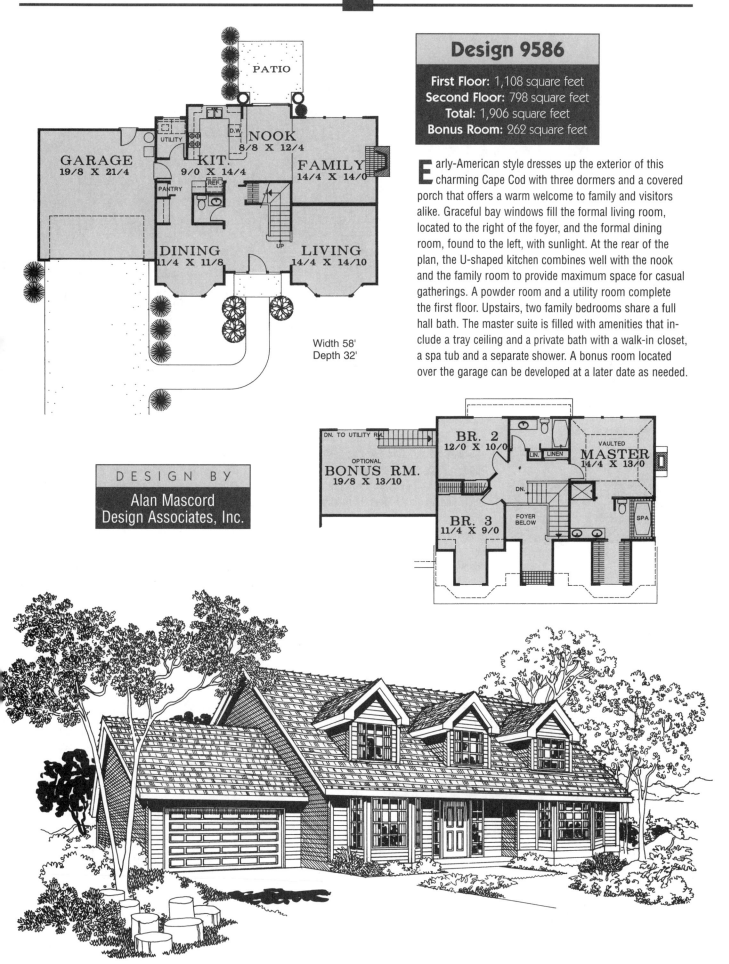

## Design 9586

**First Floor:** 1,108 square feet
**Second Floor:** 798 square feet
**Total:** 1,906 square feet
**Bonus Room:** 262 square feet

**E**arly-American style dresses up the exterior of this charming Cape Cod with three dormers and a covered porch that offers a warm welcome to family and visitors alike. Graceful bay windows fill the formal living room, located to the right of the foyer, and the formal dining room, found to the left, with sunlight. At the rear of the plan, the U-shaped kitchen combines well with the nook and the family room to provide maximum space for casual gatherings. A powder room and a utility room complete the first floor. Upstairs, two family bedrooms share a full hall bath. The master suite is filled with amenities that include a tray ceiling and a private bath with a walk-in closet, a spa tub and a separate shower. A bonus room located over the garage can be developed at a later date as needed.

Width 58'
Depth 32'

PATIO

GARAGE
19/8 X 21/4

UTILITY

D.W.

NOOK
8/8 X 12/4

KIT.
9/0 X 14/4

FAMILY
14/4 X 14/0

PANTRY

REF.

DINING
11/4 X 11/8

LIVING
14/4 X 14/10

UP

DESIGN BY
Alan Mascord
Design Associates, Inc.

DN. TO UTILITY RM.

OPTIONAL
BONUS RM.
19/8 X 13/10

BR. 2
12/0 X 10/0

LIN.   LINEN

VAULTED
MASTER
14/4 X 13/0

DN.

BR. 3
11/4 X 9/0

FOYER
BELOW

SPA

B. NATHAN.

## Design 9796

**First Floor:** 1,395 square feet
**Second Floor:** 489 square feet
**Total:** 1,884 square feet

The charm of this home is evident at first glance, but you'll especially appreciate its qualities the moment you step inside. A magnificent great room beckons with a cathedral ceiling and a fireplace with extended hearth, while sliding glass doors, framed by tall windows, provide access to the rear covered porch. A spacious open area to the right of the plan accomodates both formal and informal dining occasions. The formal dining area offers rear porch access and privacy walls that separate this area from the kitchen, which features a food preparation island and generous counter and cabinet space. The nearby bayed breakfast nook offers natural light and access to a private screened porch—ideal for casual entertaining. The second level is dedicated to the master suite which offers a luxurious bath and a sitting nook with window, but also includes a bonus room with skylights.

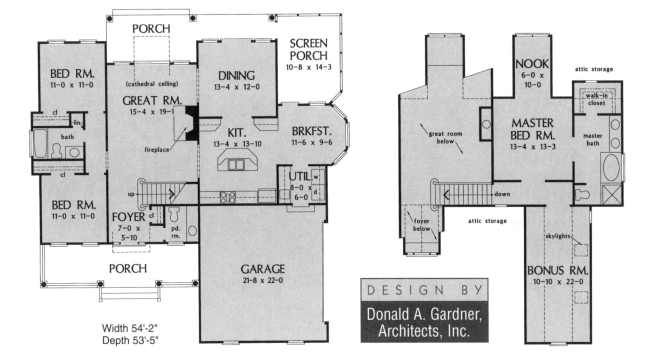

Width 54'-2"
Depth 53'-5"

DESIGN BY
**Donald A. Gardner,
Architects, Inc.**

DECK

(cathedral ceiling)

**GREAT RM.**
16-0 x 18-10

fireplace

**BED RM.**
12-2 x 13-4

cl

sto.

bath

lin.

cl

**BED RM.**
11-0 x 11-6

sto.

up

**FOYER**
9-6 x 6-8

**STUDY/ LIVING RM.**
11-0 x 12-0

porch

**BRKFST.**
12-0 x 9-8

**KIT.**
12-0 x 11-6

**DINING**
12-0 x 12-4

**MASTER BED RM.**
14-0 x 16-0

skylight

master bath

lin.

w d

walk-in closet

**UTIL.** cl

up

storage

**GARAGE**
22-8 x 19-8

(optional door location)

## Design 9799

**Square Footage:** 2,170
**Bonus Room:** 615 square feet

DESIGN BY

Donald A. Gardner,
Architects, Inc.

**B**rick accents and bright, arch-topped windows highlight the facade of this appealing home. The foyer introduces a clever interior design, starting with stylish formal living and dining rooms flanking the entry, each with a coffered ceiling and an arched, multi-pane window. The elegance continues with a cathedral ceiling in the great room which features a warming fireplace as well as rear deck access and opens to a sunny breakfast room through a columned archway. A convenient kitchen with food preparation island easily serves casual and formal dining areas. The dramatic master suite is carefully positioned to the rear of the plan for privacy and offers a coffered ceiling and access to the rear deck. A skylit bath with twin lavs, garden tub, separate shower and walk-in closet complete this lavish retreat. The second story offers 615 square feet of bonus space and a balcony overlook to the great room below.

Width 68'-10"
Depth 57'-4"

great room below

attic storage

down

(unfinished)
**BONUS**
12-2 x 17-1

down

(unfinished)
**BONUS**
12-0 x 13-6

**BONUS RM.**
22-8 x 14-5

skylights

balcony (optional)

attic storage

## Design 3662

**Square Footage:** 1,937
**Bonus Room:** 414 square feet

**L**

This transitional design wears a winsome, country look but delivers contemporary appeal. Arch-top and multi-pane windows complement gables, dormers and a columned, covered porch to create an inviting exterior. An angled entry introduces a refreshingly unique interior design, and opens to the principal living area. The great room offers a sloped ceiling, a fireplace with extended hearth, access to a patio deck retreat and built-in shelves for an entertainment center—or "build" a library. The kitchen shares a lovely feature with this room: an angled desk set against a curved half-wall with display below. Gourmet features in the kitchen includes a cooktop island, double sink and pantry—the outdoors compliments the morning nook with plenty of natural light. A satisfying master suite with sloped ceiling affords privacy and repose with a secluded sitting area and a relaxing bath with windowed garden tub, dual lavatories, compartmented toilet and walk-in closet with extra linen storage. Two family bedrooms share a full bath and a gallery hall off the living area. Plans for an optional bonus room are included.

Width 76'-4"
Depth 73'-4"

DESIGN BY
Home Planners

seat

spa

DECK

SCREEN PORCH
16-0 x 11-0
skylights

wet bar

BED RM.
12-4 x 11-8

GREAT RM.
16-0 x 17-4

fireplace

cabinets

cl

lin.

bath

cl

BED RM./ STUDY
12-0 x 12-0

FOYER
12-4 x 5-6

PORCH

BRKFST.
12-0 x 8-6

KITCHEN
12-0 x 12-8

DINING
12-0 x 13-8

up

MASTER BED RM.
13-4 x 18-8

skylights

master bath

walk-in closet

UTIL.

d- -w-

lin.

storage

GARAGE
22-0 x 20-4

storage

Width 69'-8"
Depth 67'-6"

attic storage

BONUS RM.
18-0 x 19-0

skylights

down

DESIGN BY
Donald A. Gardner,
Architects, Inc.

## Design 9734

**Square Footage:** 1,977
**Bonus Room:** 430 square feet

A two-story foyer with a Palladian window above sets the tone for this sunlit home. Columns mark the passage from the foyer to the great room, which features a centered fireplace and built-in cabinets. This room offers views and access to a rear screen porch with four skylights and a wet bar—and just a few steps away is a deck with spa. The nearby breakfast room offers a separate entrance to the rear deck and shares light from outdoor areas with the kitchen. The formal dining room offers a coffered ceiling and a Palladian window with views to the front property. A secluded master suite offers comfort and style to spare, with a skylit bath, corner whirlpool tub, generous walk-in closet and private access to the rear deck and spa. On the opposite side of the plan, a front bedroom with coffered ceiling and Palladian window could be a study. This room shares a hall bath with a secondary bedroom.

## Design 8126

**Square Footage:** 2,127
**Bonus Room:** 338 square feet

DESIGN BY
Larry E. Belk Designs

Three arched windows, shutters, and a brick facade provide just the right touch of elegance and give this home a picturesque appeal. Ten-foot ceilings in the living areas lend an open, spaciousness inside. A corner fireplace in the great room offers warmth and light to the main living areas. Guests and family alike will enjoy the rear covered patio with access to a sunny breakfast area and adjoining kitchen with snack counter. The formal dining room sits just off the foyer and opens to the great room through decorative columns. Luxurious accomodations abound in the master suite: a bath with coffered ceiling, large His and Hers closets, a whirlpool tub, a shower with a seat and knee-space vanity. Bedrooms 2 and 3 on the opposite side of the plan share a hall bath. Stairs at the front of the plan lead to an expandable area on the second floor. Please specify crawlspace or slab foundation when ordering.

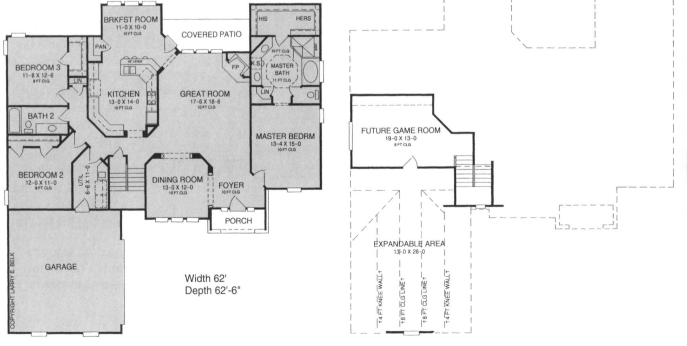

Width 62'
Depth 62'-6"

**BEDRM 3**
11-6 X 12-4

**BEDRM 2**
14-0 X 10-6

**GARAGE**
21-4 X 23-4

**BRKFST**
9-6 X 9-6
10 FT CLG

**KITCHEN**
10-6 X 14-6
10 FT CLG

**BATH 2**

LIN

PAN

**UTIL**
8-0 X 6-0

**PORCH**

FP

**GREAT ROOM**
19-4 X 17-6
11 FT CLG

ARCH

**DINING ROOM**
12-4 X 12-0
12 FT CLG

**FOYER**
10 FT CLG

**PORCH**

LIN

**MASTER BATH**

LEDGE

**MASTER BEDRM**
13-4 X 14-6
10 FT CLG

Width 60'-10"
Depth 65'

**BATH 2**

STAIRS
UP TO FUTURE
+ EXP AREA +

**BEDRM 2**
14-0 X 11-4

**UTIL**

COPYRIGHT LARRY E. BELK

↑ LINE OF WALLS FOR ROOM ABOVE ↑
↑ LINE OF 8' CLG FOR ROOM ABOVE ↑

**GARAGE**

↑ LINE OF 8' CLG FOR ROOM ABOVE ↑
↑ LINE OF WALLS FOR ROOM ABOVE ↑

DESIGN BY
**Larry E. Belk Designs**

**S**implicity embraces elegance in this traditional design, which features an entry flanked by square columns and dominated by a gable finished with dentil moulding. An angled foyer opens through columned archways to an extensive great room with fireplace which is flanked by picture windows. The formal dining room offers beautiful surroundings with columns and a graceful archway to the great room, allowing dinner guests to enjoy the glow of the fireplace. An octagonal, windowed breakfast room offers bright lights—whether in the big city or in the wide open spaces—and views galore! A roomy kitchen shares the extension of this sunny space and overlooks the great room. A distinctive master suite offers a private retreat for the homeowner, with a raised ceiling, corner windows, and a striking bath with angled tub, separate shower, twin lavatories and generous walk-in closet. Bedrooms 2 and 3 share a hall bath. Please specify crawlspace or slab foundation when ordering.

## Design 8166

**Square Footage:** 1,955
**Bonus Room:** 240 square feet

Copyright 1992 Stephen S. Fuller, Inc.

This handsome Colonial home will serve the family well for generations to come. Interesting window treatments add to livability—many of the rooms expand into bays. The living and dining rooms define the front of the house while the family room with its fireplace, the breakfast nook and the kitchen with its abundant counter space all define the back of the house. A deck serves the rear of the house and may be accessed from the family room. Upstairs, a gracious master suite offers a windowed bay and a secluded bath with a garden tub positioned within a dormer with window. Three family bedrooms share a balcony hall which overlooks the foyer, and a hall bath with double-bowl vanity. This home is designed with a basement foundation.

MASTER SUITE
15'-6" x 15'-0"

BEDROOM No.2
11'-6" x 12'-6"

BEDROOM No.4
10'-0" x 10'-0"

M. BATH

DN

OPEN TO BELOW

BATH

BEDROOM No.3
13'-0" x 13'-0"

MASTER CLOSET

BREAKFAST
11'-0" x 6'-0"

FAMILY ROOM
15'-6" x 17'-0"

LAUNDRY

KITCHEN
10'-0" X 13'-8"

PWDR

COAT

PAN.

DN

FOYER
7'-10" x 12'-4"

UP

TWO-CAR GARAGE
20'-0" x 25'-8"

LIVING ROOM
10'-2" x 13'-0"

DINING ROOM
10'-2" x 12'-0"

STOOP

Width 54'
Depth 39'

## Design 9905

**First Floor:** 1,020 square feet
**Second Floor:** 1,175 square feet
**Total:** 2,195 square feet

DESIGN BY
**Design Traditions**

# Design 9831

**Square Footage:** 2,150
**Expandable Lower Level:**
2,150 square feet

**QUOTE ONE®**
Cost to build? See page 214
to order complete cost estimate
to build this house in your area!

DESIGN BY
**Design Traditions**

Width 64'
Depth 64'-4"

This home draws its inspiration from both French and English country homes. From the foyer and across the spacious great room, French doors give a generous view of the covered rear porch. The adjoining dining room is subtly defined by the use of columns and a large triple window. The kitchen, with its generous work island, adjoins the breakfast area and keeping room with fireplace, a vaulted ceiling and an abundant use of windows. The study to the front of the first floor could be a guest room. It shares a bath with the bedroom beside it. The home is completed by a quiet master suite located at the rear. It contains a bay window, a garden tub and His and Hers vanities. Space on the lower level can be developed later.

**O**ne-story living takes a lovely traditional turn in this brick one-story home. The foyer opens to the dining room through columned arches and to the great room, creating an extensive living area with a sense of spaciousness. To the right of the plan, this area opens to a second, more casual, living area through double doors. Gourmet cooks will fully appreciate this well-appointed kitchen with large food prepartion counter and walk-in pantry. Family and friends will gather around the fireplace in the adjacent keeping room with beautiful bayed breakfast nook. To the left of the plan, two family bedrooms and a full bath share a central hall which leads to a sizable master suite with coffered ceiling, lovely bayed sitting area, and sumptuous bath with compartmented garden tub, dressing area and walk-in closet. This home is designed with a basement foundation.

DECK

SITTING AREA
12'-0" X 12'-0"

MASTER SUITE
13'-0" X 17'-6"

M.BATH

M.CLOSET

GREAT ROOM
20'-6" X 19'-0"

KITCHEN
10'-0" X 18'-0"

BREAKFAST
11'-4" X 10'-0"

KEEPING ROOM
11'-4" X 11'-0"

PNTRY

DN.

LAUNDRY

CLO.

CLO.

BATH

LIN.

BEDROOM NO. 3
12'-0" X 11'-8"

COAT

FOYER
8'-0" X 14'-4"

DINING ROOM
12'-0" X 14'-4"

TWO CAR GARAGE
21'-4" X 21'-5"

BEDROOM NO. 2
13'-10" X 12'-6"

STOOP

Width 69'
Depth 49'-6"

**QUOTE ONE**®
Cost to build? See page 214
to order complete cost estimate
to build this house in your area!

DESIGN BY
**Design Traditions**

Copyright 1992 Stephen S. Fuller, Inc.

Copyright 1992 Stephen S. Fuller.Inc.

Width 62'
Depth 61'-6"

BEDROOM NO. 3
11'-6" X 11'-0"

BATH

BEDROOM NO. 2
11'-4" X 11'-0"

SUN ROOM
12'-0" X 13'-8"

PORCH

PORCH

BREAKFAST
10'-0" X 9'-0"

LAUNDRY

KITCHEN
12'-0" X 13'-2"

FAMILY ROOM
18'-0" X 14'-0"

MASTER BATH

W.I.C.

MASTER BEDROOM
13'-4" X 15'-6"

BATH

STORAGE

DN

TWO CAR GARAGE
20'-4" X 19'-8"

DINING ROOM
11'-4" X 11'-4"

FOYER
6'-8" X 11'-10"

PORCH

DEN/GUEST BEDROOM
11'-4" X 14'-0"

DESIGN BY
Design Traditions

**QUOTE ONE®**

Cost to build? See page 214
to order complete cost estimate
to build this house in your area!

## Design 9862

**Square Footage:** 2,170

This classic cottage features a stone and wooden exterior with an arch-detailed porch and a box-bay window. From the foyer, double doors open to the den with built-in bookcases and a fireplace. A full bath is situated next to the den, allowing for an optional guest room. The family room is centrally located, just beyond the foyer. Its hearth is framed by windows overlooking the porch at the rear of the home. The master bedroom opens onto the rear porch. The master bath, with a large walk-in closet, double vanities, a corner tub and a separate shower, completes this relaxing retreat. Left of the family room awaits a sun room with access to the covered porch. A breakfast area complements the attractive and efficiently designed kitchen. Two secondary bedrooms with large closets share a full bath featuring double vanities. This home is designed with a basement foundation.

# Design Q385

**First Floor:** 1,445 square feet
**Second Floor:** 652 square feet
**Total:** 2,097 square feet

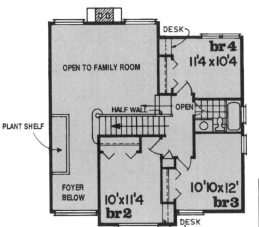

DESIGN BY
**Select Home Designs**

A portico entry, graceful arches and brick detailing provide appeal and a low-maintenance exterior for this design. A half-circle transom over the entry lights the two-story foyer while a plant shelf lines the hallway to the sunken family room. This living space holds a vaulted ceiling, masonry fireplace and French-door access to the railed patio. The nearby kitchen has a center prep island, built-in desk overlooking the family room and extensive pantries in the breakfast area. The formal dining room has a tray ceiling and access to the foyer and the central hall. The master suite is on the first level for privacy and convenience. It features a walk-in closet and lavish bath with twin vanities, whirlpool tub and separate shower. Family bedrooms are on the second floor. Bedroom 4 and Bedroom 2 boast built-in desks. Plans include details for both a basement and a crawlspace foundation.

Width 56'-8"
Depth 48'-4"

## Design Q390

**First Floor:** 1,353 square feet
**Second Floor:** 899 square feet
**Total:** 2,252 square feet
**Bonus Room:** 183 square feet

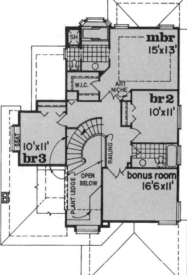

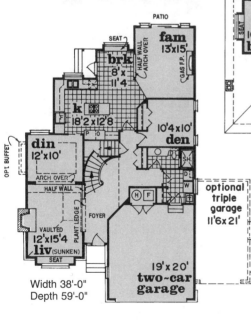

PATIO

SEAT

**brk**
8' x
11'4

HALF WALL
ARCH OVER

**fam**
13'x15'
GAS F.P.

**k**
18'2'x12'8

**din**
12'x10'

OPT. BUFFET

10'4'x10'
**den**

ARCH OVER

HALF WALL

PLANT LEDGE

FOYER

VAULTED
12'x15'4
**liv** (SUNKEN)
SEAT

optional
triple
garage
11'6 x 21'

19'x20'
**two~car
garage**

Width 38'-0"
Depth 59'-0"

SH

**mbr**
15'x13'

W.I.C.

ART
NICHE

**br2**
10'x11'

SEAT

10'x11'
**br3**

PLANT LEDGE

OPEN
BELOW

RAILING

bonus room
16'6'x11'

D E S I G N   B Y
**Select Home Designs**

This three-bedroom plan has bonus space and offers two attractive exterior finishes: horizontal siding with brick detailing or California stucco. Plans include details for both. Interior details make the floor plan unique. A plant ledge visually separates the vaulted foyer from the sunken living room. Note the fireplace and window seat here. A coffered ceiling, optional buffet recess and elegant archway distinguish the dining room. The nearby L-shaped kitchen, with center cooking island, adjoins a sunny breakfast room and large family room. A private den could serve as guest space if needed. On the second floor are three bedrooms and bonus space to develop into a fourth bedroom if needed, adding 183 square feet to the total. The master suite has a coffered ceiling and bath with raised tub and shower. Family bedrooms share a full bath. If you find that a two-car garage is not sufficient, plans include options for a triple garage. Plans include details for both a basement and crawlspace foundation.

**ALTERNATE FRONT PERSPECTIVE**

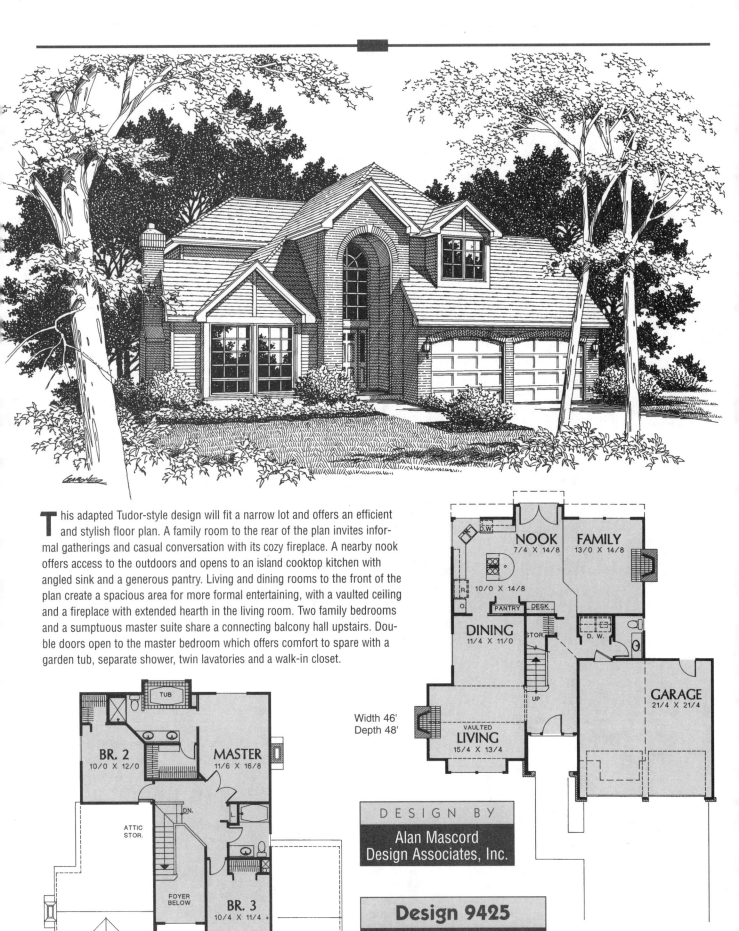

This adapted Tudor-style design will fit a narrow lot and offers an efficient and stylish floor plan. A family room to the rear of the plan invites informal gatherings and casual conversation with its cozy fireplace. A nearby nook offers access to the outdoors and opens to an island cooktop kitchen with angled sink and a generous pantry. Living and dining rooms to the front of the plan create a spacious area for more formal entertaining, with a vaulted ceiling and a fireplace with extended hearth in the living room. Two family bedrooms and a sumptuous master suite share a connecting balcony hall upstairs. Double doors open to the master bedroom which offers comfort to spare with a garden tub, separate shower, twin lavatories and a walk-in closet.

Width 46'
Depth 48'

**NOOK**
7/4 X 14/8

**FAMILY**
13/0 X 14/8

10/0 X 14/8

PANTRY DESK

**DINING**
11/4 X 11/0

**GARAGE**
21/4 X 21/4

UP

**VAULTED**
**LIVING**
15/4 X 13/4

TUB

**BR. 2**
10/0 X 12/0

**MASTER**
11/6 X 16/8

ATTIC STOR.

DN.

FOYER BELOW

**BR. 3**
10/4 X 11/4

DESIGN BY

**Alan Mascord**
**Design Associates, Inc.**

## Design 9425

**First Floor:** 1,062 square feet
**Second Floor:** 838 square feet
**Total:** 1,900 square feet

## Design 9582

**First Floor:** 972 square feet
**Second Floor:** 843 square feet
**Total:** 1,815 square feet
**Bonus Room:** 180 square feet

### DESIGN BY
**Alan Mascord Design Associates, Inc.**

A brick arch and a two-story bay window adorn the facade of this comfortable family home. Inside, the formal bayed living room and dining room combine to make entertaining a breeze. At the rear of the home, family life is easy with the open floor plan of the family room, nook and efficient kitchen. A fireplace graces the family room, and sliding glass doors access the outdoors from the nook. A powder room is conveniently located in the entry hall to make it easily accessible. Upstairs, three bedrooms include the master suite with pampering bath. A full hall bath with twin-vanities is shared by the family bedrooms. A bonus room is available for future development as a study, library or fourth bedroom.

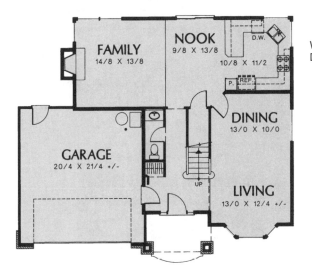

FAMILY
14/8 X 13/8

NOOK
9/8 X 13/8

D.W.

10/8 X 11/2

P.  REF.

DINING
13/0 X 10/0

GARAGE
20/4 X 21/4 +/-

UP

LIVING
13/0 X 12/4 +/-

Width 45'
Depth 37'

BR. 3
12/0 X 10/0

BR. 2
11/0 X 10/0

LIN.

NICHE

LIN.

DN.

BONUS
14/4 X 10/0

D. W.

FOYER
BELOW

MASTER
13/0 X 16/6 +/-
(9'-6" CLG.)

A combined hip and gable roof, keystones and horizontal wood siding lend an air of distinction to this lovely traditional home. The floor plan flows easily with living areas radiating from the foyer. Combined living space to the rear of the plan includes an extensive family room with warming fireplace, a bay-windowed breakfast nook with access to the rear yard, and a well-appointed kitchen with angled sink and peninsular cooktop counter. Upstairs, a master suite with a vaulted ceiling and pampering bath offer a soothing retreat with corner whirlpool spa, compartmented toilet and generous walk-in closet. Bonus space offers the possibility of a fourth bedroom. Two family bedrooms share a hall bath with compartmented tub. This plan includes an alternate side-load garage.

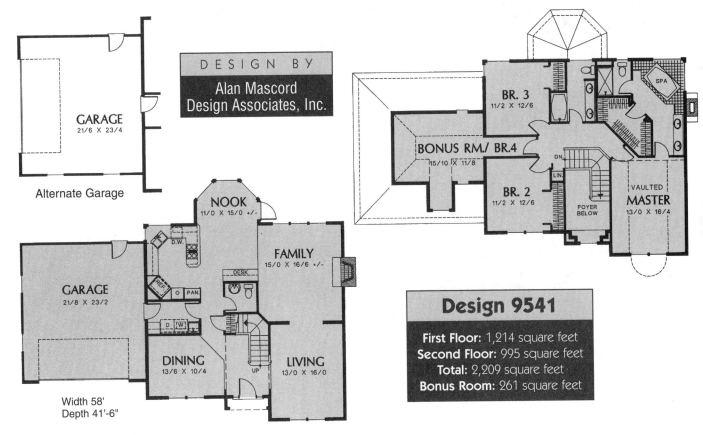

**Alternate Garage**

GARAGE 21/6 X 23/4

DESIGN BY
Alan Mascord
Design Associates, Inc.

GARAGE 21/8 X 23/2

NOOK 11/0 X 15/0 +/-

FAMILY 15/0 X 16/6 +/-

DINING 13/6 X 10/4

LIVING 13/0 X 16/0

Width 58'
Depth 41'-6"

BR. 3 11/2 X 12/6

SPA

BONUS RM/ BR.4 15/10 X 11/8

BR. 2 11/2 X 12/6

VAULTED MASTER 13/0 X 16/4

FOYER BELOW

## Design 9541

**First Floor:** 1,214 square feet
**Second Floor:** 995 square feet
**Total:** 2,209 square feet
**Bonus Room:** 261 square feet

## NOOK
9/4 X 11/0 +
(9' CLG.)

10/10 X 13/10

PAN. DESK

## FAMILY
16/10 X 14/0 +/
(9' CLG.)

## GARAGE
20/8 X 23/4

STOR.

D. W.

## DINING
13/4 X 10/0
(9' CLG.)

## DEN
10/0 X 10/0 +
(9' CLG.)

UP

## PARLOR
13/4 X 15/0
(9' CLG.)

Width 56'
Depth 42'

TUB

## BR. 4
10/0 X 11/0

## BR. 3
11/0 X 11/0

LIN.

DN.

## BONUS RM.
15/8 X 13/4

LINEN

## MASTER
VAULTED
13/4 X 17/0 +

FOYER
BELOW

## BR. 2
12/4 X 10/0

PLANT
SHELF

# Design 9477

**First Floor:** 1,308 square feet
**Second Floor:** 1,141 square feet
**Total:** 2,449 square feet
**Bonus Room:** 266 square feet

Arched windows, gables and transoms lend an air of quiet elegance to this traditional design. The interior design allows plenty of space for formal and informal occasions. To the rear of the first floor, an open living area includes the family room with warming fireplace, a sunny breakfast area and a gourmet kitchen with cooktop island counter. Double doors open to a secluded den off the foyer, with a powder room nearby. For more formal occasions, a parlor with fireplace and extended hearth leads to a formal dining area through columned arches. Upstairs, a master suite with vaulted ceiling and a spacious bath opens to a connecting hall which leads to three family bedrooms and a full bath. Bonus space could become a study or gameroom.

## DESIGN BY
## Alan Mascord
## Design Associates, Inc.

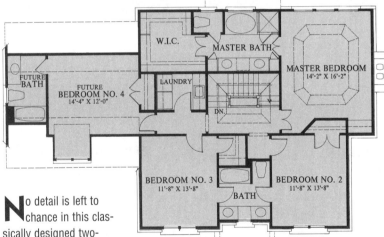

FUTURE BATH

W.I.C.

MASTER BATH

MASTER BEDROOM
14'-2" X 16'-2"

LAUNDRY

FUTURE BEDROOM NO. 4
14'-4" X 12'-0"

DN.

BEDROOM NO. 3
11'-8" X 13'-8"

BATH

BEDROOM NO. 2
11'-8" X 13'-8"

## Design 9886

**First Floor:** 1,165 square feet
**Second Floor:** 1,050 square feet
**Total:** 2,215 square feet

DESIGN BY
**Design Traditions**

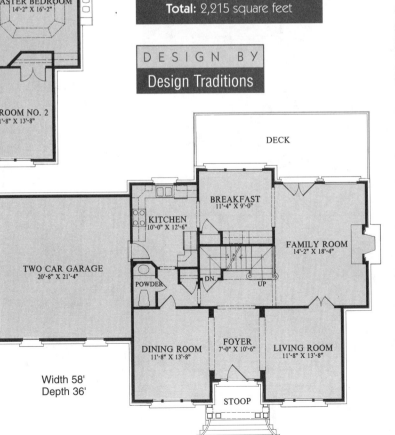

DECK

BREAKFAST
11'-4" X 9'-0"

KITCHEN
10'-0" X 12'-6"

FAMILY ROOM
14'-2" X 18'-4"

TWO CAR GARAGE
20'-8" X 21'-4"

POWDER

DN.

UP

DINING ROOM
11'-8" X 13'-8"

FOYER
7'-0" X 10'-6"

LIVING ROOM
11'-8" X 13'-8"

Width 58'
Depth 36'

STOOP

No detail is left to chance in this classically designed two-story home. A formal entry opens to the living and dining rooms through graceful arches. For more casual entertaining, the family room provides ample space for large gatherings and features a warming fireplace and access to the rear deck through double doors. A roomy breakfast area is bathed in beautiful natural light from triple windows. The adjacent L-shaped kitchen handles any occasion with ease. Upstairs, the master suite runs the width of the house and includes a generous walk-in closet and bath with knee-space vanity, twin lavatories, garden tub and separate shower. A central hall leads to two family bedrooms and a full bath as well as bonus space which offers the possibility of a future fourth bedroom and bath. This home is designed with a basement foundation.

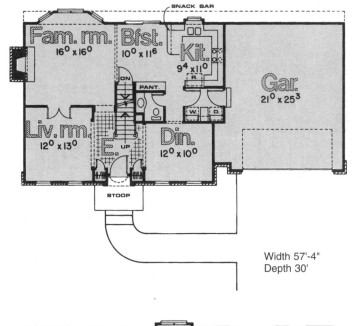

SNACK BAR

Fam. rm.
16⁰ x 16⁰

Bfst.
10⁰ x 11⁶

Kit.
9⁴ x 11⁰

Gar.
21⁰ x 25³

PANT.

Liv. rm.
12⁰ x 13⁰

UP

Din.
12⁰ x 10⁰

W. D.

STOOP

Width 57'-4"
Depth 30'

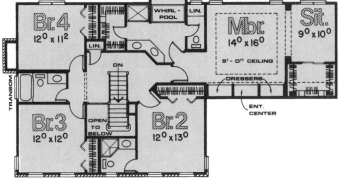

Br. 4
12⁰ x 11²

WHIRL-POOL

LIN.

LIN.

Mbr.
14⁰ x 16⁰

9' - 0" CEILING

Sit.
9⁰ x 10⁰

LIN.

TRANSOM

DN

DRESSERS

Br. 3
12⁰ x 12⁰

OPEN
TO
BELOW

Br. 2
12⁰ x 13⁰

ENT.
CENTER

## Design 9344

**First Floor:** 1,000 square feet
**Second Floor:** 1,345 square feet
**Total:** 2,345 square feet

An arched entry, shutters and a brick facade highlight the exterior of this modern, two-story Colonial home. Living and dining rooms at the front of the plan accomodate formal occasions. The rear of the plan is designed for informal gatherings, with a generous family room with warming fireplace and bayed conversation area, a bright breakfast area and a well-equipped U-shaped kitchen with snack bar. Bright windows and French doors add appeal to the living room. Upstairs, a U-shaped balcony hall overlooks the entry below and connects four bedrooms, including a master suite. This retreat features a private sitting room, two walk-in closets, compartmented bath, separate vanities and a window-brightened whirlpool tub.

DESIGN BY
**Design Basics, Inc.**

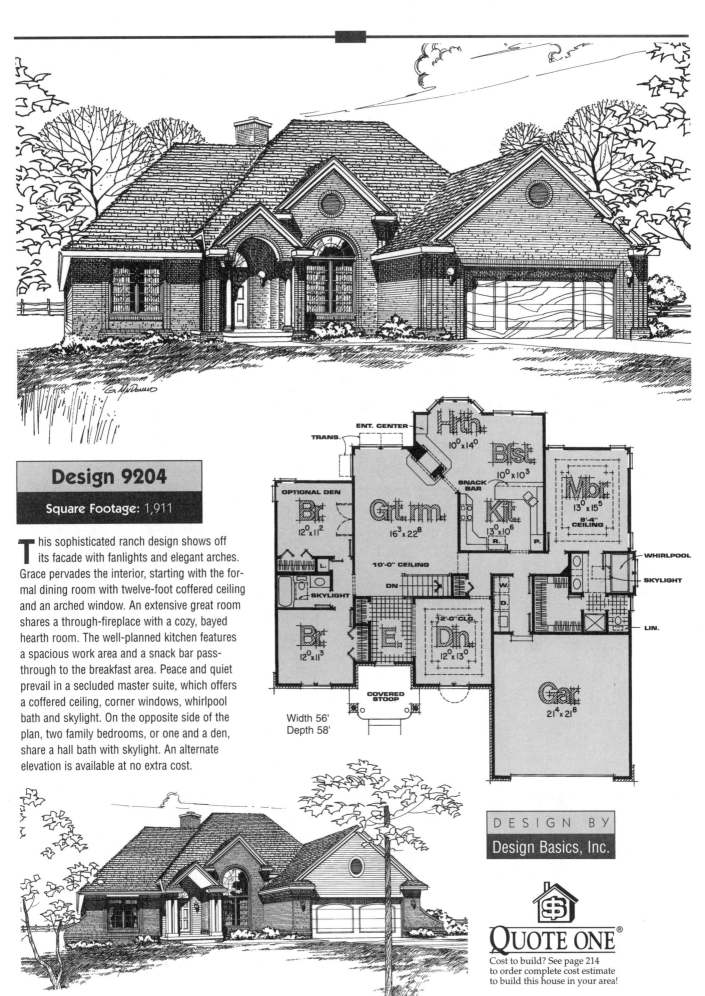

## Design 9204

**Square Footage:** 1,911

This sophisticated ranch design shows off its facade with fanlights and elegant arches. Grace pervades the interior, starting with the formal dining room with twelve-foot coffered ceiling and an arched window. An extensive great room shares a through-fireplace with a cozy, bayed hearth room. The well-planned kitchen features a spacious work area and a snack bar pass-through to the breakfast area. Peace and quiet prevail in a secluded master suite, which offers a coffered ceiling, corner windows, whirlpool bath and skylight. On the opposite side of the plan, two family bedrooms, or one and a den, share a hall bath with skylight. An alternate elevation is available at no extra cost.

Width 56'
Depth 58'

DESIGN BY
**Design Basics, Inc.**

QUOTE ONE®
Cost to build? See page 214
to order complete cost estimate
to build this house in your area!

## Design 9362

**Square Footage:** 2,172

**QUOTE ONE**®

Cost to build? See page 214
to order complete cost estimate
to build this house in your area!

**B**eautiful arches and grand rooflines announce an interior that is both spectacular and convenient. The entry leads to a magnificent great room with centered fireplace and views to the rear grounds—a perfect complement to a front-facing formal living room. The dining room with tray ceiling and double arched windows opens from the entry and is just steps away from the kitchen—which features a food preparation island, pantry, and access to a rear patio through the breakfast area. Bedroom 3 offers the possibility of a guest room at this end of the plan, with a nearby full bath. To the right of the plan, a glorious master suite, with raised ceiling and triple transoms, offers a relaxing bath with windowed whirlpool tub, twin lavatories and walk-in closet. A nearby family bedroom has access to a hall bath. The three-car garage offers extra storage space.

DESIGN BY
**Design Basics, Inc.**

Width 76'
Depth 46'

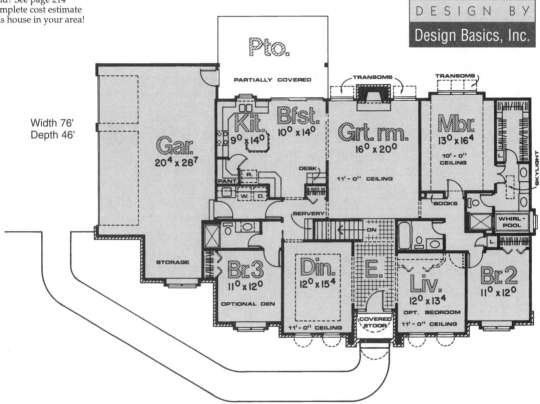

A two-level entry, varying rooflines and multipane windows add to the spectacular appeal of this three-bedroom home. To the right of the foyer, the formal dining room offers elegant columns and archways that open to the main living areas. A generous family room offers space for an optional fireplace and an abundance of light through triple windows. An angled peninsular counter in the tiled kitchen opens that area to natural light from the bayed breakfast nook and the glass doors to the covered patio. A gracious master suite is carefully placed to the rear of the plan for privacy, offering views of the rear grounds as well as a roomy tiled bath with garden tub, separate shower and walk-in closet. Two additional bedrooms share a full bath.

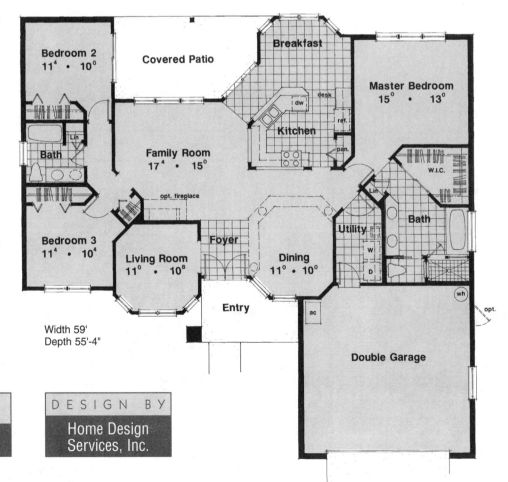

Width 59'
Depth 55'-4"

## Design 8644

**Square Footage:** 1,831

DESIGN BY
Home Design
Services, Inc.

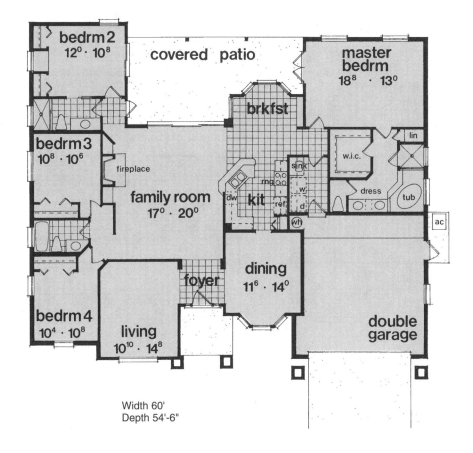

bedrm 2
12⁰ · 10⁸

covered patio

master bedrm
18⁸ · 13⁰

brkfst

bedrm 3
10⁸ · 10⁶

fireplace

family room
17⁰ · 20⁰

sink

w.i.c.

lin

dw

kit

rng

w

dress

tub

ref

d

wh

ac

bedrm 4
10⁴ · 10⁸

living
10¹⁰ · 14⁸

foyer

dining
11⁶ · 14⁰

double garage

Width 60'
Depth 54'-6"

## Design 8605

**Square Footage:** 2,171

This design offers elegance and spirit with its columned entry and fanlights, yet its floor plan has economy in mind. The foyer opens directly into the main living area—a spacious family room with fireplace and access to a rear covered patio. Vaulted ceilings maintain an aura of spaciousness throughout the living area. Bedroom 2 offers a semi-private bath and could be used as a mother-in-law suite or guest room. The secluded living room and bay-windowed dining room provide beautiful surroundings for formal entertaining. The master suite provides the best of everything, from private access to the covered patio, to handy linen storage.

DESIGN BY

Home Design
Services, Inc.

## Design 6629

**Square Footage:** 2,214

**M**ake yourself at home in this delightful one-story design. An arched entry greets family and visitors and announces a comfortable and stylish interior design. Volume ceilings highlight the main living areas, including a formal dining room and a great room with access to a rear veranda. The convenient kitchen opens to a skylit breakfast nook and offers dual access to a split veranda. The homeowner will find repose in the cozy, turreted study, offering privacy through double doors. Off to one side of the plan, a spacious master suite offers a vaulted ceiling, a bumped-out whirlpool tub, a split walk-in closet and corner windows. Secondary bedrooms on the opposite side of the plan share a full bath and a gallery hall that leads to a rear veranda.

DESIGN BY

**The Sater Design Collection**

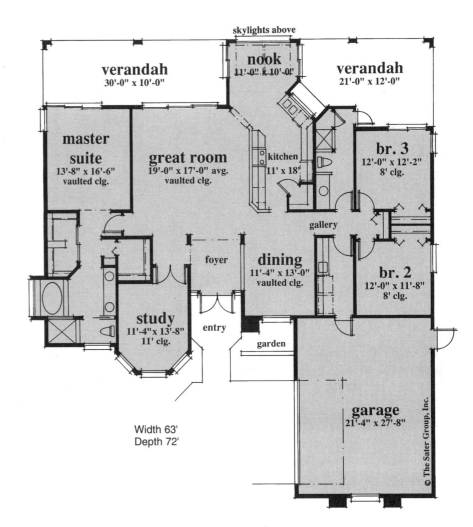

skylights above

**verandah**
30'-0" x 10'-0"

**nook**
11'-0" x 10'-0"

**verandah**
21'-0" x 12'-0"

**master suite**
13'-8" x 16'-6"
vaulted clg.

**great room**
19'-0" x 17'-0" avg.
vaulted clg.

**kitchen**
11' x 18'

**br. 3**
12'-0" x 12'-2"
8' clg.

gallery

foyer

**dining**
11'-4" x 13'-0"
vaulted clg.

**br. 2**
12'-0" x 11'-8"
8' clg.

**study**
11'-4" x 13'-8"
11' clg.

entry

garden

**garage**
21'-4" x 27'-8"

© The Sater Group, Inc.

Width 63'
Depth 72'

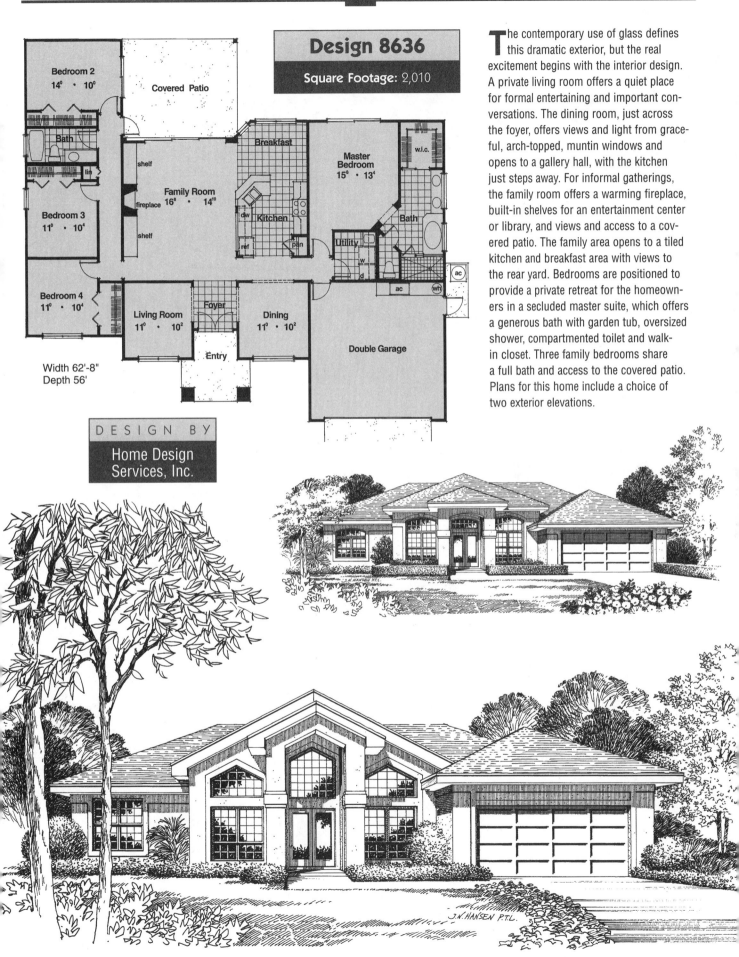

## Design 8636

**Square Footage:** 2,010

Bedroom 2
14⁰ · 10⁰

Covered Patio

Bath

Bedroom 3
11⁰ · 10⁴

Breakfast

Master Bedroom
15⁸ · 13⁴

w.l.c.

shelf

Family Room
16⁸ · 14¹⁰

fireplace

Kitchen

dw

shelf

ref

pan

Bath

Utility

w

d

ac

ac

wh

Bedroom 4
11⁰ · 10⁴

Living Room
11⁰ · 10²

Foyer

Dining
11⁰ · 10²

Double Garage

Entry

Width 62'-8"
Depth 56'

### DESIGN BY
**Home Design Services, Inc.**

The contemporary use of glass defines this dramatic exterior, but the real excitement begins with the interior design. A private living room offers a quiet place for formal entertaining and important conversations. The dining room, just across the foyer, offers views and light from graceful, arch-topped, muntin windows and opens to a gallery hall, with the kitchen just steps away. For informal gatherings, the family room offers a warming fireplace, built-in shelves for an entertainment center or library, and views and access to a covered patio. The family area opens to a tiled kitchen and breakfast area with views to the rear yard. Bedrooms are positioned to provide a private retreat for the homeowners in a secluded master suite, which offers a generous bath with garden tub, oversized shower, compartmented toilet and walk-in closet. Three family bedrooms share a full bath and access to the covered patio. Plans for this home include a choice of two exterior elevations.

## Design 8662

### Square Footage: 2,005

Vaulted and volume ceilings soar above well-designed living areas in this spectacular move-up home. Open spaces create interior vistas and invite both formal and informal gatherings. An elegant dining room, defined by columns, offers views to the front property through multi-level muntin windows. To the left of the foyer, an extensive living room offers plans for an optional fireplace as well as privacy for quiet gatherings. The great room offers a vaulted ceiling and views to outdoor areas, and opens to the breakfast room with patio access and the kitchen with angled counter. Two family bedrooms, each with a volume ceiling, and a bath with twin lavatories complete the right side of the plan. The master bedroom enjoys its own bath with a whirlpool tub, separate shower, dual vanity and compartmented toilet.

Width 58'
Depth 60'

DESIGN BY
Home Design
Services, Inc.

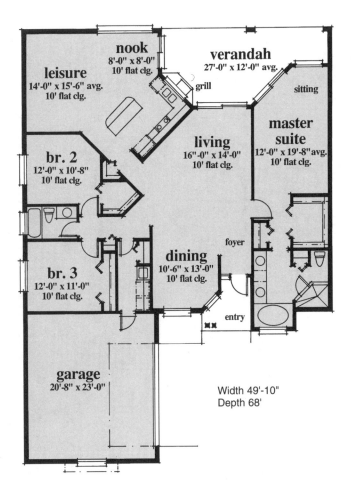

**nook**
8'-0" x 8'-0"
10' flat clg.

**leisure**
14'-0" x 15'-6" avg.
10' flat clg.

**verandah**
27'-0" x 12'-0" avg.

grill

sitting

**master suite**
12'-0" x 19'-8" avg.
10' flat clg.

**living**
16'-0" x 14'-0"
10' flat clg.

**br. 2**
12'-0" x 10'-8"
10' flat clg.

**br. 3**
12'-0" x 11'-0"
10' flat clg.

**dining**
10'-6" x 13'-0"
10' flat clg.

foyer

entry

**garage**
20'-8" x 23'-0"

Width 49'-10"
Depth 68'

## Design 6630

**Square Footage:** 1,953

A clever floor plan distinguishes this three-bedroom stucco Floridian. It features formal living and dining rooms, plus an ample leisure room with adjacent breakfast nook. The angled kitchen overlooks this casual gathering area and offers a pass-through window to a patio counter. Split sleeping quarters offer privacy to a luxurious master suite which features private access to the veranda, an angled corner shower, garden tub, dressing area and walk-in closet. Family bedrooms share a full bath on the opposite side of the plan. A handy utility room connects the living space to the two-car garage.

DESIGN BY
The Sater
Design Collection

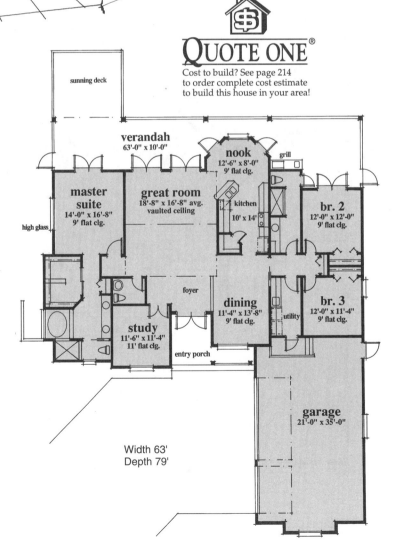

## Design 6607

**Square Footage:** 2,200

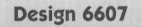
joyful marriage of indoor-outdoor living relationships endures in this spirited stucco home. An abundance of double doors and windows to the rear of the plan allows sunlight to bathe living areas with natural light. A full-length veranda and sunning deck provide the perfect area for casual entertaining—or sit and watch a beautiful sunset with your family. An open area that includes the formal dining room with decorative half-wall, the great room with vaulted ceiling and the kitchen with adjacent sunny nook creates an airy, spacious feeling. A splendid master suite offers private access to the veranda and features a double walk-in closet, a relaxing garden tub with a privacy wall, a separate shower and a double-bowl vanity.

DESIGN BY
**The Sater Design Collection**

# A TOUCH OF CLASS
## *Affordable Dream Homes*

**W**orld-class luxury homes aren't better because they're bigger—the most sensational plans build real homes that ground us, steady us and help us take root in a region. Design integrity, architectural balance and proportion, and attention to detail are part of a quality home, no matter what its size. And some of the best dream homes are the most affordable.

Lavish exteriors loaded with charm make an alluring statement but it's the quality and comfort within that really make a house step out in style. Open, bright interiors that transcend fads of the day are the true heart of a home. This selection of plans shows off some of our new ideas for interior spaces: wide kitchens, secluded dining rooms, grand great rooms, extraordinary master suites, and even a one-golf-cart garage.

Plans that may seem sprawling and untamed on paper build to cozy sanctuaries when braced with simple themes and subtle divisions of space. Design 3664 (page 179) affords private places to nestle as well as wide, open places that soar and sparkle—all with a casual elegance. And Design 3433 (page 191) combines a classic Southwestern look, earthy and spirited, with fresh ideas for indoor/outdoor relationships—from sunny sitting areas to cool breakfast *portales*.

Our plans capture the spirit and diversity of many regions. And whether the backdrop for your home is the big city or the wide open spaces, we'll help you create a home that redefines luxury. What kind of homes do innovative design, plucky creativity and timeless craftsmanship build? The possibilities could be endless.

iagonals used wisely in this Contemporary design make it a versatile choice for a variety of lot arrangements. Open planning inside creates visual appeal—the entry offers interior vistas through decorative columns and graceful arches. A fabulous great room offers a corner fireplace framed by walls of windows, which allow stunning views to outdoor areas. An exquisite formal dining room with a coffered ceiling shares the natural light of the great room. An island

kitchen with a snack bar, a planning desk, and a walk-in pantry opens to a breakfast area with bayed nook. Homeowners will retreat to the restful master suite, which offers a coffered ceiling, corner whirlpool bath, a glass-enclosed shower, twin lavatories and a walk-in closet. Two family bedrooms share a nearby full bath. The three-car garage holds extra storage space and allows access to the house through the mud/laundry room.

## Design 9250

**Square Footage:** 2,133

### DESIGN BY
**Design Basics, Inc.**

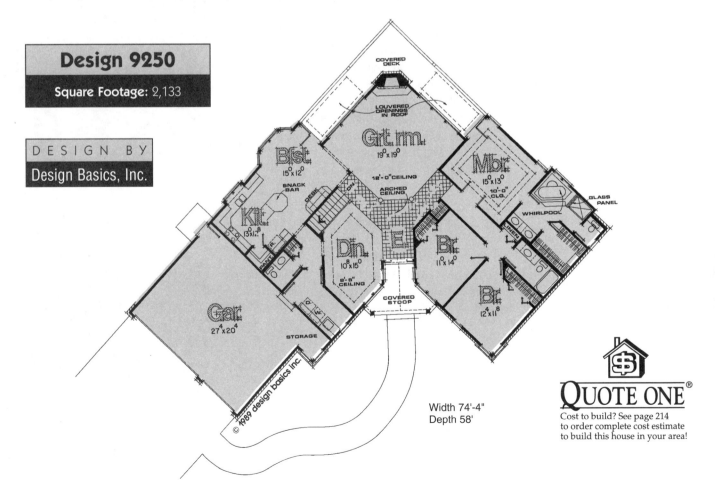

Width 74'-4"
Depth 58'

**QUOTE ONE®**
Cost to build? See page 214 to order complete cost estimate to build this house in your area!

**C**lassic keystones, quoins and stately arches create an elegant exterior and complement a grand, vaulted entry. Guests may linger in the tiled gallery off the foyer, but they'll certainly want to enjoy some of the uncommon amenities this plan has to offer. A sizable great room makes leisure and casual entertaining a pleasure, and features a handsome fireplace with extended hearth, framed by decorative niches. Plant shelves decorate this area, above triple doors to the patio retreat. The kitchen features a cooktop/utility island and built-in desk and opens to a windowed breakfast bay which allows an abundance of natural light. An eating counter accomodates quick snacks and invites family conversations. For formal occasions, this plan has a great dining room—off to one side to permit private, unhurried evening meals. Rest and relaxation await the homeowners in a sensational master suite—and for true peace and quiet, retire to an inner retreat with access to a private patio. Two family bedrooms share a private bath, and one room opens to a covered patio. A small garage designed for a one-car golf cart adjoins a roomy two-car garage.

DESIGN BY
Home Planners

**Design 3664**

Square Footage: 2,471

QUOTE ONE®
Cost to build? See page 214
to order complete cost estimate
to build this house in your area!

Width 86'-4"
Depth 80'-2"

## Design 9089

**Square Footage:** 1,849

DESIGN BY
**Larry W. Garnett & Associates, Inc.**

**QUOTE ONE®**
Cost to build? See page 214
to order complete cost estimate
to build this house in your area!

This cozy one-story design offers luxury in a compact size. A raised foyer opens to a rambling living room with centered fireplace flanked by double French doors. To the right, a formal dining room with high ceiling opens to the galley kitchen which offers a huge pantry and sunny breakfast area. The master suite with walk-in closet features a luxurious bath with garden tub and double lavatories. To the left of the plan, two family bedrooms share a hall bath.

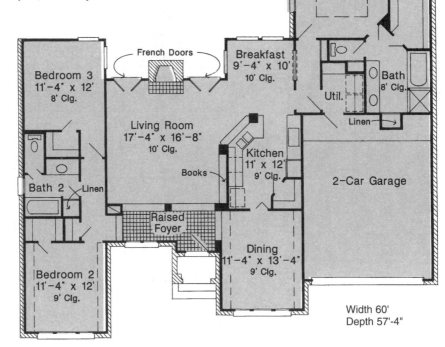

Master Bedroom
13'-4" x 16'
9' Step-Up Clg.

French Doors

Breakfast
9'-4" x 10'
10' Clg.

Bath
8' Clg.

Util.

Linen

Bedroom 3
11'-4" x 12'
8' Clg.

Living Room
17'-4" x 16'-8"
10' Clg.

Kitchen
11' x 12'
9' Clg.

Books

2-Car Garage

Bath 2

Linen

Raised
Foyer

Dining
11'-4" x 13'-4"
9' Clg.

Bedroom 2
11'-4" x 12'
9' Clg.

Width 60'
Depth 57'-4"

## Design 9846

**Square Footage:** 2,295
(without basement)

DECK

SITTING AREA
11'-4" x 6'-0"

MASTER BATH
8'-10" x 10'-6"

MASTER SUITE
13'-2" x 17'-2"

MASTER CLOSET

GREAT ROOM
20'-6" x 19'-10"

KITCHEN
10'-0" x 16'-0"

BREAKFAST
11'-4" x 7'-6"

KEEPING ROOM
13'-6" x 13'-6"

PREP ISLAND

CLOSET

BATH

LINEN

PANTRY

LAUN
7'-0" x 8'-9"

DN

BEDROOM NO.3
11'-8" x 12'-0"

BEDROOM NO.2
11'-8" x 12'-2"

STOOP

COAT

FOYER
8'-0" x 8'-0"

DINING ROOM
11'-10" x 14'-10"

TWO-CAR GARAGE
21'-4" x 21'-4"

CLOSET

Width 69'
Depth 49'-6"

PATIO

FUTURE SITTING
11'-6" x 7'-6"

FUTURE BEDROOM
16'-0" x 11'-8"

MECH./STORAGE

DRESSING

FUTURE BATH

FUTURE RECREATION
20'-6" x 20'-4"

FUTURE GAME ROOM
20'-10" x 18'-6"

WET-BAR

STORAGE

SLAB ON GRADE

**T**he abundance of details in this plan make it the finest in one-story living. The great room and formal dining room are defined by a simple column at the entry foyer—allowing for an open, dramatic sense of space. The kitchen with preparation island shares the right side of the plan with a bayed breakfast area and a keeping room with fireplace. Sleeping accommodations to the left of the plan include a master suite with sitting area, double closet and separate tub and shower. Two family bedrooms share a full bath. Additional living and sleeping space can be developed in the unfinished basement.

DESIGN BY
**Design Traditions**

**A**rch-topped and artistic window treatments complement a delightful gazebo with this Transitional plan. The octagonal library with its dramatic ceiling and cathedral windows offers a quiet retreat for family and guests. The spacious corner living room and the open kitchen with its unique circular snack-bar pass-through to the angled breakfast nook are to the rear of the plan. A charming fireplace highlights the comfortable family room. Upstairs, two bedrooms with a shared bath, and a large master suite with a walk-in closet and a corner whirlpool and shower, complete the plan.

## Design 3470

**First Floor:** 1,460 square feet
**Second Floor:** 955 square feet
**Total:** 2,415 square feet

**L** **D**

Width 70'
Depth 50'

**QUOTE ONE®**
Cost to build? See page 214
to order complete cost estimate
to build this house in your area!

DESIGN BY
**Home Planners**

## DESIGN BY
### Alan Mascord Design Associates, Inc.

**DINING**
11/0 X 14/0

**NOOK**
14/0 X 14/0
10/0 X 10/0

**BR.**

**WET BAR**

**PAN**

**DEN**
13/8 X 12/4

**SUNKEN FAMILY**
13/8 X 14/8

**TWO STORY LIVING**
13/2 X 16/10

**DN**

**DECK**

**GARAGE UNDER**

Width 50'
Depth 35'

## Design 9573

**First Floor:** 1,502 square feet
**Second Floor:** 954 square feet
**Total:** 2,456 square feet

Come home to spectacular views as well as stylish comfort with this dazzling hillside home. Inside, a carefully designed floor plan provides livability with a touch of luxury. The living room features a soaring two story ceiling and shares a see-through fireplace with the formal dining room. A secluded den offers a quiet place to study or read, as well as access to a private deck through double doors. The sunken family room also enjoys a fireplace and is near the kitchen which has a cooktop island and breakfast nook. Upstairs, a master suite with vaulted ceiling enjoys privacy, away from the two secondary bedrooms, and offers a bath with whirlpool spa, twin lavatories and walk-in closet. The family bedrooms share a full bath.

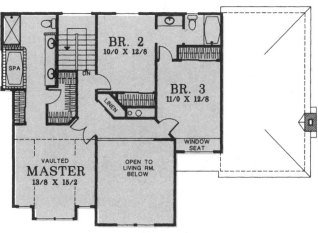

**SPA**

**BR. 2**
10/0 X 12/8

**BR. 3**
11/0 X 12/8

**LINEN**

**WINDOW SEAT**

**VAULTED MASTER**
13/8 X 15/2

**OPEN TO LIVING RM. BELOW**

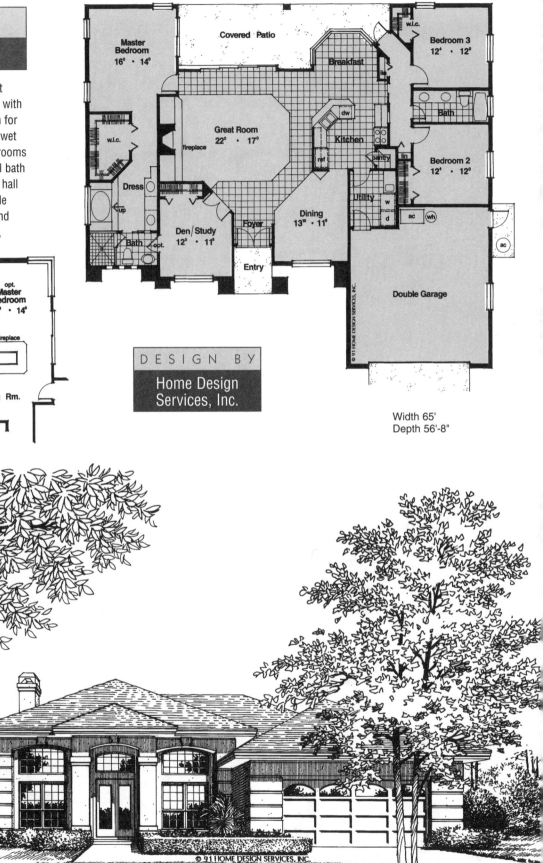

# Design 8601

**Square Footage:** 2,125

A luxurious master suite is just one of the highlights offered with this lovely plan—an alternate plan for this suite features a sitting room, wet bar and fireplace. Two family bedrooms to the right of the plan share a full bath with twin lavatories, and a gallery hall which leads to a covered patio. Tile adds interest to the living areas and surrounds a spacious great room, which offers a fireplace and access to the rear patio. A formal dining room and secluded den or study are to the front.

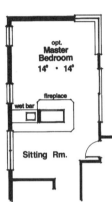

opt. **Master Bedroom** 14⁰ · 14⁰

fireplace

wet bar

**Sitting Rm.**

Master Bedroom 16⁰ · 14⁰

Covered Patio

Breakfast

Bedroom 3 12⁴ · 12⁰

w.i.c.

w.i.c.

dw

Bath

Great Room 22⁰ · 17⁰

fireplace

Kitchen

ref

pantry

Bedroom 2 12⁴ · 12⁰

Dress

Utility

up

Den/Study 12⁰ · 11⁰

opt.

Foyer

Dining 13¹⁰ · 11⁹

w

d

ac

wh

Bath

Entry

ac

Double Garage

© 91 HOME DESIGN SERVICES, INC.

DESIGN BY
**Home Design Services, Inc.**

Width 65'
Depth 56'-8"

© 91 HOME DESIGN SERVICES, INC.

J. N. HANSEN P.F.L.

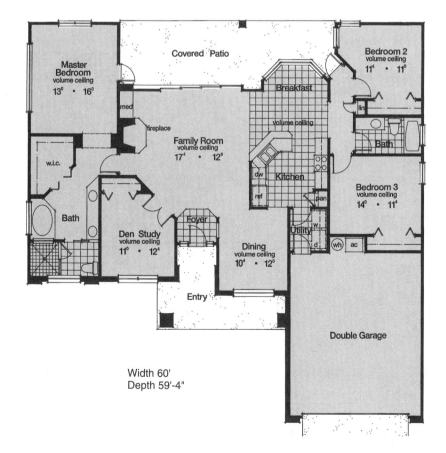

**Master Bedroom** volume ceiling 13⁰ · 16⁰

**Covered Patio**

**Bedroom 2** volume ceiling 11⁴ · 11⁰

med

fireplace

w.i.c.

**Family Room** volume ceiling 17⁴ · 12⁸

**Breakfast** volume ceiling

lin

**Bath**

**Bath**

dw **Kitchen**

ref

**Den Study** volume ceiling 11⁰ · 12⁴

**Foyer**

**Dining** volume ceiling 10⁴ · 12⁰

pan

**Bedroom 3** volume ceiling 14⁰ · 11⁴

**Utility** w

d

wh ac

**Entry**

**Double Garage**

Width 60'
Depth 59'-4"

## Design 8684

**Square Footage:** 1,898

Family living is at the core of this brick one-story home inspired by the design of Frank Lloyd Wright. To the left of the foyer, double doors open onto a den/study which could easily be converted to a nursery. The nearby master suite features a spacious bedroom and a pampering bath with a large walk-in closet, a separate shower and a relaxing tub. Centrally located, the family room with a cozy fireplace opens to a bayed breakfast nook and a well-appointed kitchen—a perfect arrangement for casual gatherings. The family sleeping wing offers two bedrooms and a full bath, plus patio access via a "kids" door.

DESIGN BY

**Home Design Services, Inc.**

**T**his elegant exterior houses a very livable plan. Every bit of space has been put to good use. The front country kitchen is a good place to begin. It is efficiently planned with its island cooktop, built-ins and pass-through to the dining room. The large great room will be the center of all family activities. Quiet times can be enjoyed in the front library. The second floor contains the sleeping zone made up of three family bedrooms and a grand master suite.

## Design 2668

**First Floor:** 1,206 square feet
**Second Floor:** 1,254 square feet
**Total:** 2,460 square feet

L

Width 52'
Depth 42'

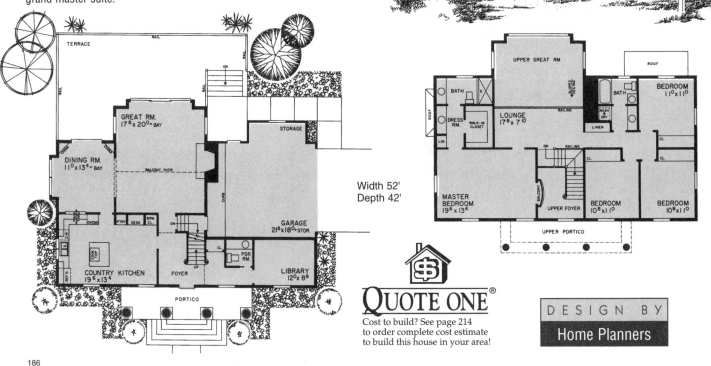

TERRACE

RAIL

GREAT RM.
17⁸ x 20⁰ + BAY

DINING RM.
11⁰ x 13⁴ + BAY

BALCONY OVER

STORAGE

GARAGE
21⁸ x 18⁰ + STOR.

COUNTRY KITCHEN
19⁶ x 13⁴

OVENS

PTRY DESK BRM. CL.

COOK TOP

FOYER

UP

PDR. RM.

LIBRARY
12⁰ x 8⁸

PORTICO

UPPER GREAT RM.

ROOF

BATH

DRESS. RM.

WALK-IN CLOSET

LOUNGE
17⁸ x 7¹⁰

RAILING

BATH

WASH & DRY

LINEN

LIN

MASTER BEDROOM
19⁶ x 13⁴

DN RAILING

BALCONY

UPPER FOYER

BEDROOM
10⁸ x 11⁰

BEDROOM
11⁰ x 11⁰

CL.

CL.

BEDROOM
10⁸ x 11⁰

UPPER PORTICO

**QUOTE ONE®**

Cost to build? See page 214 to order complete cost estimate to build this house in your area!

DESIGN BY
**Home Planners**

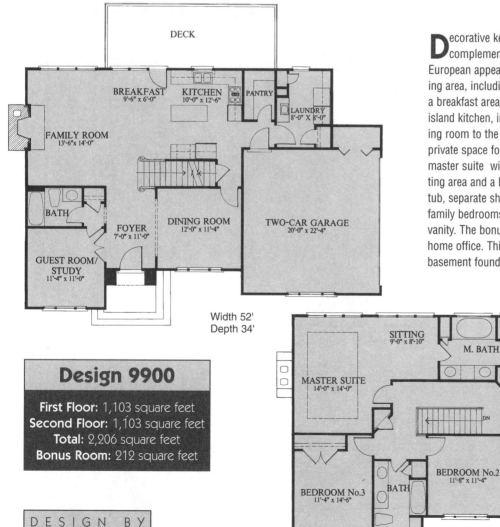

DECK

BREAKFAST
9'-6" x 6'-0"

KITCHEN
10'-0" x 12'-6"

PANTRY

LAUNDRY
8'-0" X 8'-0"

FAMILY ROOM
13'-6"x 14'-0"

BATH

FOYER
7'-0" x 11'-0"

DINING ROOM
12'-0" x 11'-4"

TWO-CAR GARAGE
20'-0" x 22'-4"

GUEST ROOM/
STUDY
11'-4" x 11'-0"

Width 52'
Depth 34'

## Design 9900

**First Floor:** 1,103 square feet
**Second Floor:** 1,103 square feet
**Total:** 2,206 square feet
**Bonus Room:** 212 square feet

DESIGN BY

Design Traditions

SITTING
9'-0" x 8'-10"

M. BATH

MASTER
CLOSET

MASTER SUITE
14'-0" x 14'-0"

UNFINISHED
BONUS

BEDROOM No.2
11'-8" x 11'-4"

BEDROOM No.3
11'-4" x 14'-6"

BATH

**D**ecorative keystones and muntin windows complement a stucco exterior, creating European appeal with this design. An open living area, including a family room with fireplace, a breakfast area with rear deck access and an island kitchen, invites casual gatherings. A dining room to the front of the plan offers more private space for formal occasions. Upstairs, a master suite with coffered ceiling offers a sitting area and a bath with dual vanity, whirlpool tub, separate shower and walk-in closet. Two family bedrooms share a full bath with dual vanity. The bonus room would make a great home office. This home is designed with a basement foundation.

## Design 3437

**First Floor:** 1,522 square feet
**Second Floor:** 800 square feet
**Total:** 2,322 square feet

**L**

This two-story Spanish Mission-style design shows character inside and out. The foyer opens to a splendid two-story gathering room through a graceful archway. To the rear of the plan, the formal dining area offers access to a rear columned porch. The first-floor master suite features a fireplace and gracious bath with walk-in closet, whirlpool, shower, dual vanities and linen storage. A second fireplace serves both the gathering room and media room or library. The kitchen with island cooktop includes a snack bar and adjoins a breakfast nook. Upstairs, two family bedrooms share a full bath, and a nearby guest room offers a private bath.

DESIGN BY
Home Planners

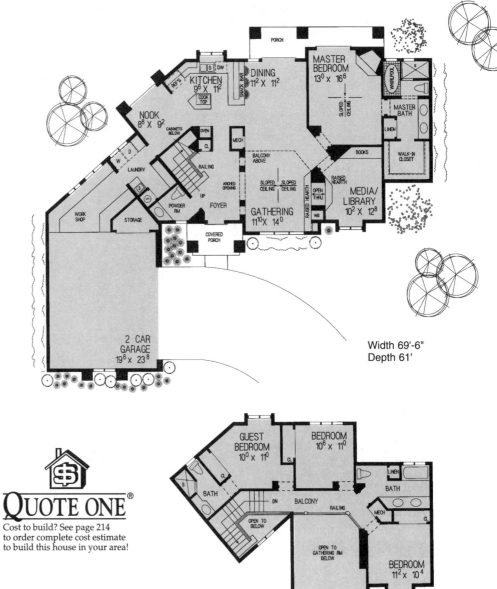

**QUOTE ONE®**
Cost to build? See page 214 to order complete cost estimate to build this house in your area!

Width 69'-6"
Depth 61'

Bedroom 2
11¹⁰ • 10⁰

Bath

lin

Covered Patio

Master Bedroom
16¹⁰ • 13⁰

w.i.c.

Nook

Bedroom 3
12⁰ • 11⁰

fireplace

Family Room
19⁰ • 15¹⁰

desk

Bath

linen

Utility

Bath

lin

Kitchen

dw

w
d

ref

pan

ac

ac

wh

Bedroom 4
12⁰ • 11⁰

Living Room
12⁸ • 10¹⁰

Foyer

Dining
12⁸ • 10¹⁰

Double Garage

Entry

Width 61'-8"
Depth 50'-4"

© '91 HOME DESIGN SERVICES, INC.

## Design 8637

**Square Footage:** 2,089

**T**his four-bedroom, three-bath home offers the finest in modern amenities. The formal living spaces have a classic split design, perfect for quiet time and conversation. The unique design of the bedroom wing affords flexibility and offers a livable environment for the family. Bedrooms 3 and 4 share their own bath while Bedroom 2 has a private bath with pool access, making it the perfect guest room. The huge family room, which opens up to the patio with twelve-foot, pocket sliding doors, has space for a fireplace and media equipment. The master suite, located just off the kitchen and nook, offers a private retreat and features a double door entry and a bed wall with glass above. The angled entry to the bath allows a dressing area near the walk-in closet. The step-down shower, private toilet room, and knee-space vanity make this a super bath!

J.N.HANSEN F.L.

## Design 3644

**Square Footage:** 2,015

# QUOTE ONE®

Cost to build? See page 214 to order complete cost estimate to build this house in your area!

DESIGN BY
Home Planners

**T**his Santa Fe-style home is as warm as a desert breeze and just as comfortable. Outside details are reminiscent of old-style adobe homes, while the interior caters to convenient living. The front covered porch leads to an open foyer. Columns define the formal dining room and the giant great room. The kitchen has an enormous pantry, a snack bar and is connected to a breakfast nook with rear patio access. Two family bedrooms are found on the right side of the plan. They share a full bathroom with twin vanities. The master suite is on the left side of the plan and has a monstrous walk-in closet and a bath with spa tub and separate shower. The home is completed with a three-car garage.

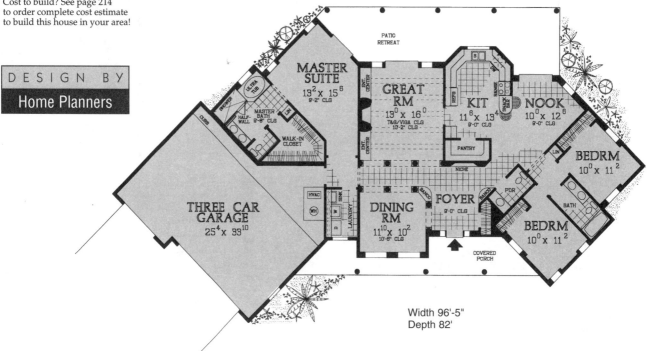

Width 96'-5"
Depth 82'

**COURTYARD**

**COVERED PORCH**

**BEDROOM** 11⁰ X 11⁰

**BATH**

**BEDROOM** 10⁶ X 11⁶

**LINEN**

**MECH**

**STOR**

**BRKFST** 9⁸ X 11⁰

**FAMILY RM** 11⁰ X 10⁴

**STOR**

**LAUNDRY RM**

**RANGE**

**KITCHEN** 10⁶ X 14⁰

**PTRY**

**OVEN**

**STOR**

**LINEN**

**PDR RM**

**DINING RM** 11⁴ X 9⁰

**COVERED PORCH**

**3 CAR GARAGE** 29⁸ X 21⁶

**SKYLIGHT**

**FOYER**

**RAISED HEARTH**

**RAISED HEARTH**

**RAISED HEARTH**

**ENTRY COURTYARD**

**LIVING RM** 12⁰ X 17⁰

**MECH**

**COVERED PORCH**

**CL**

**STUDY** 11² X 11⁰

**MASTER BEDROOM** 14⁰ X 13⁰

**WALK-IN CLOSET**

**MASTER BATH**

**LINEN**

Width 92'-7"
Depth 79'

## Design 3433

### Square Footage: 2,350

**L**

**S**anta Fe styling creates interesting angles in this one-story home. A grand entrance leads through a skylit courtyard, and opens through the foyer to a magnificent living room with a triple fireplace—shared by the dining room and an outdoor entertainment area. A gourmet kitchen with island range is designed for easy entertaining, both formal and informal. The family will enjoy gathering in the spacious breakfast room nearby, which offers access to one of the covered porches. A master suite with superior amenities offers privacy and repose to the home-owner, and a study with access to a private covered porch is nearby—perfect for enjoying the view or quiet contemplation. Two family bedrooms to the rear of the plan share a full bath and offer access to outdoor areas.

## Design 3660

**Square Footage:** 2,086

**L**

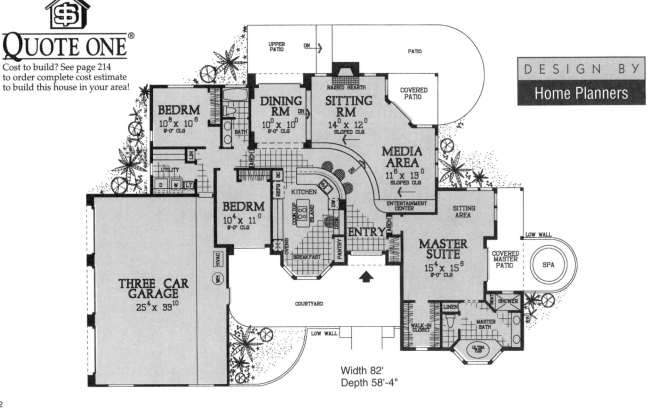

**Quote One®**

Cost to build? See page 214
to order complete cost estimate
to build this house in your area!

This home exhibits wonderful dual-use space in the sunken living room and media area. Anchoring each end of this spacious living zone is the raised-hearth fireplace and the entertainment center. The outstanding kitchen has an informal breakfast bay and looks over the snack bar to the family area. To the rear of the plan, a few steps from the kitchen and functioning with the upper patio, is the formal dining room. Through the archway are two children's bedrooms and a bath with twin vanities. At the far end of the plan is the master suite. It has a sitting area with fine, natural light. A few steps away, French doors open to the covered master patio.

DESIGN BY
**Home Planners**

UPPER PATIO

PATIO

RAISED HEARTH

COVERED PATIO

BEDRM
10⁸ x 10⁶
9'-0" CLG

DINING RM
10⁰ x 10⁰
9'-0" CLG

SITTING RM
14⁰ x 12⁰
SLOPED CLG

MEDIA AREA
11⁶ x 13⁰
SLOPED CLG

BATH

UTILITY

KITCHEN

BEDRM
10⁴ x 11⁰
9'-0" CLG

ENTERTAINMENT CENTER

SITTING AREA

ENTRY

THREE CAR GARAGE
25⁴ x 39¹⁰

BREAKFAST

PANTRY

MASTER SUITE
15⁴ x 15⁸
9'-0" CLG

COVERED MASTER PATIO

LOW WALL

SPA

COURTYARD

LINEN

SEAT

SHOWER

WALK-IN CLOSET

MASTER BATH

LOW WALL

ULTRA TUB

Width 82'
Depth 58'-4"

Width 90'-2"
Depth 69'-10"

Varying roof planes of colorful tile surfaces make a dramatic statement. Privacy fences add appeal and help form the front courtyard and side private patio. Nine-foot ceilings enhance the feeling of spaciousness inside. The kitchen has an island cooktop, built-in ovens, a nearby walk-in pantry and direct access to the outdoor covered patio. The living room is impressive with its a centered fireplace with long raised hearth. The ceiling is eighteen feet high and permits a fine view of the second-floor loft. It, too, functions through French doors with the rear patio. At the opposite end of the plan is the master bedroom. It has a walk-in closet with shoe storage, twin lavatories in the bath, plus a whirlpool and stall shower. Not to be overlooked is the access to the private patio and the rear patio. The two children's bedrooms each have direct access to a bath with twin lavatories.

## Quote One®

Cost to build? See page 214 to order complete cost estimate to build this house in your area!

DESIGN BY
**Home Planners**

### Design 3628

**First Floor:** 1,731 square feet
**Second Floor:** 554 square feet
**Total:** 2,285 square feet

## Design 3657

**Square Footage:** 2,344

**QUOTE ONE®**

Cost to build? See page 214
to order complete cost estimate
to build this house in your area!

A magnificent arched entry announces splendid planning with this Floridian design. The tiled foyer invites guests toward a gracious gathering room with fireplace and views to the rear grounds—although they may want to linger on the front covered patio. Decorative half-walls define the formal dining area which offers rear patio access. The nearby kitchen is equipped to serve formal and infor-mal occasions, and even features a snack counter for mini-meals. An office or guest room in this area, with a nearby powder room, accomodates visitors. An archway off the foyer leads to sleeping quarters, which include an outstanding master suite with His and Hers walk-in closets, step-down shower, knee-space vanity, and whirlpool tub. Two family bedrooms off a gallery hall share a full bath.

DESIGN BY
**Home Planners**

Width 97'-2"
Depth 57'-4"

QUOTE ONE®

Cost to build? See page 214
to order complete cost estimate
to build this house in your area!

## Design 3661

**Square Footage:** 2,385

**L**

A vaulted entry and tall muntin windows complement a classic stucco exterior on this Floridian-style home. Inside, an entry gallery opens to a great room which offers generous views to the rear property and columned access to a patio retreat. Niches, built-ins and half-walls decorate and help define this area. The nearby kitchen features an island cooktop counter and a cozy snack bar. The formal dining room offers privacy and natural light from a bay window. A secluded master wing soothes the homeowner with a sumptuous bath, a walk-in closet and an inner retreat with access to a covered patio. The wing also features an office with triple windows—this room could accomodate a guest, with double doors for privacy and a nearby bath. A private garage designed for a one-car golf cart adjoins a full-size two-car garage.

Width 76'-6"
Depth 77'-4"

© The Sater Group, Inc.

## Design 6614

**Square Footage:** 2,282

Two elevations are yours to choose from in this stunning sun country home. An octagon-shaped dining room with a tray ceiling opens to a living area with generous views to the outdoors as well as rear lanai access. A graceful archway announces an informal area which includes a leisure room with fireplace and built-in shelves, a sunny breakfast nook and a roomy kitchen with angled island counter. The right side of the plan offers two family bedrooms and a full bath. To the left, a master suite with sitting area and lanai access offers His and Hers walk-in closets and a luxurious bath with double-bowl vanity, angled spa and separate shower.

DESIGN BY

The Sater Design Collection

**lanai** 33'-0" x 10'-0"

high glass

mitered glass

fireplace

built ins

**leisure** 14'-8" x 19'-4" 10' clg.

**br. 2** 10'-8" x 15'-0" 10' clg.

mitered glass

**nook** 9'-0" x 9'-0"

sitting

**master suite** 13'-0" x 18'-6" 10' clg.

**living** 14'-0" x 14'-0" 12' clg.

arch

desk

**dining** 12'-4" x 15'-0" tray clg.

util.

**br. 3** 10'-8" x 14'-8" 10' clg.

foyer

entry

storage

**garage** 20'-8" x 28'-4"

© The Sater Group, Inc.

Width 60'
Depth 75'

© The Sater Group, Inc.

# COMPLETE RETREATS
## *Hardworking Vacation Homes*

**W**ho hasn't dreamed of a getaway cabin in the woods, on a lakeshore or perched on a secluded hilltop? Rustic retreats surrounded by wilderness beckon with promises of regeneration and a respite from commutes and cubicles—and a taste of the American dream. Frank Lloyd Wright said that living deep in nature called our democratic spirit out of the confusion of the city and planted it in *terra firma*.

Vacation-home builders today may be seeking solace, or simply a second home—a change of atmosphere and view. Perhaps a gathering place for family and friends for holidays and vacations. One Home Planners customer wanted a fishing lodge for business guests; others just want a place to escape the beeps and bumps of city life. Some hardworking couples build their dream home as a vacation spot then eventually retire there.

Imagine Design 2488 (page 198) on Walden Pond—of course, we've offered a few improvements to the great American classic cabin. Ours has personality, all right, and all the charm it takes to transport its inhabitants to simpler times. But we've thrown in some additional square footage, a few 21st-Century amenities and a splash of pizazz for good measure.

So linger in the shade of a cool front porch, light a fire in the fireplace, sit and read a good book (we offer lots of them—please see pages 222-223). But, most importantly, lead a better life nestled in a Home Planners vacation home you'd be sad to leave.

Photo by Lazlo Regos

*This home, as shown in the photograph, may differ from the actual blueprints.*
*For more detailed information, please check the floor plans carefully.*

## Design 2488

**First Floor:** 1,113 square feet
**Second Floor:** 543 square feet
**Total:** 1,656 square feet

**D**

A cozy cottage tailor-made for a country lifestyle! This winsome design performs equally well serving active families as a leisure-time retreat or a retirement cottage that provides a quiet haven. As a year-round home, the upstairs with its two sizable bedrooms, full bath and lounge area overlooking the gathering room comfortably holds family and guests. The second floor may also be used to accommodate a home office, a study, a sewing room, a music area or a hobby room. No matter what the lifestyle, this design functions well.

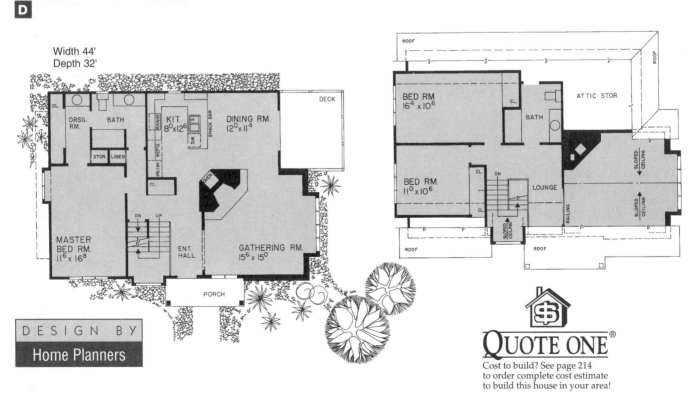

Width 44'
Depth 32'

DESIGN BY
Home Planners

## Design 3331

**First Floor:** 1,115 square feet
**Second Floor:** 690 square feet
**Total:** 1,805 square feet

**L**

This compact design is an ideal vacation retreat—with three spacious bedrooms and two full baths, it's actually bigger than it looks! Living areas include a two-story gathering room with warming fireplace and sloped ceiling, a formal dining room and a deck for outdoor eating and entertaining. The well-equipped kitchen is ready for any occasion. A main floor master bedroom offers a large bath with twin lavatories, while upstairs, two family bedrooms share a full bath. An upstairs lounge offers a private balcony.

DESIGN BY
**Home Planners**

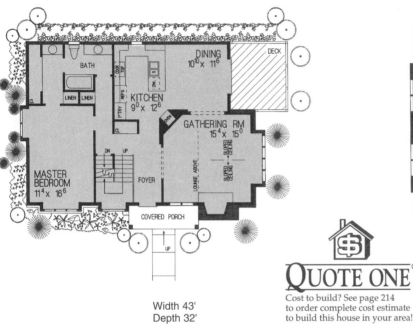

Width 43'
Depth 32'

**QUOTE ONE®**
Cost to build? See page 214
to order complete cost estimate
to build this house in your area!

*This home, as shown in the photograph, may differ from the actual blueprints. For more detailed information, please check the floor plans carefully.*

*Photo by Bob Greenspan*

## Design 3680

**First Floor:** 1,093 square feet
**Second Floor:** 580 square feet
**Total:** 1,673 square feet

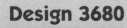

**B**rackets and balustrades on front and rear covered porches spell old-fashioned country charm on this rustic retreat. Warm evenings will invite family and guests outdoors for watching sunsets and stars. In cooler weather, the raised-hearth fireplace will make the great room a cozy place to gather. The nearby well-appointed kitchen serves both snack bar and breakfast nook. Two family bedrooms and a full bath complete the main level. Upstairs, a master bedroom with sloped ceiling offers a secluded window seat and a complete bath with garden tub, separate shower and twin lavatories. The adjacent loft/study overlooks the great room and shares the glow of the fireplace.

QUOTE ONE®

Cost to build? See page 214 to order complete cost estimate to build this house in your area!

DESIGN BY
**Home Planners**

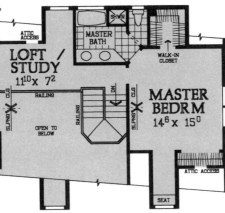

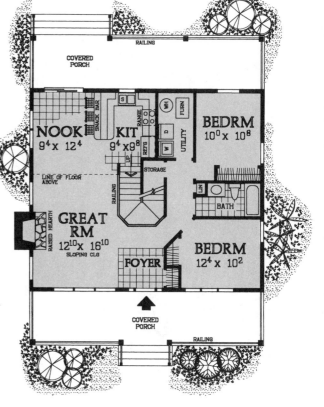

Width 36'
Depth 52'

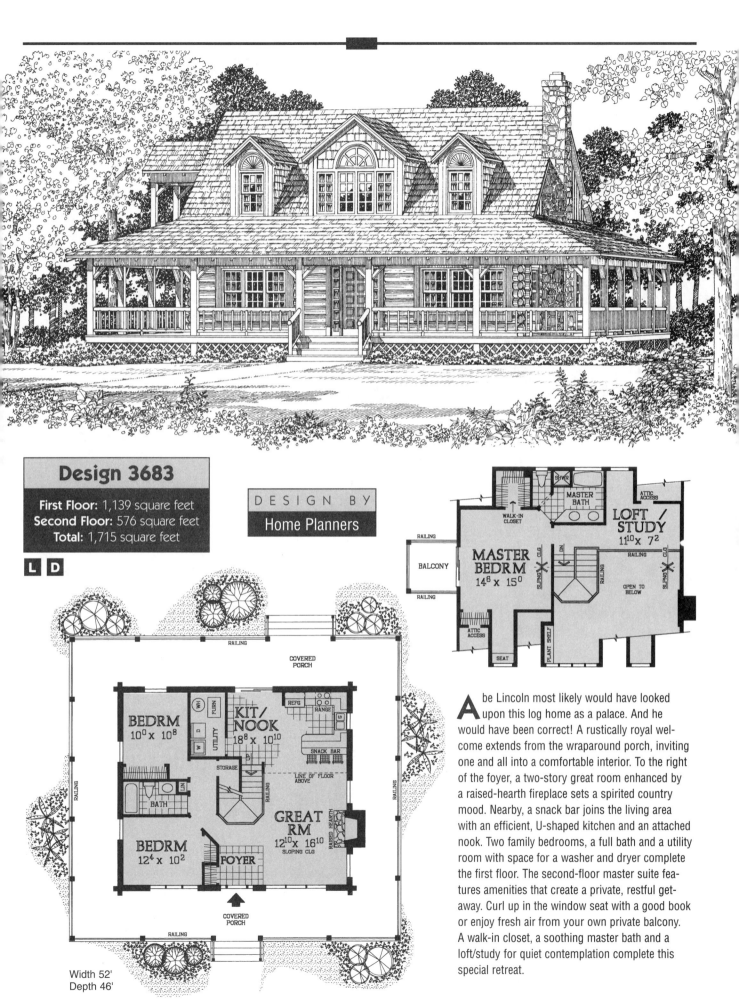

## Design 3683

**First Floor:** 1,139 square feet
**Second Floor:** 576 square feet
**Total:** 1,715 square feet

**L D**

DESIGN BY
**Home Planners**

Abe Lincoln most likely would have looked upon this log home as a palace. And he would have been correct! A rustically royal welcome extends from the wraparound porch, inviting one and all into a comfortable interior. To the right of the foyer, a two-story great room enhanced by a raised-hearth fireplace sets a spirited country mood. Nearby, a snack bar joins the living area with an efficient, U-shaped kitchen and an attached nook. Two family bedrooms, a full bath and a utility room with space for a washer and dryer complete the first floor. The second-floor master suite features amenities that create a private, restful getaway. Curl up in the window seat with a good book or enjoy fresh air from your own private balcony. A walk-in closet, a soothing master bath and a loft/study for quiet contemplation complete this special retreat.

Width 52'
Depth 46'

## Design 1499

**Main Level:** 896 square feet
**Upper Level:** 298 square feet
**Lower Level:** 896 square feet
**Total:** 2,090 square feet

Three living levels accomodate family needs with a delightful informality. A dormitory balcony overlooks the main level living room which offers deck access. Hours fly by in this relaxing retreat—you'll be tempted to live here! A well-equipped kitchen will easily accomodate meals. The plan offers sleeping quarters on each of the three levels—two bedrooms and a dormitory—plus extra space for games and recreation. Two full baths, a laundry room and extra storage space complete the plan.

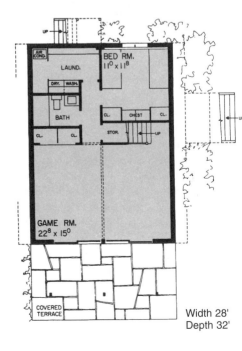

Width 28'
Depth 32'

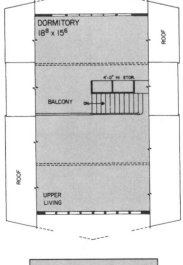

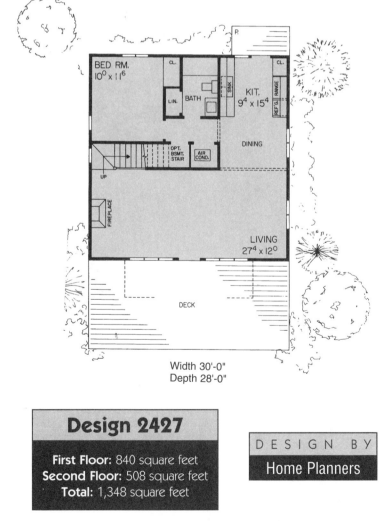

BED RM.
10⁰ x 11⁶

KIT.
9⁴ x 15⁴

BATH

LIN.

CL.

CL.

SINK

REF'G.

RANGE

P.

DINING

OPT.
BSMT.
STAIR

AIR
COND.

UP

FIREPLACE

LIVING
27⁴ x 12⁰

DECK

Width 30'-0"
Depth 28'-0"

## Design 2427

**First Floor:** 840 square feet
**Second Floor:** 508 square feet
**Total:** 1,348 square feet

DESIGN BY
Home Planners

**G**ood things come in small packages! The size and shape of this design will help hold down construction costs without sacrificing livability. A spacious living room accomodates leisurely gatherings and offers a fireplace and access to a front deck. The kitchen serves a dining area and offers convenient amenities as well as a back porch. Perhaps the most carefree characteristic is the balcony, off the master bedroom on the second level. Also on the second floor is the three-bunk dormitory. Panels through the knee walls give access to an abundant storage area.

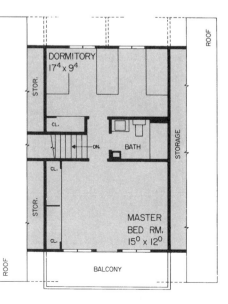

DORMITORY
17⁴ x 9⁴

STOR.

STOR.

STOR.

CL.

CL.

CL.

DN.

BATH

STORAGE

MASTER
BED RM.
15⁰ x 12⁰

ROOF

ROOF

BALCONY

**P**erfect as a second home or a vacation getaway, this home offers many amenities. A wall of windows graces the living room, presenting wonderful views of the surrounding countryside and access to the wraparound terrace. A kitchen area is located at one end of the living room for ease in serving meals. Two bedrooms and a full bath complete the first floor. Upstairs, a large dormitory with plenty of closet space is available for children or guests.

## Design 3658

**First Floor:** 784 square feet
**Second Floor:** 275 square feet
**Total:** 1,059 square feet

L D

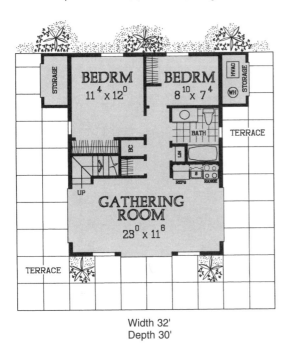

BEDRM 11⁴ x 12⁰

BEDRM 8¹⁰ x 7⁴

STORAGE

HVAC WH STORAGE

BATH

TERRACE

UP

GATHERING ROOM 23⁰ x 11⁸

TERRACE

Width 32'
Depth 30'

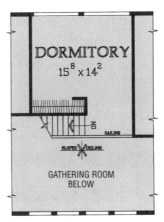

DORMITORY 15⁸ x 14²

DN RAILING

SLOPED CEILING

GATHERING ROOM BELOW

**QUOTE ONE**®

Cost to build? See page 214 to order complete cost estimate to build this house in your area!

DESIGN BY
**Home Planners**

B. NATHAN.

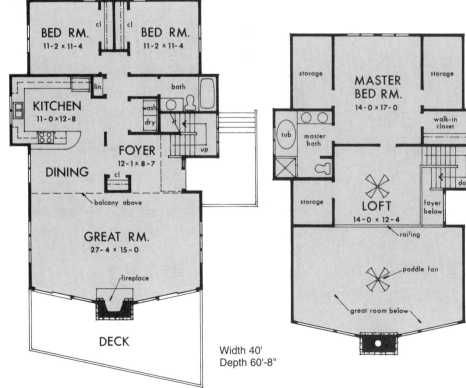

BED RM.
11-2 x 11-4

BED RM.
11-2 x 11-4

cl  cl

lin.

KITCHEN
11-0 x 12-8

bath

wash
dry

FOYER
12-1 x 8-7

up

DINING

cl

balcony above

GREAT RM.
27-4 x 15-0

fireplace

DECK

Width 40'
Depth 60'-8"

storage

storage

MASTER
BED RM.
14-0 x 17-0

tub

master
bath

walk-in
closet

storage

LOFT
14-0 x 12-4

down

foyer
below

railing

paddle fan

great room below

## Design 9630

**First Floor:** 1,374 square feet
**Second Floor:** 608 square feet
**Total:** 1,982 square feet

This rustic three-bedroom vacation home allows for casual living both inside and out. The two-level great room offers dramatic space for entertaining, with windows to the sloped roof maximizing the outdoor views. A natural rock fireplace dominates this room. Bedrooms on the first floor share a full bath. The second floor holds the master bedroom with spacious master bath and walk-in closet. A large loft area overlooks the great room and entrance foyer.

### DESIGN BY
**Donald A. Gardner, Architects, Inc.**

## Design 9697

**First Floor:** 1,039 square feet
**Second Floor:** 583 square feet
**Total:** 1,622 square feet

Charming and compact, this delightful two-story plan fits primary and secondary living needs. For the small family or empty-nester, it has all the room necessary for day-to-day activities. For the vacation home builder, it functions as a cozy retreat with fireplace and outdoor living spaces. Note that the master suite is on the first floor, away from two secondary bedrooms. The kitchen area has an island and attached dining area with boxed window. A two-story great room allows plenty of room for entertaining and relaxing.

### DESIGN BY
**Donald A. Gardner, Architects, Inc.**

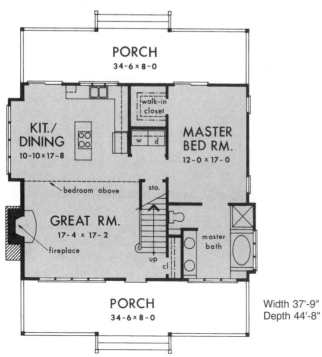

PORCH
34-6 × 8-0

KIT./DINING
10-10 × 17-8

walk-in closet

MASTER BED RM.
12-0 × 17-0

w   d

bedroom above

sto.

GREAT RM.
17-4 × 17-2

fireplace

up

cl

master bath

PORCH
34-6 × 8-0

Width 37'-9"
Depth 44'-8"

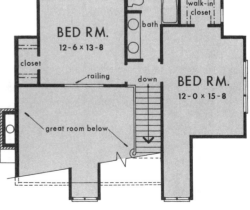

BED RM.
12-6 × 13-8

bath

walk-in closet

closet

railing

down

great room below

BED RM.
12-0 × 15-8

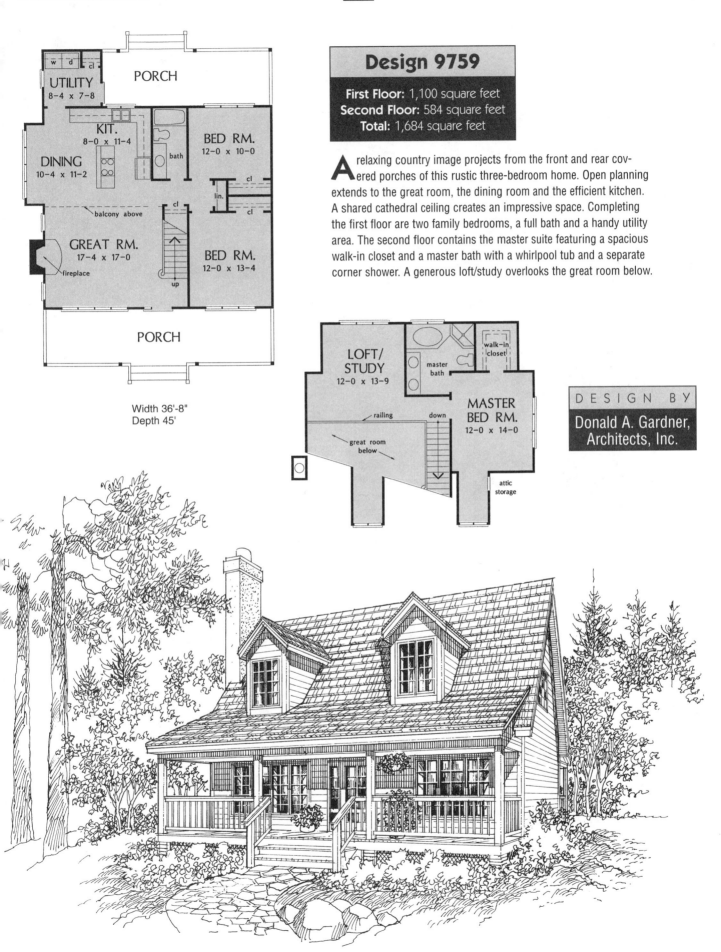

PORCH

UTILITY
8-4 x 7-8

KIT.
8-0 x 11-4

DINING
10-4 x 11-2

BED RM.
12-0 x 10-0

bath

cl

lin.

cl

balcony above

cl

GREAT RM.
17-4 x 17-0

fireplace

BED RM.
12-0 x 13-4

up

PORCH

Width 36'-8"
Depth 45'

## Design 9759

**First Floor:** 1,100 square feet
**Second Floor:** 584 square feet
**Total:** 1,684 square feet

A relaxing country image projects from the front and rear covered porches of this rustic three-bedroom home. Open planning extends to the great room, the dining room and the efficient kitchen. A shared cathedral ceiling creates an impressive space. Completing the first floor are two family bedrooms, a full bath and a handy utility area. The second floor contains the master suite featuring a spacious walk-in closet and a master bath with a whirlpool tub and a separate corner shower. A generous loft/study overlooks the great room below.

LOFT/
STUDY
12-0 x 13-9

walk-in
closet

master
bath

railing

down

great room
below

MASTER
BED RM.
12-0 x 14-0

attic
storage

DESIGN BY
Donald A. Gardner,
Architects, Inc.

207

## Design 9663

**First Floor:** 1,002 square feet
**Second Floor:** 336 square feet
**Total:** 1,338 square feet

A mountain retreat, this rustic home features covered porches front and rear. Open living is enjoyed in a great room and kitchen/dining room combination. Here, a fireplace provides the focal point and a warm welcome that continues into the L-shaped island kitchen. The cathedral ceiling that graces the great room gives an open, inviting sense of space. Two bedrooms—one with a walk-in closet—and a full bath on the first level are complemented by a master suite on the second level which includes a walk-in closet and deluxe bath. There is also attic storage on the second level. Please specify basement or crawlspace foundation when ordering.

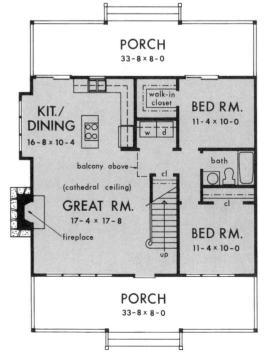

PORCH
33-8 × 8-0

walk-in closet

KIT./ DINING
16-8 × 10-4

BED RM.
11-4 × 10-0

w d

balcony above

bath

cl

(cathedral ceiling)

GREAT RM.
17-4 × 17-8

cl

fireplace

BED RM.
11-4 × 10-0

up

PORCH
33-8 × 8-0

Width 36'-8"
Depth 44'-8"

## DESIGN BY

**Donald A. Gardner, Architects, Inc.**

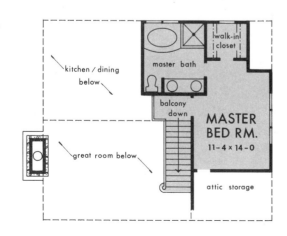

kitchen / dining below

walk-in closet

master bath

balcony down

MASTER BED RM.
11-4 × 14-0

great room below

attic storage

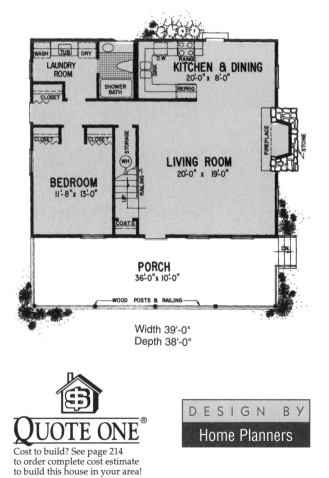

Width 39'-0"
Depth 38'-0"

## Design 4061

**First Floor:** 1,036 square feet
**Second Floor:** 273 square feet
**Total:** 1,309 square feet

**D**

**T**his charming farmhouse design will be economical to build and a pleasure to occupy. Like most vacation homes, this design features an open plan. The large living area includes a living room, a dining room and a massive stone fireplace. A partition separates the kitchen from the living room. The first floor also holds a bedroom, a full bath and a laundry room. Upstairs is a spacious sleeping loft overlooking the living room. Don't miss the large front porch—this will be a favorite spot for relaxing.

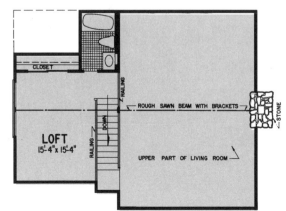

## Quote One®

Cost to build? See page 214 to order complete cost estimate to build this house in your area!

**DESIGN BY**
Home Planners

## Design 8901

**Square Footage:** 582

**P**erfect for narrow lots, lakeside or otherwise, this Victorian-style cottage will serve as a wonderful retreat. The covered front porch leads to a bright living room and dining room area. A handy closet stores coats and outer wear. The U-shaped kitchen includes a windowed sink area and access to the bay-windowed dining area. The bedroom features views out two sides and lots of closet space, and is convenient to the full bath with natural light. There's even room for a washer and dryer in the two-car garage.

DESIGN BY
**Larry W. Garnett & Associates, Inc.**

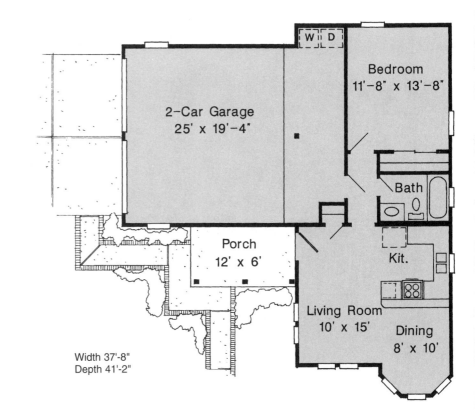

W | D

Bedroom
11'-8" x 13'-8"

2-Car Garage
25' x 19'-4"

Bath

Kit.

Porch
12' x 6'

Living Room
10' x 15'

Dining
8' x 10'

Width 37'-8"
Depth 41'-2"

*This home, as shown in the photograph, may differ from the actual blueprints. For more detailed information, please check the floor plans carefully.*

Photo by Andrew D. Lautman

Width 48'
Depth 38'

## Design 3699

**First Floor:** 1,356 square feet
**Second Floor:** 490 square feet
**Total:** 1,846 square feet

Split-log siding and a rustic balustrade create country charm with this farmhouse-style retreat. An open living area features a natural stone fireplace and a cathedral ceiling with exposed rough-sawn beam and brackets. A generous kitchen and dining area complement the living area and share the warmth of the fireplace. A master bedroom with complete bath, and a nearby family bedroom with hall bath complete the main floor. Upstairs, a spacious loft affords extra sleeping space—or provides a hobby/recreation area—and offers a full bath.

# When You're Ready To Order . . .

## Let Us Show You Our Home Blueprint Package.

Building a home? Planning a home? Our Blueprint Package has nearly everything you need to get the job done right, whether you're working on your own or with help from an architect, designer, builder or subcontractors. Each Blueprint Package is the result of many hours of work by licensed architects or professional designers.

## QUALITY

Hundreds of hours of painstaking effort have gone into the development of your blueprint set. Each home has been quality-checked by professionals to insure accuracy and buildability.

## VALUE

Because we sell in volume, you can buy professional-quality blueprints at a fraction of their development cost. With our plans, your dream home design costs only a few hundred dollars, not the thousands of dollars that custom architects charge.

## SERVICE

Once you've chosen your favorite home plan, you'll receive fast, efficient service whether you choose to mail or fax your order to us or call us toll free at 1-800-521-6797. For customer service, call toll free 1-888-690-1116.

## SATISFACTION

Over 50 years of service to satisfied home plan buyers provide us unparalleled experience and knowledge in producing quality blueprints. What this means to you is satisfaction with our product and performance.

## ORDER TOLL FREE 1-800-521-6797

After you've looked over our Blueprint Package and Important Extras on the following pages, simply mail the order form on page 221 or call toll free on our Blueprint Hotline: 1-800-521-6797. We're ready and eager to serve you. For customer service, call toll free 1-888-690-1116.

Each set of blueprints is an interrelated collection of detail sheets which includes components such as floor plans, interior and exterior elevations, dimensions, cross-sections, diagrams and notations. These sheets show exactly how your house is to be built.

## *Among the sheets included may be:*

### Frontal Sheet
This artist's sketch of the exterior of the house gives you an idea of how the house will look when built and landscaped. Large ink-line floor plans show all levels of the house and provide an overview of your new home's livability, as well as a handy reference for deciding on furniture placement.

### Foundation Plan
This sheet shows the foundation layout includ-

*SAMPLE PACKAGE*

ing support walls, excavated and unexcavated areas, if any, and foundation notes. If slab construction rather than basement, the plan shows footings and details for a monolithic slab. This page, or another in the set, may include a sample plot plan for locating your house on a building site.

## Detailed Floor Plans
These plans show the layout of each floor of the house. Rooms and interior spaces are carefully dimensioned and keys are given for cross-section details provided later in the plans. The positions of electrical outlets and switches are shown.

## House Cross-Sections
Large-scale views show sections or cut-aways of the foundation, interior walls, exterior walls, floors, stairways and roof details. Additional cross-sections may show important changes in

floor, ceiling or roof heights or the relationship of one level to another. Extremely valuable for construction, these sections show exactly how the various parts of the house fit together.

## Interior Elevations
Many of our drawings show the design and placement of kitchen and bathroom cabinets, laundry areas, fireplaces, bookcases and other built-ins. Little "extras," such as mantelpiece and wainscoting drawings, plus moulding sections, provide details that give your home that custom touch.

## Exterior Elevations
These drawings show the front, rear and sides of your house and give necessary notes on exterior materials and finishes. Particular attention is given to cornice detail, brick and stone accents or other finish items that make your home unique.

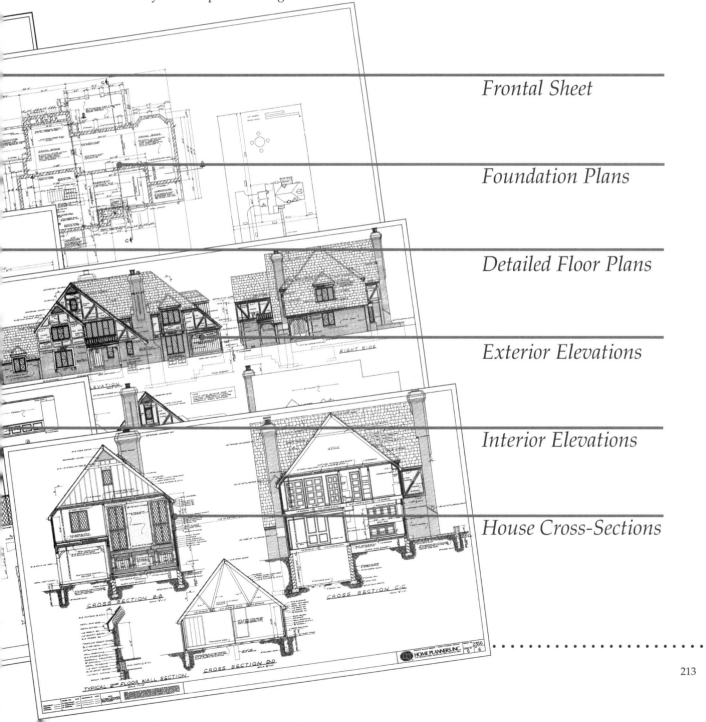

*Frontal Sheet*

*Foundation Plans*

*Detailed Floor Plans*

*Exterior Elevations*

*Interior Elevations*

*House Cross-Sections*

# *I*mportant Extras To Do The Job Right!

*Introducing eight important planning and construction aids developed by our professionals to help you succeed in your home-building project.*

## MATERIALS LIST

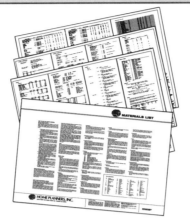

(Note: Because of the diversity of local building codes, our Materials List does not include mechanical materials.)

For many of the designs in our portfolio, we offer a customized materials take-off that is invaluable in planning and estimating the cost of your new home. This Materials List outlines the quantity, type and size of materials needed to build your house (with the exception of mechanical system items). Included are framing lumber, windows and doors, kitchen and bath cabinetry, rough and finish hardware, and much more. This handy list helps you or your builder cost out materials and serves as a reference sheet when you're compiling bids. A Materials List cannot be ordered before blueprints are ordered.

## SPECIFICATION OUTLINE

This valuable 16-page document is critical to building your house correctly. Designed to be filled in by you or your builder, this book lists 166 stages or items crucial to the building process. It provides a comprehensive review of the construction process and helps in making choices of materials. When combined with the blueprints, a signed contract, and a schedule, it becomes a legal document and record for the building of your home.

## QUOTE ONE®

### Summary Cost Report / Materials Cost Report

A new service for estimating the cost of building select designs, the Quote One® system is available in two separate stages: The Summary Cost Report and the Materials Cost Report.

Make even more informed decisions about your home-building project with the second phase of our package, our Materials Cost Report. This tool is invaluable in planning and estimating the cost of your new home. The material and installation (labor and equipment) cost is shown for each of over 1,000 line items provided in the Materials List (Standard grade) which is included when you purchase this estimating tool. It allows you to determine building costs for your specific zip-code area and for your chosen home design. Space is allowed for additional estimates from contractors and subcontractors, such as for mechanical materials, which are not included in our packages. This invaluable tool is available for a price of $110 ($120 for a Schedule E plan) which includes a Materials List. A Materials Cost Report cannot be ordered before blueprints are ordered.

The Summary Cost Report is the first stage in the package and shows the total cost per square foot for your chosen home in your zip-code area and then breaks that cost down into various categories showing the costs for building materials, labor and installation. The total cost for the report (which includes three grades: Budget, Standard and Custom) is just $19.95 for one home, and additionals are only $14.95. These reports allow you to evaluate your building budget and compare the costs of building a variety of homes in your area.

The Quote One® program is continually updated with new plans. If you are interested in a plan that is not indicated as Quote One®, please call and ask our sales reps, they will be happy to verify the status for you. To order these invaluable reports, use the order form on page 221 or call 1-800-521-6797.

# Plan-A-Home®

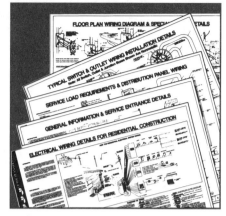

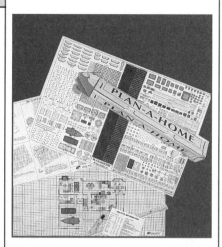

## PLUMBING

The Blueprint Package includes locations for all the plumbing fixtures in your new house, including sinks, lavatories, tubs, showers, toilets, laundry trays and water heaters. However, if you want to know more about the complete plumbing system, these 24x36-inch detail sheets will prove very useful. Prepared to meet requirements of the National Plumbing Code, these six fact-filled sheets give general information on pipe schedules, fittings, sump-pump details, water-softener hookups, septic system details and much more. Color-coded sheets include a glossary of terms.

## ELECTRICAL

The locations for every electrical switch, plug and outlet are shown in your Blueprint Package. However, these Electrical Details go further to take the mystery out of household electrical systems. Prepared to meet requirements of the National Electrical Code, these comprehensive 24x36-inch drawings come packed with helpful information, including wire sizing, switch-installation schematics, cable-routing details, appliance wattage, door-bell hookups, typical service panel circuitry and much more. Six sheets are bound together and color-coded for easy reference. A glossary of terms is also included.

**Plan-A-Home®** is an easy-to-use tool that helps you design a new home, arrange furniture in a new or existing home, or plan a remodeling project. Each package contains:

- **More than 700 reusable peel-off planning symbols** on a self-stick vinyl sheet, including walls, windows, doors, all types of furniture, kitchen components, bath fixtures and many more.

- **A reusable, transparent, 1/4-inch scale planning grid** that matches the scale of actual working drawings (1/4-inch equals 1 foot). This grid provides the basis for house layouts of up to 140x92 feet.

- **Tracing paper** and a protective sheet for copying or transferring your completed plan.

- **A felt-tip pen,** with water-soluble ink that wipes away quickly.

Plan-A-Home® lets you lay out areas as large as a 7,500 square foot, six-bedroom, seven-bath house.

## CONSTRUCTION

The Blueprint Package contains everything an experienced builder needs to construct a particular house. However, it doesn't show all the ways that houses can be built, nor does it explain alternate construction methods. To help you understand how your house will be built—and offer additional techniques—this set of drawings depicts the materials and methods used to build foundations, fireplaces, walls, floors and roofs. Where appropriate, the drawings show acceptable alternatives. These six sheets will answer questions for the advanced do-it-yourselfer or home planner.

## MECHANICAL

This package contains fundamental principles and useful data that will help you make informed decisions and communicate with subcontractors about heating and cooling systems. The 24x36-inch drawings contain instructions and samples that allow you to make simple load calculations and preliminary sizing and costing analysis. Covered are today's most commonly used systems from heat pumps to solar fuel systems. The package is packed full of illustrations and diagrams to help you visualize components and how they relate to one another.

## To Order, Call Toll Free 1-800-521-6797

To add these important extras to your Blueprint Package, simply indicate your choices on the order form on page 221 or call us Toll Free 1-800-521-6797 and we'll tell you more about these exciting products. For customer service, call toll free 1-888-690-1116.

# D *The Deck Blueprint Package*

Many of the homes in this book can be enhanced with a professionally designed Home Planners' Deck Plan. Those home plans highlighted with a D have a matching or corresponding deck plan available which includes a Deck Plan Frontal Sheet, Deck Framing and Floor Plans, Deck Elevations and a Deck Materials List. A Standard Deck Details Package, also available, provides all the how-to information necessary for building *any* deck. Our Complete Deck Building Package contains 1 set of Custom Deck Plans of your choice, plus 1 set of Standard Deck Building Details all for one low price. Our plans and details are carefully prepared in an easy-to-understand format that will guide you through every stage of your deck-building project. This page contains a sampling of 12 of the 25 different Deck layouts to match your favorite house. See page 218 for prices and ordering information.

| | | |
|---|---|---|
| **SPLIT-LEVEL SUN DECK**<br>Deck Plan D100 | **BI-LEVEL DECK WITH COVERED DINING**<br>Deck Plan D101 | **WRAP-AROUND FAMILY DECK**<br>Deck Plan D104 |
| **DECK FOR DINING AND VIEWS**<br>Deck Plan D107 | **TREND SETTER DECK**<br>Deck Plan D110 | **TURN-OF-THE-CENTURY DECK**<br>Deck Plan D111 |
| **WEEKEND ENTERTAINER DECK**<br>Deck Plan D112 | **CENTER-VIEW DECK**<br>Deck Plan D114 | **KITCHEN-EXTENDER DECK**<br>Deck Plan D115 |
| **SPLIT-LEVEL ACTIVITY DECK**<br>Deck Plan D117 | **TRI-LEVEL DECK WITH GRILL**<br>Deck Plan D119 | **CONTEMPORARY LEISURE DECK**<br>Deck Plan D120 |

# L The Landscape Blueprint Package

For the homes marked with an L in this book, Home Planners has created a front-yard landscape plan that matches or is complementary in design to the house plan. These comprehensive blueprint packages include a Frontal Sheet, Plan View, Regionalized Plant & Materials List, a sheet on Planting and Maintaining Your Landscape, Zone Maps and Plant Size and Description Guide. These plans will help you achieve professional results, adding value and enjoyment to your property for years to come. Each set of blueprints is a full 18" x 24" in size with clear, complete instructions and easy-to-read type. Six of the 40 front-yard Landscape Plans to match the most popular home plans are shown below.

## Regional Order Map

Most of the Landscape Plans shown on these pages are available with a Plant & Materials List adapted by horticultural experts to eight different regions of the country. Please specify Geographic Region when ordering your plan. See pages 218-219 for prices and regional availability. When you're ready to order, please turn to page 221.

| Region | 1 | Northeast |
|--------|---|-----------|
| Region | 2 | Mid-Atlantic |
| Region | 3 | Deep South |
| Region | 4 | Florida & Gulf Coast |
| Region | 5 | Midwest |
| Region | 6 | Rocky Mountains |
| Region | 7 | Southern California & Desert Southwest |
| Region | 8 | Northern California & Pacific Northwest |

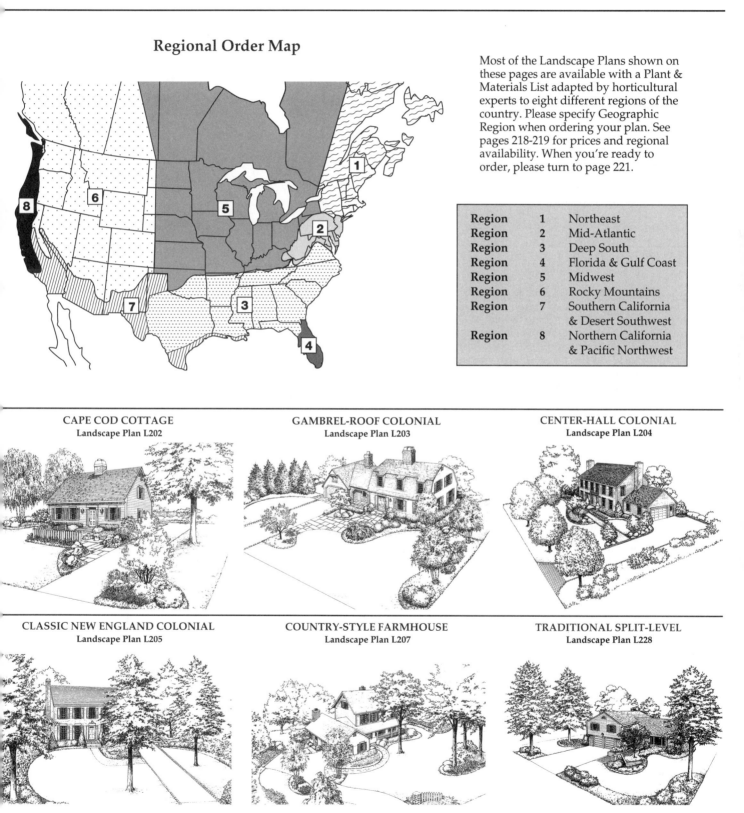

**CAPE COD COTTAGE**
Landscape Plan L202

**GAMBREL-ROOF COLONIAL**
Landscape Plan L203

**CENTER-HALL COLONIAL**
Landscape Plan L204

**CLASSIC NEW ENGLAND COLONIAL**
Landscape Plan L205

**COUNTRY-STYLE FARMHOUSE**
Landscape Plan L207

**TRADITIONAL SPLIT-LEVEL**
Landscape Plan L228

# Price Schedule & Plans Index

## House Blueprint Price Schedule
(Prices guaranteed through December 31, 1999)

| Tier | 1-set Study Package | 4-set Building Package | 8-set Building Package | 1-set Reproducible Sepias | Home Customizer® Package |
|---|---|---|---|---|---|
| A | $390 | $435 | $495 | $595 | $645 |
| B | $430 | $475 | $535 | $655 | $705 |
| C | $470 | $515 | $575 | $715 | $765 |
| D | $510 | $555 | $615 | $775 | $825 |
| E | $630 | $675 | $735 | $835 | $885 |

Prices for 4- or 8-set Building Packages honored only at time of original order.
Reverse blueprints (mirror image) with 4- or 8-set order.........$50 fee per order
Additional identical blueprints (standard of reverse) in same order ....$50 per set
Additional sets ordered within one year of original purchase...........$50 per set
Specification Outlines .........................................................................$10 each
Materials Lists (available only for those designers listed below):
▲ Home Planners Designs.................................................................$50
† Design Basics Designs.....................................................................$75
◆ Donald Gardner Designs.................................................................$50
■ Design Traditions Designs .............................................................$50
✳ Alan Mascord Designs....................................................................$50
≠ Larry W. Garnett Designs...............................................................$50
❖ The Sater Design Collection ...........................................................$50

Materials Lists for "E" price plans are an additional $10.

## Deck Plans Price Schedule

**CUSTOM DECK PLANS**

| Price Group | Q | R | S |
|---|---|---|---|
| 1 Set Custom Plans | $25 | $30 | $35 |

| | | |
|---|---|---|
| Additional identical sets | $10 each | |
| Reverse sets (mirror image) | $10 each | |

**STANDARD DECK DETAILS**
1 Set Generic Construction Details ....................$14.95 each

**COMPLETE DECK BUILDING PACKAGE**

| Price Group | Q | R | S |
|---|---|---|---|
| 1 Set Custom Plans, plus 1 Set Standard Deck Details | $35 | $40 | $45 |

## Landscape Plans Price Schedule

| Price Group | X | Y | Z |
|---|---|---|---|
| 1 set | $35 | $45 | $55 |
| 3 sets | $50 | $60 | $70 |
| 6 sets | $65 | $75 | $85 |

| | | |
|---|---|---|
| Additional Identical Sets | | $10 each |
| Reverse Sets (mirror image) | | $10 each |

# Index

To use the Index below, refer to the design number listed in numerical order (a helpful page reference is also given). Note the price index letter and refer to the House Blueprint Price Schedule above for the cost of one, four or eight sets of blueprints or the cost of a reproducible sepia. Additional prices are shown for identical and reverse blueprint sets, as well as a very useful Materials List for some of the plans. Also note in the Index below those plans that have matching or complementary Deck Plans or Landscape Plans. Refer to the schedules above for prices of these plans. All Home Planners' plans can be customized with Home Planners' Home Customizer® Package. These plans are indicated below with this symbol: ◖. See page 221 for information. Some plans are also part of our Quote One® estimating service and are indicated by this symbol: ◙. See page 214 for more information.

**To Order:** Fill in and send the order form on page 221—or call toll free 1-800-521-6797 or 520-297-8200. FAX: 800-244-6699 or 520-544-3086.

| DESIGN | PRICE | PAGE | CUSTOMIZABLE | QUOTE ONE® | DECK | DECK PRICE | LANDSCAPE | LANDSCAPE PRICE | REGIONS |
|---|---|---|---|---|---|---|---|---|---|
| ▲1499 | B | 202 | ◖ | | | | | | |
| ▲2427 | A | 203 | ◖ | | | | | | |
| ▲2488 | A | 198 | ◖ | ◙ | D102 | Q | | | |
| ▲2490 | A | 63 | ◖ | ◙ | | | | | |
| ▲2520 | B | 144 | ◖ | | D105 | R | L201 | Y | 1-3,5,6,8 |
| ▲2563 | B | 38 | ◖ | ◙ | D114 | R | L201 | Y | 1-3,5,6,8 |
| ▲2622 | A | 33 | ◖ | ◙ | D103 | R | L200 | X | 1-3,5,6,8 |
| ▲2661 | A | 36 | ◖ | ◙ | D113 | R | L202 | X | 1-3,5,6,8 |
| ▲2668 | B | 186 | ◖ | | | | L214 | Z | 1-3,5,6,8 |
| ▲2682 | A | 34 | ◖ | | D115 | Q | L200 | X | 1-3,5,6,8 |
| ▲2711 | B | 62 | ◖ | ◙ | D105 | R | L229 | Y | 1-8 |
| ▲2774 | B | 147 | ◖ | ◙ | D100 | Q | L207 | Z | 1-6,8 |
| ▲2776 | B | 81 | ◖ | ◙ | D113 | R | L207 | Z | 1-6,8 |
| ▲2822 | A | 116 | ◖ | ◙ | | | L229 | Y | 1-8 |
| ▲2826 | B | 117 | ◖ | ◙ | D116 | R | | | |
| ▲2864 | A | 9 | ◖ | ◙ | D100 | Q | L225 | X | 1-3,5,6,8 |
| ▲2871 | B | 10 | ◖ | | D117 | S | | | |
| ▲2875 | B | 121 | ◖ | ◙ | D113 | R | L236 | Z | 3,4,7 |
| ▲2878 | B | 8 | ◖ | ◙ | D112 | R | L200 | X | 1-3,5,6,8 |
| ▲2905 | A | 32 | ◖ | ◙ | D121 | S | L229 | Y | 1-8 |
| ▲2913 | B | 11 | ◖ | ◙ | D124 | S | | | |
| ▲2927 | B | 115 | ◖ | ◙ | D100 | Q | | | |
| ▲2947 | B | 12 | ◖ | ◙ | D112 | R | L200 | X | 1-3,5,6,8 |
| ▲2948 | B | 120 | ◖ | ◙ | | | | | |
| ▲2964 | B | 60 | ◖ | ◙ | | | | | |
| ▲2973 | B | 126 | ◖ | | | | L223 | Z | 1-3,5,6,8 |
| ▲2974 | A | 67 | ◖ | ◙ | | | L223 | Z | 1-3,5,6,8 |
| ▲3309 | B | 127 | ◖ | ◙ | | | L209 | Y | 1-6,8 |
| ▲3316 | A | 76 | ◖ | ◙ | | | L202 | X | 1-3,5,6,8 |
| ▲3331 | A | 199 | ◖ | ◙ | | | L203 | X | 1-3,5,6,8 |
| ▲3332 | B | 13 | ◖ | ◙ | | | L200 | X | 1-3,5,6,8 |
| ▲3340 | B | 90 | ◖ | ◙ | | | L224 | Y | 1-3,5,6,8 |
| ▲3376 | B | 124 | ◖ | ◙ | D114 | R | L205 | Y | 1-3,5,6,8 |
| ▲3385 | C | 61 | ◖ | ◙ | D100 | Q | L207 | Z | 1-6,8 |
| ▲3431 | B | 122 | ◖ | ◙ | | | | | |
| ▲3433 | C | 191 | ◖ | ◙ | | | L213 | Z | 1-8 |
| ▲3437 | C | 188 | ◖ | ◙ | | | L212 | Z | 1-8 |
| ▲3458 | C | 57 | ◖ | ◙ | D105 | R | L222 | X | 1-3,5,6,8 |
| ▲3460 | A | 15 | ◖ | ◙ | | | L200 | X | 1-3,5,6,8 |
| ▲3461 | B | 80 | ◖ | ◙ | | | L204 | Y | 1-3,5,6,8 |
| ▲3466 | B | 44 | ◖ | ◙ | D110 | R | L207 | Z | 1-6,8 |
| ▲3470 | C | 182 | ◖ | ◙ | D114 | R | L211 | Y | 1-8 |
| ▲3487 | B | 41 | ◖ | ◙ | | | L209 | Y | 1-6,8 |
| ▲3491 | B | 43 | ◖ | ◙ | D111 | S | L215 | Z | 1-6,8 |

| DESIGN | PRICE | PAGE | CUSTOMIZABLE | QUOTE ONE® | DECK | DECK PRICE | LANDSCAPE | LANDSCAPE PRICE | REGIONS |
|---|---|---|---|---|---|---|---|---|---|
| ▲ 3499 | B | 39 | ✓ | ✓ | D111 | S | L283 | X | 1-8 |
| ▲ 3569 | B | 118 | ✓ | ✓ | D105 | R | L238 | Y | 3,4,7,8 |
| ▲ 3600 | X | 56 | ✓ | ✓ | | | L200 | X | 1-3,5,6,8 |
| ▲ 3609 | C | 143 | ✓ | ✓ | D100 | Q | L224 | Y | 1-3,5,6,8 |
| ▲ 3619 | B | 83 | ✓ | ✓ | D111 | S | L207 | Z | 1-6,8 |
| ▲ 3620 | B | 70 | ✓ | ✓ | | | | | |
| ▲ 3628 | C | 193 | ✓ | ✓ | | | | | |
| ▲ 3643 | B | 123 | ✓ | ✓ | | | L237 | Y | 7 |
| ▲ 3644 | B | 190 | ✓ | ✓ | | | | | |
| ▲ 3651 | C | 40 | ✓ | ✓ | D112 | R | L235 | Z | 1-3,5,6,8 |
| ▲ 3652 | B | 45 | ✓ | ✓ | D105 | R | L220 | Y | 1-3,5,6,8 |
| ▲ 3654 | C | 129 | ✓ | ✓ | | | L292 | X | 1-8 |
| ▲ 3655 | B | 6 | ✓ | ✓ | | | L205 | Y | 1-3,5,6,8 |
| ▲ 3657 | C | 194 | ✓ | ✓ | | | | | |
| ▲ 3658 | B | 204 | ✓ | ✓ | D102 | Q | L202 | X | 1-3,5,6,8 |
| ▲ 3659 | B | 7 | ✓ | ✓ | | | L290 | Y | 1-8 |
| ▲ 3660 | B | 192 | ✓ | ✓ | | | L236 | Z | 3,4,7 |
| ▲ 3661 | C | 195 | ✓ | ✓ | | | L288 | Z | 1-8 |
| ▲ 3662 | B | 152 | ✓ | ✓ | | | L287 | Z | 1-8 |
| ▲ 3664 | C | 179 | ✓ | ✓ | | | L287 | Z | 1-8 |
| ▲ 3677 | B | 142 | ✓ | ✓ | D110 | R | L222 | Y | 1-3,5,6,8 |
| ▲ 3678 | B | 77 | ✓ | ✓ | | | L282 | X | 1-8 |
| ▲ 3680 | B | 200 | ✓ | ✓ | D111 | S | L282 | X | 1-8 |
| ▲ 3681 | B | 71 | ✓ | ✓ | D111 | S | L282 | X | 1-8 |
| ▲ 3682 | B | 50 | ✓ | ✓ | D111 | S | L282 | X | 1-8 |
| ▲ 3683 | B | 201 | ✓ | ✓ | D111 | S | L292 | X | 1-8 |
| ▲ 3687 | B | 66 | ✓ | ✓ | D110 | R | L282 | X | 1-8 |
| ▲ 3699 | B | 211 | ✓ | ✓ | D115 | Q | L292 | X | 1-8 |
| ▲ 4061 | A | 209 | ✓ | ✓ | D115 | Q | | | |
| 6600 | B | 42 | | | | | | | |
| ❖ 6607 | D | 176 | | ✓ | | | | | |
| 6614 | C | 196 | | | | | | | |
| 6629 | D | 172 | | | | | | | |
| 6630 | B | 175 | | | | | | | |
| † 7236 | C | 135 | | | | | | | |
| † 7305 | C | 64 | | | | | | | |
| † 7306 | C | 137 | | | | | | | |
| 7494 | C | 87 | | | | | | | |
| † 7601 | C | 16 | | | | | | | |
| † 7607 | C | 54 | | | | | | | |
| ◆ 7611 | C | 55 | | | | | | | |
| 8064 | B | 138 | | | | | | | |
| 8126 | C | 154 | | | | | | | |
| 8136 | D | 139 | | | | | | | |
| 8155 | C | 112 | | | | | | | |
| 8166 | B | 155 | | | | | | | |
| 8176 | B | 99 | | | | | | | |
| 8177 | B | 14 | | | | | | | |
| 8180 | B | 23 | | | | | | | |
| 8181 | B | 24 | | | | | | | |
| 8183 | B | 27 | | | | | | | |
| 8229 | B | 22 | | | | | | | |
| 8601 | B | 184 | | | | | | | |
| 8605 | B | 171 | | | | | | | |
| 8633 | B | 119 | | | | | | | |
| 8636 | B | 173 | | | | | | | |
| 8637 | B | 189 | | | | | | | |
| 8644 | B | 170 | | | | | | | |
| 8662 | B | 174 | | | | | | | |
| 8684 | B | 185 | | | | | | | |
| 8901 | A | 210 | | | | | | | |
| ≠ 8923 | D | 101 | | ✓ | | | | | |
| 8993 | D | 82 | | | | | | | |
| 8997 | C | 78 | | | | | | | |
| 8998 | C | 79 | | | | | | | |
| ≠ 9001 | D | 51 | | ✓ | | | | | |
| ≠ 9012 | D | 130 | | ✓ | | | | | |
| ≠ 9028 | C | 25 | | ✓ | | | | | |
| ≠ 9055 | D | 128 | | ✓ | | | | | |
| ≠ 9060 | C | 68 | | | | | | | |
| ≠ 9063 | D | 69 | | ✓ | | | | | |
| ≠ 9088 | C | 94 | | ✓ | | | | | |
| ≠ 9089 | C | 180 | | ✓ | | | | | |
| ≠ 9161 | C | 95 | | ✓ | | | | | |
| 9182 | C | 100 | | | | | | | |
| 9196 | D | 146 | | | | | | | |
| † 9201 | C | 102 | | ✓ | | | | | |
| † 9202 | C | 103 | | | | | | | |
| † 9204 | D | 168 | | ✓ | | | | | |
| † 9206 | C | 134 | | ✓ | | | | | |
| † 9235 | C | 19 | | ✓ | | | | | |
| † 9238 | C | 46 | | ✓ | | | | | |
| † 9250 | C | 178 | | ✓ | | | | | |
| † 9251 | D | 133 | | ✓ | | | | | |
| † 9252 | C | 132 | | ✓ | | | | | |
| † 9282 | C | 31 | | | | | | | |
| † 9310 | C | 136 | | ✓ | | | | | |
| † 9344 | D | 167 | | | | | | | |
| † 9362 | C | 169 | | ✓ | | | | | |
| ✱ 9425 | B | 162 | | | | | | | |
| ✱ 9437 | D | 89 | | | | | | | |
| ✱ 9437A | D | 89 | | | | | | | |
| ✱ 9459 | B | 47 | | | | | | | |
| ✱ 9477 | C | 165 | | | | | | | |
| ✱ 9497 | C | 148 | | | | | | | |
| ✱ 9509 | B | 18 | | | | | | | |
| ✱ 9516 | B | 30 | | | | | | | |
| ✱ 9518 | B | 20 | | | | | | | |
| ✱ 9541 | C | 164 | | | | | | | |
| ✱ 9557 | C | 85 | | ✓ | | | | | |
| ✱ 9573 | C | 183 | | | | | | | |
| ✱ 9582 | C | 163 | | | | | | | |
| ✱ 9585 | C | 131 | | | | | | | |
| 9586 | C | 149 | | | | | | | |
| ✱ 9588 | C | 86 | | | | | | | |
| ✱ 9593 | B | 21 | | | | | | | |
| ◆ 9606 | C | 49 | | ✓ | | | | | |
| ◆ 9619 | D | 91 | | | | | | | |
| ◆ 9621 | C | 74 | | ✓ | | | | | |
| ◆ 9630 | C | 205 | | | | | | | |
| ◆ 9645 | C | 75 | | ✓ | | | | | |
| ◆ 9661 | C | 114 | | ✓ | | | | | |
| ◆ 9662 | C | 84 | | ✓ | | | | | |
| ◆ 9663 | B | 208 | | | | | | | |
| ◆ 9697 | B | 206 | | | | | | | |
| ◆ 9712 | D | 145 | | ✓ | | | | | |
| ◆ 9734 | C | 153 | | ✓ | | | | | |
| ◆ 9742 | C | 140 | | ✓ | | | | | |
| ◆ 9747 | C | 53 | | ✓ | | | | | |
| ◆ 9749 | C | 73 | | ✓ | | | | | |
| ◆ 9759 | C | 207 | | ✓ | | | | | |
| ◆ 9764 | C | 17 | | ✓ | | | | | |
| ◆ 9771 | C | 72 | | | | | | | |
| ◆ 9773 | D | 141 | | ✓ | | | | | |
| ◆ 9779 | C | 52 | | ✓ | | | | | |
| ◆ 9780 | C | 48 | | ✓ | | | | | |
| ◆ 9796 | C | 150 | | | | | | | |
| ◆ 9799 | D | 151 | | | | | | | |
| ■ 9812 | C | 106 | | ✓ | | | | | |
| ■ 9813 | C | 58 | | ✓ | | | | | |
| ■ 9831 | C | 157 | | ✓ | | | | | |
| ■ 9840 | B | 98 | | ✓ | | | | | |
| ■ 9842 | C | 107 | | ✓ | | | | | |
| ■ 9846 | C | 181 | | ✓ | | | | | |
| ■ 9849 | B | 28 | | ✓ | | | | | |
| ■ 9853 | C | 93 | | ✓ | | | | | |
| ■ 9862 | C | 159 | | ✓ | | | | | |
| ■ 9872 | B | 26 | | ✓ | | | | | |
| ■ 9874 | B | 105 | | ✓ | | | | | |
| ■ 9877 | C | 108 | | ✓ | | | | | |
| ■ 9884 | C | 104 | | ✓ | | | | | |
| ■ 9885 | C | 158 | | ✓ | | | | | |
| 9886 | C | 166 | | ✓ | | | | | |
| ■ 9892 | C | 111 | | ✓ | | | | | |
| ■ 9893 | C | 109 | | ✓ | | | | | |
| ■ 9894 | B | 96 | | ✓ | | | | | |
| 9895 | B | 97 | | | | | | | |
| 9900 | C | 187 | | | | | | | |
| 9902 | B | 29 | | | | | | | |
| 9905 | C | 156 | | | | | | | |
| 9907 | C | 110 | | | | | | | |
| ■ 9914 | B | 59 | | ✓ | | | | | |
| 9915 | B | 113 | | | | | | | |
| 9950 | C | 92 | | | | | | | |
| Q220 | C | 88 | | | | | | | |
| Q385 | D | 160 | | | | | | | |
| Q390 | C | 161 | | | | | | | |

# Before You Order . . .

Before filling out the coupon at right or calling us on our Toll-Free Blueprint Hotline, you may want to learn more about our services and products. Here's some information you will find helpful.

## Quick Turnaround

We process and ship every blueprint order from our office within two business days. Because of this quick turnaround, we won't send a formal notice acknowledging receipt of your order.

## Our Exchange Policy

Since blueprints are printed in response to your order, we cannot honor requests for refunds. However, we will exchange your entire first order for an equal number of blueprints at a price of $50 for the first set and $10 for each additional set; $70 total exchange fee for 4 sets; $100 total exchange fee for 8 sets . . . *plus* the difference in cost if exchanging for a design in a higher price bracket or *less* the difference in cost if exchanging for a design in lower price bracket. One exchange is allowed within a year of purchase date. **(Sepias and reproducibles are not refundable, returnable or exchangeable.)** All sets from the first order must be returned before the exchange can take place. Please add $18 for postage and handling via Regular Service; $30 via Priority Service; $40 via Express Service. Returns and cancellations are subject to a 20% restocking fee, shipping and handling charges are not refundable.

## About Reverse Blueprints

If you want to build in reverse of the plan as shown, we will include any number of reverse blueprints (mirror image) from a 4- or 8-set package for an additional fee of $50. Although lettering and dimensions will appear backward, reverses will be a useful aid if you decide to flop the plan.

## Revising, Modifying and Customizing Plans

The wide variety of designs available in this publication allows you to select ideas and concepts for a home to fit your building site and match your family's needs, wants and budget. Like many homeowners who buy these plans, you and your builder, architect or engineer may want to make changes to them. Some minor changes may be made by your builder, but we recommend that most changes be made by a licensed architect or engineer. If you need to make alterations to a design that is customizable, you need only order our Home Customizer® Package to get you started. As set forth below, we cannot assume any responsibility for blueprints which have been changed, whether by you, your builder or by professionals selected by you or referred to you by us, because such individuals are outside our supervision and control.

## Architectural and Engineering Seals

Some cities and states are now requiring that a licensed architect or engineer review and "seal" a blueprint, or officially approve it, prior to construction due to concerns over energy costs, safety and other factors. Prior to application for a building permit or the start of actual construction, we strongly advise that you consult your local building official who can tell you if such a review is required.

## About the Designers

The architects and designers whose work appears in this publication are among America's leading residential designers. Each plan was designed to meet the requirements of a nationally recognized model building code in effect at the time and place the plan was drawn. Because national building codes change from time to time, plans may not comply with any such code at the time they are sold to a customer. In addition, building officials may not accept these plans as final construction documents of record as the plans may need to be modified and additional drawings and details added to suit local conditions and requirements. We strongly advise that purchasers consult a licensed architect or engineer, and their local building official, before starting any construction related to these plans.

## Local Building Codes and Zoning Requirements

At the time of creation, our plans are drawn to specifications published by the Building Officials and Code Administrators (BOCA) International, Inc.; the Southern Building Code Congress (SBCCI) International, Inc.; the International Conference of Building Officials; or the Council of American Building Officials (CABO). Our plans are designed to meet or exceed national building standards. Because of the great differences in geography and climate throughout the United States and Canada, each state, county and municipality has its own building codes, zone requirements, ordinances and building regulations. Your plan may need to be modified to comply with local requirements regarding snow loads, energy codes, soil and seismic conditions and a wide range of other matters. In addition, you may need to obtain permits or inspections from local governments before and in the course of construction. Prior to using blueprints ordered from us, we strongly advise that you consult a licensed architect or engineer—and speak with your local building official—before applying for any permit or beginning construction. We authorize the use of our blueprints on the express condition that you strictly comply with all local building codes, zoning requirements and other applicable laws, regulations, ordinances and requirements. **Notice:** Plans for homes to be built in Nevada must be re-drawn by a Nevada-registered professional. Consult your building official for more information on this subject.

## Foundation and Exterior Wall Changes

Most of our plans are drawn with either a full or partial basement foundation. Depending on your specific climate or regional building practices, you may wish to change this basement to a slab or crawlspace. Most professional contractors and builders can easily adapt your plans to alternate foundation types. Likewise, most can easily change 2x4 wall construction to 2x6, or vice versa.

## Disclaimer

We and the designers we work with have put substantial care and effort into the creation of our blueprints. However, because we cannot provide on-site consultation, supervision and control over actual construction, and because of the great variance in local building requirements, building practices and soil, seismic, weather and other conditions, WE CANNOT MAKE ANY WARRANTY, EXPRESS OR IMPLIED, WITH RESPECT TO THE CONTENT OR USE OF OUR BLUEPRINTS, INCLUDING BUT NOT LIMITED TO ANY WARRANTY OF MERCHANTABILITY OR OF FITNESS FOR A PARTICULAR PURPOSE.

## Terms and Conditions

These designs are protected under the terms of United States Copyright Law and may not be copied or reproduced in any way, by any means, unless you have purchased Sepias or Reproducibles which clearly indicate your right to copy or reproduce. We authorize the use of your chosen design as an aid in the construction of one single family home only. You may not use this design to build a second or multiple dwellings without purchasing another blueprint or blueprints or paying additional design fees.

## How Many Blueprints Do You Need?

A single set of blueprints is sufficient to study a home in greater detail. However, if you are planning to obtain cost estimates from a contractor or subcontractors—or if you are planning to build immediately—you will need more sets. Because additional sets are cheaper when ordered in quantity with the original order, make sure you order enough blueprints to satisfy all requirements. The following checklist will help you determine how many you need:

____ Owner

____ Builder (generally requires at least three sets; one as a legal document, one to use during inspections, and at least one to give to subcontractors)

____ Local Building Department (often requires two sets)

____ Mortgage Lender (usually one set for a conventional loan; three sets for FHA or VA loans)

____ TOTAL NUMBER OF SETS

---

# Have You Seen Our Newest Designs?

Home Planners is one of the country's most active home design firms, creating nearly 100 new plans each year. At least 50 of our latest creations are featured in each edition of our New Design Portfolio. You may have received a copy with your latest purchase by mail. If not, or if you purchased this book from a local retailer, just return the coupon below for your FREE copy. Make sure you consider the very latest of what Home Planners has to offer.

## Yes! Please send my FREE copy of your latest New Design Portfolio.

Offer good to U.S. shipping address only.

Name _____

Address _____

City_____State_____Zip _____

**HOME PLANNERS, LLC**
Wholly owned by Hanley-Wood, Inc.
3275 WEST INA ROAD, SUITE 110
TUCSON, ARIZONA 85741

Order Form Key

| TB44 |

## Toll Free 1-800-521-6797

Regular Office Hours:
8:00 a.m. to 8:00 p.m. Eastern Time, Monday through Friday
Our staff will gladly answer any questions during regular office hours. Our answering service can place orders after hours or on weekends.

If we receive your order by 4:00 p.m. Eastern Time, Monday through Friday, we'll process it and ship within two business days. When ordering by phone, please have your charge card ready. We'll also ask you for the Order Form Key Number at the bottom of the coupon.

By FAX: Copy the Order Form on the next page and send it on our FAX line: 1-800-224-6699 or 1-520-544-3086.

## Canadian Customers
### Order Toll-Free 1-800-561-4169

For faster service and plans that are modified for building in Canada, customers may now call in orders directly to our Canadian supplier of plans and charge the purchase to a charge card. Or, you may complete the order form at right, adding the current exchange rate to all prices and mail in Canadian funds to:

**The Plan Centre** 60 Baffin Place
Unit 5
Waterloo, Ontario N2V 1Z7

**OR:** Copy the Order Form and send it via our Canadian FAX line: 1-800-719-3291.

# The Home Customizer®

"This house is perfect...if only the family room were two feet wider." Sound familiar? In response to the numerous requests for this type of modification, Home Planners has developed **The Home Customizer® Package**. This exclusive package offers our top-of-the-line materials to make it easy for anyone, anywhere to customize any Home Planners design to fit their needs. Check the index on pages 218-219 for those plans which are customizable.

Some of the changes you can make to any of our plans include:

- exterior elevation changes
- kitchen and bath modifications
- roof, wall and foundation changes
- room additions and more!

**The Home Customizer® Package** includes everything you'll need to make the necessary changes to your favorite Home Planners design. The package includes:

- instruction book with examples
- architectural scale and clear work film
- erasable red marker and removable correction tape
- ¼"-scale furniture cutouts
- 1 set reproducible, erasable Sepias
- 1 set study blueprints for communicating changes to your design professional
- a copyright release letter so you can make copies as you need them
- referral letter with the name, address and telephone number of the professional in your region who is trained in modifying Home Planners designs efficiently and inexpensively.

The price of the **Home Customizer® Package** ranges from $645 to $885, depending on the price schedule of the design you have chosen. **The Home Customizer® Package** will not only save you 25% to 75% of the cost of drawing the plans from scratch with a custom architect or engineer, it will also give you the flexibility to have your changes and modifications made by our referral network or by the professional of your choice. Now it's even easier and more affordable to have the custom home you've always wanted.

**ORDER TOLL FREE!**
For information about any of our services or to order call
**1-800-521-6797 or 520-297-8200.**
Browse our website:
**www.homeplanners.com**

---

## BLUEPRINTS ARE NOT REFUNDABLE
## EXCHANGES ONLY

---

**For Customer Service,
call toll free 1-888-690-1116.**

---

# ORDER FORM

**HOME PLANNERS, LLC**
Wholly owned by Hanley-Wood, Inc.
3275 WEST INA ROAD, SUITE 110
TUCSON, ARIZONA 85741

**THE BASIC BLUEPRINT PACKAGE**
Rush me the following (please refer to the Plans Index and Price Schedule in this section):

| | | |
|---|---|---|
| _____ | Set(s) of blueprints for plan number(s) _____. | $_____ |
| _____ | Set(s) of sepias for plan number(s) _____. | $_____ |
| _____ | Home Customizer® Package for plan(s)_____. | $_____ |
| _____ | Additional identical blueprints (standard or reverse) in same order @ $50 per set. | $_____ |
| _____ | Reverse blueprints @ $50 fee per order. | $_____ |

**IMPORTANT EXTRAS**
Rush me the following:

_____ Materials List: $50 (Must be purchased with Blueprint set.)
$75 Design Basics. Add $10 for a Schedule E-G plan Materials List.$_____
_____ **Quote One®** Summary Cost Report @ $19.95 for 1, $14.95 for each additional, for plans _____ $_____
Building location: City _____Zip Code _____
_____ **Quote One®** Materials Cost Report @ $110 Schedule A-D; $120 Schedule E for plan_____ $_____
(Must be purchased with Blueprints set.)
Building location: City _____Zip Code_____
_____ Specification Outlines @ $10 each. $_____
_____ Detail Sets @ $14.95 each; any two for $22.95; any three for $29.95; all four for $39.95 (save $19.85). $_____
❏ Plumbing ❏ Electrical ❏ Construction ❏ Mechanical
(These helpful details provide general construction advice and are not specific to any single plan.)
_____ Plan-A-Home® @ $29.95 each. $_____
**DECK BLUEPRINTS**
_____ Set(s) of Deck Plan _____ $_____
_____ Additional identical blueprints in same order @ $10 per set. $_____
_____ Reverse blueprints @ $10 per set. $_____
_____ Set of Standard Deck Details @ $14.95 per set. $_____
_____ Set of Complete Building Package (Best Buy!)
Includes Custom Deck Plan _____.
(See Index and Price Schedule)
Plus Standard Deck Details $_____
**LANDSCAPE BLUEPRINTS**
_____ Set(s) of Landscape Plan _____. $_____
_____ Additional identical blueprints in same order @ $10 per set. $_____
_____ Reverse blueprints @ $10 per set. $_____
Please indicate the appropriate region of the country for
Plant & Material List. (See Map on page 217): Region _____

| POSTAGE AND HANDLING | 1-3 sets | 4+ sets |
|---|---|---|
| Signature is required for all deliveries. **DELIVERY** (Requires street address - No P.O. Boxes) | | |
| •Regular Service (Allow 7-10 business days delivery) | ❏ $15.00 | ❏ $18.00 |
| •Priority (Allow 4-5 business days delivery) | ❏ $20.00 | ❏ $30.00 |
| •Express (Allow 3 business days delivery) | ❏ $30.00 | ❏ $40.00 |
| **CERTIFIED MAIL** If no street address available. (Allow 7-10 days delivery) | ❏ $20.00 | ❏ $30.00 |
| **OVERSEAS DELIVERY** Note: All delivery times are from date Blueprint Package is shipped. | fax, phone or mail for quote | |

**POSTAGE (From box above)** $_____
**SUB-TOTAL** $_____
**SALES TAX** (AZ, MI & WA residents, please add appropriate state and local sales tax.) $_____
**TOTAL (Sub-total and tax)** $_____

**YOUR ADDRESS (please print)**
Name _____
Street _____
City _____State_____Zip _____
Daytime telephone number (_____) _____

**FOR CREDIT CARD ORDERS ONLY**
Please fill in the information below:
Credit card number _____
Exp. Date: Month/Year _____
Check one ❏ Visa ❏ MasterCard ❏ Discover Card ❏ American Express

Signature _____
Please check appropriate box: ❏ Licensed Builder-Contractor
❏ Homeowner

**ORDER TOLL FREE!**
1-800-521-6797 or 520-297-8200

Order Form Key
TB44

# Helpful Books & Software

Home Planners wants your building experience to be as pleasant and trouble-free as possible. That's why we've expanded our library of Do-It-Yourself titles to help you along. In addition to our beautiful plans books, we've added books to guide you through specific projects as well as the construction process. In fact, these are titles that will be as useful after your dream home is built as they are right now.

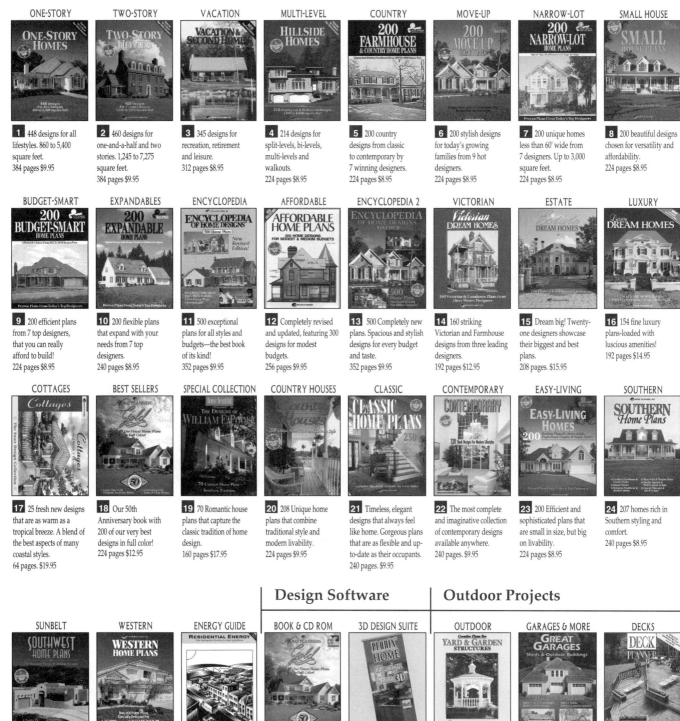

**ONE-STORY**

**1** 448 designs for all lifestyles. 860 to 5,400 square feet. 384 pages $9.95

**TWO-STORY**

**2** 460 designs for one-and-a-half and two stories. 1,245 to 7,275 square feet. 384 pages $9.95

**VACATION**

**3** 345 designs for recreation, retirement and leisure. 312 pages $8.95

**MULTI-LEVEL**

**4** 214 designs for split-levels, bi-levels, multi-levels and walkouts. 224 pages $8.95

**COUNTRY**

**5** 200 country designs from classic to contemporary by 7 winning designers. 224 pages $8.95

**MOVE-UP**

**6** 200 stylish designs for today's growing families from 9 hot designers. 224 pages $8.95

**NARROW-LOT**

**7** 200 unique homes less than 60' wide from 7 designers. Up to 3,000 square feet. 224 pages $8.95

**SMALL HOUSE**

**8** 200 beautiful designs chosen for versatility and affordability. 224 pages $8.95

**BUDGET-SMART**

**9** 200 efficient plans from 7 top designers, that you can really afford to build! 224 pages $8.95

**EXPANDABLES**

**10** 200 flexible plans that expand with your needs from 7 top designers. 240 pages $8.95

**ENCYCLOPEDIA**

**11** 500 exceptional plans for all styles and budgets—the best book of its kind! 352 pages $9.95

**AFFORDABLE**

**12** Completely revised and updated, featuring 300 designs for modest budgets. 256 pages $9.95

**ENCYCLOPEDIA 2**

**13** 500 Completely new plans. Spacious and stylish designs for every budget and taste. 352 pages $9.95

**VICTORIAN**

**14** 160 striking Victorian and Farmhouse designs from three leading designers. 192 pages $12.95

**ESTATE**

**15** Dream big! Twenty-one designers showcase their biggest and best plans. 208 pages. $15.95

**LUXURY**

**16** 154 fine luxury plans-loaded with luscious amenities! 192 pages $14.95

**COTTAGES**

**17** 25 fresh new designs that are as warm as a tropical breeze. A blend of the best aspects of many coastal styles. 64 pages. $19.95

**BEST SELLERS**

**18** Our 50th Anniversary book with 200 of our very best designs in full color! 224 pages $12.95

**SPECIAL COLLECTION**

**19** 70 Romantic house plans that capture the classic tradition of home design. 160 pages $17.95

**COUNTRY HOUSES**

**20** 208 Unique home plans that combine traditional style and modern livability. 224 pages $9.95

**CLASSIC**

**21** Timeless, elegant designs that always feel like home. Gorgeous plans that are as flexible and up-to-date as their occupants. 240 pages. $9.95

**CONTEMPORARY**

**22** The most complete and imaginative collection of contemporary designs available anywhere. 240 pages. $9.95

**EASY-LIVING**

**23** 200 Efficient and sophisticated plans that are small in size, but big on livability. 224 pages $8.95

**SOUTHERN**

**24** 207 homes rich in Southern styling and comfort. 240 pages $8.95

## Design Software

## Outdoor Projects

**SUNBELT**

**25** 215 Designs that capture the spirit of the Southwest. 208 pages  $10.95

**WESTERN**

**26** 215 designs that capture the spirit and diversity of the Western lifestyle. 208 pages $9.95

**ENERGY GUIDE**

**27** The most comprehensive energy efficiency and conservation guide available. 280 pages $35.00

**BOOK & CD ROM**

**28** Both the Home Planners Gold book and matching Windows™ CD ROM with 3D floorplans. $24.95

**3D DESIGN SUITE**

**29** Home design made easy! View designs in 3D, take a virtual reality tour, add decorating details and more. $59.95

**OUTDOOR**

**30** 42 unique outdoor projects. Gazebos, strombellas, bridges, sheds, playsets and more! 96 pages $7.95

**GARAGES & MORE**

**31** 101 Multi-use garages and outdoor structures to enhance any home. 96 pages $7.95

**DECKS**

**32** 25 outstanding single-, double- and multi-level decks you can build. 112 pages $7.95

## Landscape Designs

| EASY CARE | FRONT & BACK | BACKYARDS | BEDS & BORDERS | BATHROOMS | KITCHENS | HOUSE CONTRACTING | WINDOWS & DOORS |

**33** 41 special landscapes designed for beauty and low maintenance. 160 pages $14.95

**34** The first book of do-it-yourself landscapes. 40 front, 15 backyards. 208 pages $14.95

**35** 40 designs focused solely on creating your own specially themed backyard oasis. 160 pages $14.95

**36** Practical advice and maintenance techniques for a wide variety of yard projects. 160 pages. $14.95

**37** An innovative guide to organizing, remodeling and decorating your bathroom. 96 pages $10.95

**38** An imaginative guide to designing the perfect kitchen. Chock full of bright ideas to make your job easier. 176 pages $14.95

**39** Everything you need to know to act as your own general contractor...and save up to 25% off building costs. 134 pages $14.95

**40** Installation techniques and tips that make your project easier and more professional looking. 80 pages $7.95

| ROOFING | FRAMING | VISUAL HANDBOOK | BASIC WIRING | PATIOS & WALKS | TILE | TRIM & MOLDING |

**41** Information on the latest tools, materials and techniques for roof installation or repair. 80 pages $7.95

**42** For those who want to take a more-hands on approach to their dream. 319 pages $19.95

**43** A plain-talk guide to the construction process; financing to final walk-through, this book covers it all. 498 pages $19.95

**44** A straight forward guide to one of the most misunderstood systems in the home. 160 pages $12.95

**45** Clear step-by-step instructions take you from the basic design stages to the finished project. 80 pages $7.95

**46** Every kind of tile for every kind of application. Includes tips on use installation and repair. 176 pages $12.95

**47** Step-by-step instructions for installing baseboards, window and door casings and more. 80 pages $7.95

## Additional Books Order Form

To order your books, just check the box of the book numbered below and complete the coupon. We will process your order and ship it from our office within 48 hours. Send coupon and check (in U.S. funds).

**YES!** Please send me the books I've indicated:

| | | |
|---|---|---|
| ☐ 1:VO . . . . . . . . . . $9.95 | ☐ 25:SW . . . . . . . . $10.95 | |
| ☐ 2:VT . . . . . . . . . . $9.95 | ☐ 26:WH . . . . . . . . . $9.95 | |
| ☐ 3:VH . . . . . . . . . . $8.95 | ☐ 27:RES . . . . . . . . $35.00 | |
| ☐ 4:VS . . . . . . . . . . $8.95 | ☐ 28:HPGC . . . . . . $24.95 | |
| ☐ 5:FH . . . . . . . . . . $8.95 | ☐ 29:PLANSUITE . . $59.95 | |
| ☐ 6:MU . . . . . . . . . $8.95 | ☐ 30:YG . . . . . . . . . $7.95 | |
| ☐ 7:NL . . . . . . . . . . $8.95 | ☐ 31:GG . . . . . . . . $7.95 | |
| ☐ 8:SM . . . . . . . . . . $8.95 | ☐ 32:DP . . . . . . . . $7.95 | |
| ☐ 9:BS . . . . . . . . . . $8.95 | ☐ 33:ECL . . . . . . . $14.95 | |
| ☐ 10:EX . . . . . . . . . $8.95 | ☐ 34:HL . . . . . . . . $14.95 | |
| ☐ 11:EN . . . . . . . . . $9.95 | ☐ 35:BYL . . . . . . . $14.95 | |
| ☐ 12:AF . . . . . . . . . $9.95 | ☐ 36:BB . . . . . . . . $14.95 | |
| ☐ 13:E2 . . . . . . . . . $9.95 | ☐ 37:CDB . . . . . . . $10.95 | |
| ☐ 14:VDH . . . . . . $12.95 | ☐ 38:CKI . . . . . . . $14.95 | |
| ☐ 15:EDH . . . . . . $15.95 | ☐ 39:SBC . . . . . . . $14.95 | |
| ☐ 16:LD2 . . . . . . $14.95 | ☐ 40:CGD . . . . . . . $7.95 | |
| ☐ 17:CTG . . . . . . $19.95 | ☐ 41:CGR . . . . . . . $7.95 | |
| ☐ 18:HPG . . . . . . $12.95 | ☐ 42:SRF . . . . . . . $19.95 | |
| ☐ 19:WEP . . . . . . $17.95 | ☐ 43:RVH . . . . . . . $19.95 | |
| ☐ 20:CN . . . . . . . . $9.95 | ☐ 44:CBW . . . . . . . $12.95 | |
| ☐ 21:CS . . . . . . . . $9.95 | ☐ 45:CGW . . . . . . . $7.95 | |
| ☐ 22:CM . . . . . . . . $9.95 | ☐ 46:CWT . . . . . . . $12.95 | |
| ☐ 23:EL . . . . . . . . $8.95 | ☐ 47:CGT . . . . . . . $7.95 | |
| ☐ 24:SH . . . . . . . . $8.95 | | |

**Canadian Customers**
**Order Toll-Free 1-800-561-4169**

Additional Books Sub-Total . . . . . . . . . . $_____
ADD Postage and Handling . . . . . . . . . . $ 4.00
Sales Tax: (AZ, MI & WA residents, please add appropriate state and local sales tax.) . . . . $_____
YOUR TOTAL (Sub-Total, Postage/Handling, Tax) . . $_____

**YOUR ADDRESS** (Please print)

Name _____

Street _____

City _____ State _____ Zip _____

Phone (_____) _____ — _____

**YOUR PAYMENT**
Check one: ☐ Check ☐ Visa ☐ MasterCard ☐ Discover Card
☐ American Express
Required credit card information:

Credit Card Number _____

Expiration Date (Month/Year) _____ / _____

Signature Required _____

**Home Planners, LLC**
**Wholly owned by Hanley-Wood, Inc.**
3275 W. Ina Road, Suite 110, Dept. BK, Tucson, AZ 85741

TB44

Design 3662, page 152

# OVER 3 MILLION BLUEPRINTS SOLD

*"We instructed our builder to follow the plans including all of the many details which make this house so elegant…Our home is a fine example of the results one can achieve by purchasing and following the plans which you offer…Everyone who has seen it has assured us that it belongs in 'a picture book.' I truly mean it when I say that my home 'is a DREAM HOUSE.'"*

S.P.
Anderson, SC

*"We have had a steady stream of visitors, many of whom tell us this is the most beautiful home they've seen. Everyone is amazed at the layout and remarks on how unique it is. Our real estate attorney, who is a Chicago dweller and who deals with highly valued properties, told me this is the only suburban home he has seen that he would want to live in."*

W. & P.S.
Flossmoor, IL

*"Your blueprints saved us a great deal of money. I acted as the general contractor and we did a lot of the work ourselves. We probably built it for half the cost! We are thinking about more plans for another home. I purchased a competitor's book but my husband wants only your plans!"*

K.M.
Grovetown, GA

*"We are very happy with the product of our efforts. The neighbors and passersby appreciate what we have created. We have had many people stop by to discuss our house and kindly praise it as being the nicest house in our area of new construction. We have even had one person stop and make us an unsolicited offer to buy the house for much more than we have invested in it."*

K. & L.S.
Bolingbrook, IL

*"The traffic going past our house is unbelievable. On several occasions, we have heard that it is the 'prettiest house in Batvia.' Also, when meeting someone new and mentioning what street we live on, quite often we're told, 'Oh, you're the one in the yellow house with the wrap-around porch! I love it!'"*

A.W.
Batvia, NY

*"I have been involved in the building trades my entire life…Since building our home we have built two other homes for other families. Their plans from local professional architects were not nearly as good as yours. For that reason we are ordering additional plan books from you."*

T.F.
Kingston, WA

*"The blueprints we received from you were of excellent quality and provided us with exactly what we needed to get our successful home-building project underway. We appreciate your invaluable role in our home-building effort."*

T.A.
Concord, TN